ALSO BY JEFF HOBBS

Show Them You're Good

The Short and Tragic Life of Robert Peace

The Tourists

Children of the State

STORIES OF SURVIVAL AND HOPE
IN THE JUVENILE JUSTICE SYSTEM

JEFF HOBBS

SCRIBNER

New York London Toronto Sydney New Delhi

Scribner
An Imprint of Simon & Schuster, Inc.
1230 Avenue of the Americas
New York, NY 10020

First Scribner hardcover edition January 2023

SCRIBNER and design are registered trademarks of The Gale Group, Inc.,
used under license by Simon & Schuster, Inc., the publisher of this work.

For information about special discounts for bulk purchases, please contact Simon &
Schuster Special Sales at 1-866-506-1949 or business@simonandschuster.com.

The Simon & Schuster Speakers Bureau can bring authors to your live event.
For more information or to book an event, contact the Simon & Schuster Speakers
Bureau at 1-866-248-3049 or visit our website at www.simonspeakers.com.

Manufactured in the United States of America

1   3   5   7   9   10   8   6   4   2

Library of Congress Cataloging-in-Publication Data

Names: Hobbs, Jeff, 1980– author.
Title: Children of the state : survival and hope in the
juvenile justice system / Jeff Hobbs.
Description: First Scribner hardcover edition. | New York : Scribner, [2023]
Identifiers: LCCN 2022020137 (print) | LCCN 2022020138 (ebook) |
ISBN 9781982116361 (hardcover) | ISBN 9781982116385 (ebook)
Subjects: LCSH: Juvenile delinquents—United States—Case studies. | Juvenile
delinquents—Rehabilitation—United States—Case studies. | Juvenile justice,
Administration of—United States—Case studies.
Classification: LCC HV9104 .H63 2023 (print) | LCC HV9104 (ebook) |
DDC 364.360973—dc23/eng/20220615
LC record available at https://lccn.loc.gov/2022020137
LC ebook record available at https://lccn.loc.gov/2022020138

ISBN 978-1-9821-1636-1
ISBN 978-1-9821-1638-5 (ebook)

To "Mama" Rose Villalon, and to the constellation of educators, counselors, therapists, coordinators, mentors, volunteers, and families who devote their lives and spirits every day to the most imperiled youth among us

It was the evident purpose of the founders of the first juvenile courts to save, to redeem, and to protect every delinquent child for the benefit of himself and of society and of the state. . . . If these principles are not applied to the juvenile court, the result will be that in the future, as in the past, distressed children, broken in body and mind, must travel along the trail of tears that leads finally to their destruction.

—Judge Charles W. Hoffman, speaking to the first
Conference on Juvenile-Court Standards, June 21, 1921

AUTHOR'S NOTE

◆

A YOUNG MAN, about seventeen years old, sauntered into a class-room where another young man was idly waiting for English language arts class to start. He took a boxer's crouch and landed a powerful, undefended right cross on the waiting boy's face. The crack of knuckle bones against cheekbone was audible throughout the room. The boy who'd received the blow appeared simultaneously dazed and emotionally wounded as he stumbled backward and tripped over a desk, half his face already bright red beneath the skin as blood rushed there. Without pause, the attacker launched himself forward with the leverage of both height and surprise to continue the assault, ferociously barraging with head and body blows. Ultimately, three large, well-trained adults were required to wrest him off and out of the room, while his victim lay in the fetal position, reduced by the violence to trying only to protect his head.

Meanwhile, I was starfished against a wall in order to stay out of everyone's way. I'd been invited to speak about books and writing to this class in San Francisco's Woodside Learning Center. The facility was more broadly known as the Juvenile Justice Center, the city's equivalent of county jail for youth. The pure force of the attack was stunning, as was its targeted quickness. In one moment, the classroom had been peaceful. In the next, it was taut with ferocity. And the adults in the room whose jobs were to prevent this exact thing from happening had been powerless to do so—really through no fault of their own. As a result, the unit was secured, all the boys living there locked in their rooms, and class was canceled. The teachers who had arranged the visit seemed frustrated but not terribly surprised.

I visited Woodside a few times in the years that followed, as well as a number of other juvenile facilities in various cities—to lead a book club discussion, maybe, or assist a creative writing class. Each place was physically different with its own ecosystem of educators, guards, counselors, spaces, and schedules. Each place was sad. Each place was striking in just how young and fragile its residents appeared, how even the loud, brash ones seemed to exist in a constant retreat within themselves, and how they strived to find rare, small moments of joy in the simplest observations while denying the grim long-term consequences of their plights. A veteran juvenile hall history teacher once told me, when I asked as to his aspirations for his students after they were released, "I used to have high hopes for them leaving here and graduating from high school and maybe even college. Now, I mainly just hope that, within five years of leaving, my students aren't dead. Even if they're in adult prison, but still alive, I consider that a success." This teacher, who ate his lunch every day in a nearby woodsy area while listening to the birds in order to manage the constant heartache of his work, added, "Frankly, the track record with that is not great."

As these various visits accumulated, I realized that people without direct experience in juvenile halls tended to have no idea that these buildings contained schools—that the young people detained inside them attended core academic classes every day and accumulated credits toward graduation. Most people instead seemed conditioned to equate juvenile hall with prison, youth offenders with inmates, educators and counselors with guards. These misconceptions and the casual nature with which they are perpetuated in our society seemed insidious and unjust.

After deciding to write about what it felt like to be an incarcerated juvenile and to teach incarcerated juveniles in America, I spent significant time in each of three spaces within the juvenile justice system. Two of them were secure placement facilities, and the third was a highly regarded diversion program.

Ferris School is the sole youth residential detention facility in the state of Delaware and has been for 102 years. Kids there—all boys, though a separate, lower-security facility for girls is on an adjacent campus—have been sentenced to be held at Ferris generally for three, six, nine, or twelve months. The entire building, including the sector devoted to education, operates under the purview of the state's Department of Services for Children, Youth & Their Families. This book follows a student named Josiah Wright through his yearlong incarceration there.

Woodside, already mentioned, is a court facility housing San Francisco's juvenile arrestees awaiting sentencing before a judge but deemed unfit to be free in the interim. The structure is connected to the juvenile court building, and students are placed there for anywhere from a couple days to many months depending on the progress of their various cases. There is one living unit for girls and two for boys. The residential program is managed by the Juvenile Probation Department. The educational sector is run by the San Francisco Unified School District. This book focuses on the work and trials of educators there, mainly through the experience of an English language arts teacher named Megan Mercurio and the school principal, Chris Lanier.

Exalt Youth is a New York City–based nonprofit dedicated to helping young people who have had serious contact with the legal system avoid further contact while reclaiming forward movement in their lives. The intensive, four-month program involves classroom experience, a paid internship, and immersive prep for various life challenges such as job interviews and regular school days. The majority of Exalt students are referred by professionals within the legal system (probation officers, lawyers, and even policemen) hoping to divert kids from further incarceration. This book observes the challenges of transitioning from juvenile hall back into the outside world through the experience of Ian Alvaro and his Exalt teacher Alex Griffith.

I had prior connections with each of these entities (I also grew up about ten minutes from Ferris School and remember being intimidated playing against its football and basketball teams as a JV player at a nearby private school), which eased the process of obtaining the access and permissions needed to write honestly about the people inside—not that this was remotely easy, just slightly less complicated. I also felt that these programs together formed an expansive view of the national landscape of juvenile incarceration: East Coast and West Coast; short- and long-term imprisonment; small city and large city; the experience of young people and the adults guiding them before, during, and post-incarceration. It would be disingenuous to assert that these places and this work offer a complete representation of juvenile justice in America, but I believe that these pages illuminate a tremendous range of incident and relevance.

Beginning in August of 2019, I spent roughly one week per month at each location. During those weeks, while subject to the limitations inherent to a locked facility, I observed and participated in almost every part of the school day, usually beginning with either yoga or some other form of exercise around 7:00 a.m. and ending in the evening after dinner, when most students began retreating to their rooms and their books and reflections. The vast majority of my time was spent in classrooms: English, math, social studies, and so on.

In early March of 2020, the in-facility research ended abruptly due to the COVID-19 pandemic. I'd spent about seven months working intensively and had been planning on at least five more when everything closed. Over the months that followed, I kept in close touch with teachers and parents via phone and email. I was unable to contact students still in confinement due to technological regulations. Nearly all of these young people were released during the pandemic shutdown, after which we were in touch by phone, Zoom, and in person once again.

Everyone I spent time with was made aware of the purpose of my presence. Every nonpublic person who is named in these pages gave written permission. Those under eighteen during the period of research also provided permission from parents or guardians.

I did not attend individual therapy sessions or family visitations. Certain portions of those intensely private moments were reported to me afterward, with permission of all involved.

I did not record on video or audio any of my experiences inside the facilities (devices were not permitted past security, and I did not want to put undue pressure on staff by requesting a waiver). I relied instead on written notes taken in real time and recorded interviews conducted later.

Reprinting of poems and other student writings has all been done with permission.

Many of those written about here are black, Latinx, and female. They also span generations and socioeconomic classes. These pages detail the human experiences these people entrusted to me—a white male—over hundreds of hours of voluntary sharing, as well as some of the feelings these experiences generated. I know these people well and care about them, but I can't fully understand their interiors and I don't claim to. For this reason, and also out of fundamental respect for the courage required to participate in a project like this, each prominent character has read and expressed comfort with my rendering of his or her story prior to publication.

Some names and identifying details have been changed.

Book I

———————◆———————

Residence

Chapter 1

◆

August 2019

F ROM THE FRONT, the building looked very much like a school: redbrick walls with grooved aluminum roofing painted evergreen, one story high except for the arched gymnasium, an American flag hanging from the tall pole outside the lobby, a short boxwood hedge broken at points by a picnic bench or flower bed. No tall fences wrapped the structure's perimeter, no armed and armored humans safeguarded the doors, no iron bars fortified its windows. The edifice and surroundings were entirely unremarkable, such that an unknowing passerby would have been hard-pressed to identify Ferris School as a secure facility for court-committed male youths—or, colloquially, a juvenile hall.

For almost eleven months that facility had been within view from Josiah Wright's bedroom window. He'd spent most of what would have been his junior year of high school living down the hill from Ferris School in a cluster of low-security residential units called the Cottages. They housed criminally prosecuted juveniles in the state of Delaware deemed unsuitable for probation but not deserving of full detention. The Cottages were over a hundred years old and looked like quaint college dorms, with porticos over the entryways. Inside, Josiah had shared space with a constantly rotating group of twelve other boys. The kids there had, like Josiah, been arrested for property crimes or other nonviolent offenses. They had some degree of autonomy within their highly structured days. They could portion themselves during meals, use the outdoor basketball court, change the channel on the shared TV when they wished, and have monitored access to a closet of books and art supplies. They were being held by the state under the order of the court system, which felt terrible, but that feeling was generally ameliorated by the knowledge that life could be worse: they could be in *jail*. Jail was inside Ferris School, the building up the hill with the green roof that they saw every day but never had to enter.

Josiah was about to enter that building now. Two days after his release from the Cottages, he'd been arrested again. His crime involved serious violence, and so he'd been adjudicated to Ferris School for one year, which would be his eighteenth year on earth.

* * *

AFTER SERVING HIS term in the Cottages, Josiah had been released on probation to his mother's home near downtown Wilmington, Delaware. For a full day, he'd been thrilled to be there. The small bedroom he shared with his younger brother and sister, ages thirteen and nine, respectively, had felt roomy. He took an hour-long shower. He sized himself up in the mirror, still missing the long braids that had been shorn off at the outset of his detainment, exposing his birdishly sharp face. He left his stuff strewn across the floor. He stayed awake texting with friends until three in the morning—his friends regarding him as a conquering hero—and then slept until almost noon. His mother made pancakes and perfectly burnt bacon and, for practically the first time in his imprinted memory, was unconditionally nice to him. The world lay all before him, fresh and washed and free.

By the second day, Josiah began to feel severely unhappy. His mom and siblings complained about the long shower, the stuff on the floor, the late nights and the late mornings. He had to meet with his probation officer accompanied by his mother, who was irritated at having to miss work. The building downtown was grim and crowded, the waiting room filled with irritated mothers missing work. Some probation officers considered themselves counselors or educators, impassioned by the idea of mending fractured childhoods. Josiah was assigned to the other kind, a tired, disinterested older man who seemed a little hungover or just depressed. The man didn't apologize for being forty-five minutes behind schedule, or ask Josiah how he was feeling after such an extended time away from home, or seem concerned with much at all beyond the packet of forms to be signed and the rigid instructions to be given. Josiah had to make his probation meetings every single time and go to school every single day. He could not drink alcohol or smoke weed. He had to be home when random checks occurred. Any truancy or violations would trigger a court review.

"What if someone does a random check and I'm, like, at the store getting something for my mom?" Josiah ventured to ask. "Could there be a fifteen-minute heads-up or something? Could somebody just text me?"

The PO breathed out and smirked at Josiah as if he were just another kid challenging authority, just another kid who wouldn't last long outside. His mother grunted and flicked Josiah in the flank with her knuckles. The whole experience in this building seemed to be transporting her back to the helpless ire that had seized her after Josiah's first arrest a year ago, to the raving question laden with blame that she'd asked aloud more than once: *Why has God afflicted me with this child?*

"Be home for random checks," the PO repeated.

Outside the building, the paperwork finished, Josiah's mother leaned both hands against a random parked car, her purse dangling from her elbow and her head hanging toward the sidewalk. While she took deep breaths, her lips formed words rapidly but made no sound. Though he was outside and wearing street clothes with a fully idle afternoon ahead of him, Josiah was feeling no less confined than he'd felt living in the Cottages. The feeling increased that night when his mother commanded him to watch his younger siblings—whom he'd been thrilled to see at first and had then grown exponentially more annoyed by each minute since—while she went out "with some friends," meaning with a man. Still awake late that night, he listened to her trip inside and stumble around for a time, swearing at herself and at him and at the world. Then he did what every counselor and teacher and therapist in the Cottages had strongly advised him not to do upon release: he copied a few old friends onto a text chain and asked what they were doing tomorrow. The following morning, while his mother slept off her hangover and his siblings played a video game, he simply left without any word as to where he was going, whom with, or how long he expected to be gone. For the first time in a very, very long time, he felt liberated.

Now, three weeks later, the van that had taken him directly from his court date drove past the Cottages. A group of kids idled around a picnic table outside in the muggy August heat. He knew a few of them from his time there, and an innocent part of him wanted to slap his hands against the windows and holler. But his older, harder self—the self that had just been found guilty of property destruction and assault—sat quietly instead and gazed forlornly at their laughing, suntouched faces. He didn't want them to see where he was going. The van drove on up the hill to Ferris School for his intake process. For what had transpired on the day he'd fled his home to hang out with friends, he'd been sentenced to twelve months.

The building looked very different from the rear, where the van dropped him to be escorted inside, than from the quaint front. The walls back here were built from unpainted gray cinder blocks. The concrete formed two wide cylindrical structures that jutted from the main body and were clearly engineered to contain people inside. In a few moments, they would be containing him.

The initial intake was fast but not painless. Josiah was the only new arrival, and he had some familiarity with the procedures. He first had to listen to a lecture regarding what was expected of him and what he should expect. The security staff member who lectured him was a tall black woman with close-cropped hair and a goofy sense of humor. Security staff here were employees of Youth Rehabilitative Services (YRS) and were mainly responsible for keeping order. They wore black uniforms, and no matter how sensitive they were or how meaningful their relationships with the kids, they were still looked at as guards or jailers. This YRS counselor worked in the Cottages as well, so Josiah knew her and liked her. Still, she addressed him formally as "Resident Wright." She seemed unsurprised that he was back so soon.

"I ain't even gonna ask what you did this time because I don't want to know and you're probably not gonna tell me the truth anyway." She looked over his intake sheet for the fourth or fifth time. "Twelve months," she grumbled, reading his sentence and shaking her head. "My goodness, Resident Wright. Just, *why?*"

Josiah shrugged. Over the next year of his life, he was determined to give as little of himself as possible to the system and those helping to run it. He had come here alone and he would survive here alone. He repeated these words to himself over and over.

The YRS counselor was telling him about the disciplinary points system. He already had some knowledge of how it worked, but the rules she described seemed much tighter than they'd been in the Cottages. Each student at Ferris began each day with twenty-five points. Staff members took points away at their own discretion for infractions. Speaking out of turn to an adult was minus three points, swearing or being outside of an assigned area was five points, threatening a peer was ten, threatening an adult was all twenty-five. One could earn points back by cleaning common areas, being particularly engaged in a classroom, and being generally helpful—but only in small chunks of one or two points, and also at staff discretion. The points balance at the end of the day affected how much dessert a person could have, how early he had to be in his room, time permitted in the gym, team sports participation, and other small perks. And the points system was tied to a system of time-outs, in which markedly disruptive kids could be given either five- or thirty-minute time-outs, during which they had to stand alone facing a wall. While the YRS counselor explained all this, Josiah fell into a pattern of alternately nodding his head and grunting, "Mm-hm," even as he ceased listening entirely.

He spent some time in the nurse's office. She weighed him, measured him, and took his blood pressure. It was all routine and non-invasive until she took out a clipboard and began asking him questions. They began rotely enough—"How often do you exercise?" "How many glasses of milk do you drink a day?"—but then segued into the areas of substance abuse and mental health. She asked about alcohol, marijuana, and opioids. She asked if he ever heard voices.

"Yeah, my brain." He was growing angry, and it was overcoming him quickly, and he didn't know why. He felt like a just-lit firecracker that might or might not go off.

"Wright," the counselor uttered sternly as a warning.

"I don't get the question," he said defiantly. "Having thoughts *is* hearing voices."

The nurse checked a box, though he couldn't see which one.

"That was a poor start, Resident Wright," the counselor said to him afterward in the hallway. He was now wearing his Ferris-issued uniform, what everyone referred to as Bob Barkers, for reasons he didn't understand since he had never heard of anyone named Bob Barker. The clothes he would be wearing every day consisted of a maroon cotton T-shirt, khaki slacks made of a slightly stretchy, synthetic, rip-proof fabric, and black Under Armour sneakers, which were actually comfortable. He'd missed dinner, but the counselor had called ahead to have a plate saved for him in the cafeteria. He ate his chicken slices, plain white rice, and slurry of unidentifiable greens alone in the large room.

The din from the adjacent living units—those cinder-block cylinders he'd passed—reverberated through the walls, behind which the current lot of Ferris School residents were having their rec time before lights out. The noise was a general racket punctuated now and again by high-pitched voices trying to land a joke or proclaiming victory in some game or arguing with staff that they didn't do whatever they were in trouble for. Josiah, knowing that he was about to be living in the center of that noise for a long time, tried his best to tune it out and enjoy these last moments of relative quiet. He sat facing the windows that lined the back of the cafeteria. Outside, it was dark beyond the reach of the facility's perimeter lights, and he stared into the blackness and tried to discern shapes outside: a squirrel or bird, maybe, or even just a tree, or anything that signified life existing beyond these rigid, sterile spaces. But Josiah saw only his semi-reflection in the glass.

Then the counselor walked him the thirty feet from the cafeteria to the Hive, which was what most students called the module of the building that contained the sleeping quarters and rec area, due to its rotunda shape. Adults called this space "the cluster." Beneath the domed ceiling, maybe fifteen boys ranging from thirteen to eighteen years old idled in different areas. A checkers game set up on a card table seemed to be causing most of the noise he'd heard. Two kids were reading magazines in big deep chairs (furnished not for comfort, but because they were too heavy to be thrown). Four others sat in the same pose with their arms crossed and their chins to their chests, as if nodding off. The floor was covered in a rubbery material, and Josiah's sneakers made an awful squelching noise on it. The space smelled like over a dozen teenaged boys lived in it.

He already recognized six people—not people he knew well or liked much, but familiar faces from both the Cottages and around his neighborhood. Josiah nodded while purposefully fixing his face into a cold glower. Kids entered juvenile hall in different modes: some casually or even jovially, others angry, some depressed, some eager to join groups and others obsessively guarded of their own space, most seeming bored. The only way no one ever tried to act was scared, even though fear could be the most difficult feeling to hide. Josiah aimed for absolute stoicism.

A few kids greeted him as he passed—"Yo!" "What up?" "I heard you maybe shot somebody?!"—but most met him only with head nods.

He didn't really respond to anyone. His room was up a flight of stairs, toward the end of a walkway overlooking the rec area. He was aware that others below were tracking him. They fixated on anything novel here, anything that signified change. Even a light bulb that had gone out caused some stir. For maybe the next day or two, Josiah represented something new and worthy of attention. That was why, once the thick metal door opened into a space the size of a modest walk-in closet, with a shelf, cot, and narrow vertical slit in the cinder-block wall, he stayed there for the remaining forty-five minutes before lights out.

He sat on the cot and stared at the wall and roughly rubbed his hands down his face over and over. He was angry. And he was scared. And he was also already crushingly bored. And he knew that by tomorrow, his peers here would have all heard that he was beginning a yearlong stint just a few weeks after finishing a yearlong stint. They would give him grief about it and magnify the reality that two years of his childhood would be spent in state care. They would dig hard and deep into his weakest points. So he would need to figure out how not to fight, because being categorized as a fighter at the outset made things hard with the YRS staff and therapists. More important, such behavior made its way back to the judge who had sent him here and would be receiving regular reports of his time here. He would need to control anger and frustration and shame, though he had no training to do so. He sat in the bright, unnatural fluorescence that flooded the stark room. He practiced taking deep breaths. He shuddered involuntarily a few times. Then the lights went out.

*　　*　　*

He curled up tightly when he tried to sleep, and he struggled to ignore the faint, eerie sounds of friction that were a nocturnal fixture here—perhaps made by a rodent in the walls, or someone rustling in his sleep in the grip of a terrible dream in the next room, or a gust of wind outside, or creaks within the joists of an old building, or some incessant skittering within his own soul. Along with shutting out the sounds, he tried to ground his restless sadness, to understand that it didn't belong to him alone, that in this moment in the middle of his first night, he shared it with each kid in the rows and columns of cot-size quarters on either side of him as well as above and below. Maybe he shared it, in the curious elasticity of time in this place, with the boy who had slept on this mattress in this room before he'd been sent here, and the boy who'd slept here before that boy, and the boy who would sleep here after Josiah had left, and the boy who would sleep here after that boy. Maybe they were all lying awake in the same spot at different temporal points, wondering what hour it was, wondering what those wretched vibrations were, wondering when it would be light again, wondering what they had done to be here in this helpless state, wondering what had been done to them. Maybe that shared ordinariness, that signal of his utter inconsequence in the world inside and outside these walls, was the true terror that struck him most potently in the hours before dawn.

*   *   *

JOSIAH HAD A rough time staying awake in class, not only because he could barely sleep at night and the class content seemed built from a middle school curriculum, but because whatever he did or didn't learn within these forty-five-minute blocks did not appear to have any bearing at all on his life. Josiah was contemplating the loss of his childhood due to a few seconds' worth of terrible decision-making. Meanwhile, his juvenile hall English teacher was talking about transition words. Josiah had already oozed forward onto the desktop a few times, angling his head so that the teacher couldn't see his closed eyes. But with only three other students in the class, discretion was impossible. The YRS counselor on duty in the classroom kept waking him up and pleading, "C'mon, man, I don't want to have to take points away." Josiah would grunt back and struggle to sit upright for a minute or two before beginning to sag again. This was the first class of the day and six more were to follow; this was the first day of his confinement with 364 to follow.

He wondered if he was sentenced to spend all of it like this: falling into a daze, being jarred back into the utter mundanity of the present, falling into a daze again . . .

The teacher, a soft-spoken woman in her fifties, was explaining how words such as *although* and *nevertheless* could make a run-on sentence grammatically correct by connecting independent clauses. "Can you think of any other words like this that we would call transition words?" she asked the class generally. No one moved or spoke. Josiah felt his eyelids begin to flutter again. She looked at him. "Resident Wright, can you think of any transition words not listed on the board?"

"I don't really understand these words," he grumbled.

She briefly re-explained what a conjunctive adverb accomplished. "It works kind of like a bridge, if that makes sense."

It didn't, but he scanned the walls, which were covered with various peppy English-themed posters. He'd learned this trick in elementary school: whenever he blanked on a spelling or the use of a certain bit of punctuation, he would search the classroom for an example. After a moment he said, *"However."*

"However—that's a good example. Thank you, Mr. Wright."

About halfway through the English period, another student entered the room. He was of average height but heavy, his hair rolled into floppy twists that fell halfway down his forehead. He walked in a sort of glide. Josiah had not met Resident Bosley yet, but had heard him because Bosley talked incessantly and loudly. All night until the moment the lights were shut off, and then all morning from the moment they clanked on, Bosley was talking. For the most part, he ragged on others for the way they wore their Bob Barkers or for smelling bad or making a lame joke. His voice was at once high-pitched and booming. Josiah could barely stand him.

Bosley immediately looked at his points sheet over the YRS counselor's shoulder as he passed by. His face scrunched in manufactured outrage and confusion as he pointed at the paper before the counselor could quickly flip it over to hide the marks.

"I didn't even do that. I didn't cuss that time. How could I lose points for that?"

"I don't know." The counselor shrugged. This counselor, a heavyset white man in his twenties, was nearing the end of a double shift: sixteen hours overnight, many of those hours spent arguing with teenagers about their point sheets. He was exhausted. "I wasn't in that class. I believe it, though."

"But I didn't!" Bosley pleaded. Self-righteous indignation had rigidified his soft features. "I didn't say shit that whole class! I just listened and worked!"

"Sit down, Mr. Bosley. Or do you want more points off?"

Josiah had been in the building for about twelve hours, and he'd already witnessed about that many arguments over points being taken off. The points system seemed intended to standardize order and punishment across all the various school spaces, to give consistency to the most volatile element of a detention facility: discipline. What it really seemed to do was provide a fixation for boys compulsively searching for reasons to feel wronged.

Bosley made an elaborate performance of raising his hands in submission, walking to his desk, sitting straight, and facing the teacher with his pencil at the ready. But he scowled throughout and couldn't keep himself from adding, "I'm just saying, though, this ain't right. I didn't say any bad words. All I did was tear the sign off the wall." Bosley didn't specify which sign he'd torn down, or why, or how he could feel so resentful for losing points over it.

Bosley wasn't even in this English class. Technically, he was supposed to be earning his science credits. But Ferris didn't offer science classes due to its staffing budget, physical space, and the dangers inherent to the equipment needed, such as heavy textbooks and measuring containers. Those classes were taken via computer. Bosley signed in to the laptop given him, clamped headphones over his ears, and was soon watching episodes of *Wild Kratts*, an animal-centric cartoon aimed at toddlers.

Amid the disruption of Bosley's entrance, Josiah had laid his head down again upon his arms and fallen fully asleep.

*   *   *

THUS FAR IN his childhood, Josiah had witnessed three deaths, two of them murders, the first when he was maybe seven years old. He'd been under the care of some older cousins that day, and they'd left him on the stoop of an unfamiliar row house while they went inside, probably to smoke weed. Josiah had sat there, watching a group of boys and girls across the street, none much older than he, sell drugs. A plain-looking sedan had pulled up, and one of the kids leaned inside it. The others kept talking, laughing, stepping to the music playing from a window overhead. The *crack-crack* resounded like concrete being split by a mallet, and all the kids on the block bolted in different directions, disappearing around corners and down alleys and over fences. The car rumbled away almost casually. The boy who'd been leaning into the car was now on his back on the sidewalk, directly across the street from where Josiah sat, maybe thirty feet away. The boy's arms were extended and his wide-open eyes seemed to peer straight upward even though the sun was blindingly bright overhead. One of his legs was twitching. Gore from his head crept across a slanted sidewalk slab. Josiah felt for a few moments as if he were the only waking human being on the street to witness this other human being's final moments. Then his cousins cautiously emerged and heads began peeking out of windows, and soon the police were there messing around the body. No one ever asked Josiah any questions about what he'd seen.

Six years later, at age thirteen, while playing basketball with friends in Walnut Park, his eyes had happened to be pointing directly at a picnic table on the far side of the park where a car slowed down by a group. Again the stark cracking sounds reverberated and Josiah's gaze had lingered just long enough to see one person's body—a young woman's body—thoroughly lacerated by bullets. Then he and his friends bolted and eventually reenacted the event many times over a pizza, complete with Josiah miming the shooter and his pal playing the role of the woman, convulsing with both the impact of the bullets and his own desensitized laughter.

The other death Josiah had witnessed had not involved the loss of life, but had carried the same irreversible finality. It had taken place the earliest in his life, too, but still resounded. He was four years old when his father left. He didn't remember the man well. Josiah's mother rarely spoke about him except in random, scornful mutterings. Josiah recalled vaguely a presence and a voice. He did remember with some vividness the way his mother had baked him cookies and let him eat as many as he wanted before telling him in an almost chillingly matter-of-fact tone that his father had left. Over the weeks and months that followed, maybe Josiah had asked if the man was ever coming home, and maybe his mother had elaborated on the situation—or not. Josiah didn't hold on to any details around losing his father except the cookies and his mother's demeanor. He later understood that his father had left Delaware completely, which was the same as leaving Josiah's entire universe. But throughout his childhood, whenever he'd seen a man he didn't recognize in the neighborhood (which wasn't often, since he knew most of the men in the neighborhood), he couldn't help wondering if the man could be his father returned home. It never was his father, just as the ghosts people sometimes claimed to have seen of departed loved ones were never real. Over time, he came to treat his fatherlessness—outwardly, anyway—the same way his mother had treated the man's leaving: with a shrug and the occasional bitter, empty aside.

And in frequent meetings with the therapeutic staff during his year in the Cottages, that was still how Josiah treated most instances of loss and lacking in his life: it was just shit that happened where he lived, bad luck that touched a lot of people and had touched him. And it was how he was trying to treat his newly assigned year at Ferris School: shit that happened, bad luck.

*   *   *

"My eyes hurt," murmured a younger student toward the teacher, waking Josiah up again.

"Move closer to the board," she gently prodded. Her accent was pure Delawarean, with its compressed vowel sounds. "Then you won't have to squint."

"No, the back of my eyes." The window facing outside was large but thick and tinted such that the outdoor skies looked perpetually overcast, which exacerbated the brightness of the fluorescent lights within. Eyes were hurting all the time.

"We'll see about getting you a Tylenol or something once class is over."

The boy clenched the upper half of his face tightly and plunked his head facedown on the desk with some force. He grimaced and blurted, "I have to use the bathroom."

"Class is over in ten minutes."

"I'm about to explode, man."

"You've already been twice." The teacher happened to make eye contact with Josiah and casually rolled her eyes as if to say, *See what we deal with?* He, too, was bothered by the whining and couldn't help but smile in some small commiseration.

Bosley paused his video and began plying the YRS counselor for details surrounding the weekend's drama: a minor uprising by students in one of the Cottages. The incident had begun with someone dumping a bottle of water on a stairwell and escalated to a radio summons for "All staff available." The boys locked in the school building had somewhat enjoyed watching from the windows as the men and women tasked with guarding them, not all of the staff in great physical shape, huffed across the wide grass lawns toward the Cottages. Regardless of what had actually transpired, that something out of the ordinary *had* transpired was thrilling.

Josiah was hearing about this incident for the first time. Because he had such a personal connection with the Cottages—which were less than a hundred yards away but somehow felt worlds distant—he woke up fully for the first time all period and listened.

"Was you there?" Bosley asked the counselor.

With a cool pride, the counselor replied, "Yeah, I was there. I was up here and then the call came in and I had to sprint all the way down the hill."

"Was they all fighting?"

"Not by the time I got there."

"But they was fighting before?"

"Yeah. Big-time. I had to put a kid in a headlock." The counselor mimed the hold he'd used.

"Oh, shit."

The teacher snapped her fingers a few times in reference to the lesson: "You know, you guys have to learn this stuff if you're going to earn credits."

Bosley pointed to her simple list of transitional words, eyes now beaming with a sudden indignation. "You act like our life revolves around those words." He pointed to the sheets on the counselor's desk. "Our lives only revolve around points!" He'd spoken in the tone of a peroration, a wise and angered man on a pedestal summating their plight. A long, quiet moment passed.

Then the teacher nodded and agreed in a rare moment of accord. "I know. The point system is horrible. It's reductive. It doesn't even teach you how to add. I'm sorry."

Bosley suddenly slammed his laptop closed, folded his arms on top of it, and laid down his head. "Whatever. I don't even care about school. I'm dropping out when I go home."

"That's a shame. When is that?"

"Probably March."

"Well, it's still September. You got a while in this building. You might as well do something."

From his pillowed position, Bosley grinned. "I do bitches and make dollars."

The two other kids snickered, and Josiah joined them. The teacher met his eyes once more, this time in minor disappointment. *I guess you're just like the rest of them*, she seemed to say now. He was wounded, just ever so slightly. Whatever bit of brain chemistry caused students to desire to please their teachers, Josiah possessed a modest dose of it. But he was also relieved that genuine laughter was possible here.

Bosley opened the computer again and eagerly resumed watching the cartoon scientists morph into exotic animals to outwit the villains. Josiah nodded toward him to get his attention and said, "Yo, my little sister is into that show. She's, like, six." Josiah had subtracted three years from his sister's actual age to make the jab strike harder. But Bosley appeared unaffected: without irony, he grinned and returned a thumbs-up.

*   *   *

THE "EDUCATION" SECTOR of Ferris School composed only a small fraction of the greater residential facility: an L-shaped hallway with five classrooms, a cluster of administrative offices, a kitchen for home ec, and a library. The library was set within the shape's elbow, and the other spaces were organized around it. The library was large, about forty feet square. Three of its walls were windows peering into the surrounding hallways. Against the one solid wall, five bulky shelves contained a couple hundred books. The majority of the space was an open floor surrounded by chairs and was used mainly for visiting speakers and other large group gatherings. This was where Sarah Martin, Ferris's school counselor, conducted many of her student meetings.

More adults worked inside Ferris School than there were kids being detained there. YRS counselors were physically with the boys during both day and night shifts and were involved with every aspect of residential life. Teachers worked fairly regular hours in their classrooms. The sports coach had been leading the various exercise and athletic programs for more than twenty years. Multiple psychologists treated boys individually and led group therapy sessions that might focus on fatherlessness, peer pressure, the concept of restorative justice, and many other complicated areas. A Family Crisis Specialist communicated with parents and guardians regarding different students' challenges and accomplishments inside, and they also worked to ensure a stable living situation upon release. An Education Transition Specialist was responsible for tracking a student's academic credits and placing him in a school program where he could succeed. In the administrative wing, teams of people dealt with the judicial and law enforcement piece of each student's narrative. Others managed public relations. Community liaisons organized visitors, presentations, and enrichment activities. A Pentecostal minister had been coordinating volunteers and generally looking after the boys here for almost forty years. Ferris students were intensively cared for.

Sarah Martin had been working here for a year and three months when Josiah met with her for the first time at the beginning of his second week in Ferris. He recognized her because every single morning she stood at the doorway to the education sector and gave each Ferris student a fist pound as they filed inside for classes. Her job in its heart was to help each boy at Ferris engage with the education he would receive here. For many, the task was natural and relatively smooth. For others, anything involving school was simply a dirge. For a few, the process was brutal. She was in her early forties, with roan-colored hair pulled back in a tight ponytail and the smiley demeanor of a kind, cool aunt. The first thing she noticed about Josiah was how cosmically annoyed he seemed, as if he were dealing with abysmal service at a restaurant.

Josiah had focused his initial days here on projecting a contained, impenetrable front as a defense mechanism against the often-cruel humor of teenaged boys. Behind that armor, he felt fragile, hypersensitive, and wronged. The woman sitting down with him now, with her too-nice smile and laptop computer, seemed to exacerbate this complicated plait of psychologies.

On the other side of the windows, YRS staff were hustling boys up and down the halls into their assigned classrooms with the usual commotion of commands. Josiah believed that they were all staring at him through the glass and snickering. He sat far back from the table as if to track all the passersby, his eyes darting around and glaring through the Plexiglas.

In truth, no one outside the library really registered Josiah's being there, and Ms. Martin resented the space for this illusion of unwanted exposure. Confinement had this effect on nearly all the kids, made them feel as if their movements and behaviors were of extreme significance, or at least curiosity, to everyone around them. As a result self-consciousness pervaded the spaces, in some cases bordering on narcissism, which could make Ms. Martin's job difficult.

"I'm just going to ask a few questions, if that's all right, and you don't have to answer any you don't want to. I'm not writing any of this down. I'm not grading or measuring anything. I don't have any forms and nothing goes back to the judge. This is just get-to-know-you kind of stuff."

"But you don't know me," he said.

"That's sort of the point," she replied.

He lifted his head pointedly. "What do you do here again?"

"I help students keep track of schoolwork and look at different possibilities for when you get out of here."

"I'm not getting out for, like, a year."

"I'm sorry." She seemed earnest. "I can't sugarcoat that. But the more time we have to plan, the better." She then added, "Especially if you're thinking about college."

"College?" Josiah made an abrupt cackling noise, followed by a dismissive *pshaa*.

Ms. Martin asked about any brothers or sisters he had, and what his favorite sport was, and what his favorite subject was at school. She had all his background paperwork and high school transcripts furnished by the school's Transition Specialist.

They entered a tepid back-and-forth. Josiah had gauged this woman as nice enough and decided that she wasn't aiming to exploit him or fool him in some way. Without dropping his veneer of childish irritation, he indulged her questions with one-word, often one-syllable answers. But the interchange still qualified as a dialogue, and that was Ms. Martin's primary goal for the meeting. Her secondary goal was to see if she could draw a smile. She felt that she might have come close a few times.

A part of Josiah's consciousness had always desired to be a good student and progress quietly through the milestones of youth and not trouble anyone. A different part of him had come to believe that the world and most of the people in it were conspiring to get one over on him, that this was happening constantly and invisibly within even the most innocuous interactions, that he would be doomed by it if he didn't combat it. The latter sector had been governing his actions for a while now, making any engagement with this teacher seem like a question of integrity.

Josiah suddenly pronounced himself exhausted and laid his head on the table, eyes closed. Ms. Martin let him feign sleep for a while. He seemed all right. She guessed that he was not nearly as hard as he depicted himself to be, and that he knew he wasn't, and that this knowledge caused him to invest even more effort in the facade. This negative feedback loop operated within many, many boys here at Ferris. It operated within some boys at her previous job at a private Christian high school. It operated, she guessed, within boys all over America. Yet each individual boy believed his particular brand of severity to be unique, and she'd learned to treat each as if that belief were true.

Ms. Martin regained his attention by pulling a Myers-Briggs personality test onto her laptop screen. The short questionnaire was a useful icebreaker for her purposes, and its modest measure of self-reflection helped set a positive tone for their work moving forward. She explained that the test was unofficial and for him alone; he did not have to bother with it if he didn't want to. But Josiah was intrigued.

He'd been evaluated many times by therapists, and they tended to ask repetitive questions and then keep their reports to themselves. The idea of generating his own report felt like a nifty curiosity. That he whisked through the test in less than fifteen minutes told Ms. Martin that he possessed some ability to focus on a task, and also that he was literate.

Once finished, he leaned back, stretched his arms, and ran his hands down his face. He groaned as if a tremendous chore had just been completed. He cracked a number of knuckles in his fingers and waited for her to strike the key that would tally the results.

"You said you weren't giving me any tests?"

She appeared uncomfortable for a moment, as if he'd truly caught her in a wrong. "You're right," she finally said. "I see how it feels to you like I tried to trick you. I'm sorry. I just thought this would be sort of fun. It's like an internet quiz."

He appreciated the way she'd admitted her error without dispute. Adults didn't generally do that.

She pressed the Return button and the program instantaneously categorized Josiah as INFJ: introverted, intuitive, feeling, judging. He had no idea what any of the components meant. "Did I do good?"

"It's not a good-or-bad sort of test. I'd have to check, but I think this is, like, one of the rarest personality types out of all of them."

"Is that good though?"

He eagerly listened to her read a description of his designation from her thumbnail sheet: " 'Advocates read others well and easily see behind the mask that people unconsciously wear. Ironically, however, INFJs may struggle to understand themselves. Their reactions and behavior sometimes confuse even their own sharp intuition.' " She looked up at him. Once again he'd fallen into a silent, peevish pose. "Does any of this sound like it describes you?"

He shrugged, which was his typical auto-response—but then he thought for a few seconds and offered a tentative nod. "It does, a little."

"These are not one hundred percent accurate; they're just supposed to make people think a little bit about themselves. Sometimes, they're a little silly."

"It sounds kind of right," he said with a new and sudden surety. "I really don't understand myself a lot of the time."

Chapter 2

◆

October 2019

HISTORICALLY, JUVENILE JUSTICE systems have been designed and managed on the state level, but the fundamental sequence of becoming entangled in these systems has remained fairly constant across America in the recent past: seven distinct points of legal contact, the cascading of which could transport any child like Josiah Wright from home to jail.

The first legal contact was most often with police on the street or in school, where resource officers were common in low-income, urban neighborhoods. Whatever the behavior was that drew police attention—a drug exchange, a fight, being black and hanging out with friends, or (statistically most likely) a property crime—the officer had to decide if it merited an arrest.

In the event of an arrest, the second contact was the booking process: police at the station chose whether to detain the arrestee or instead attempt to release him or her to a guardian.

If the person was detained, then the striking of the computer keys that logged the arrest as an official case in the judicial system was the third contact.

The fourth contact involved probation officers and juvenile court attorneys, who decided whether a trial ought to commence or if the youth in question—and society at large—would be better served by diversion into a community-service or treatment program.

If the case moved toward a trial, the fifth contact occurred when a county attorney chose whether to file a petition—meaning, to prosecute the youth formally—or again opt for a path of diversion.

At this moment, a corollary decision needed to be made regarding the offender's placement throughout the legal process. If the youth was considered a danger to society or if no parent or guardian was willing to provide care, then the youth spent this time in an interim confinement facility. This was the sixth contact.

These lead-up processes could take a few days or a few months, and if each decision along the way culminated in a hearing before a judge, then this adjudication itself might last a few minutes. During those minutes—the seventh and final legal contact in the modern juvenile court—a judge reviewed a summary of all the information compiled regarding the reason for the arrest, the offender's history and family situation, and the general threat or lack thereof the young person represented. The judge then decided either to dismiss charges, release the youth into probation, or send the youth to confinement.

The entire current system, with all of its various opportunities for diversion or dismissal, was somewhat designed to avoid a trial and sentencing. The contact involved a binary yes/no decision of whether the youth should be shuffled closer to a jail sentence or provided nonpunitive resources. Each possession of money for fees and penalties, direct parental support, and professional legal advocacy all helped tip any one of those decisions toward clemency. The lack of those three commodities, plus centuries of racism and classism in America, explained why, in any given juvenile hall, virtually every detainee was poor. Within cities and diverse communities, virtually every detainee was a person of color. In this vital systemic sense, precious little has changed in this land's juvenile halls over the past thirty years.

However, much has changed on other important fronts. Over the past decade, roughly 1 million minors have been arrested in America per year, and any single day found around 30,000 of them locked up in secure placement facilities. The high turnover within such facilities meant that in the modern era some 150,000 young people spent time in jail, even if only for an afternoon, in the span of a year.

That number represented a halving of the youth incarceration levels recorded during the waning days of the "tough on crime" movement in the late 1990s. Nationwide, detainments of youth for nontrafficking drug offenses and status violations have been steadily falling. Average lengths of detainment have shortened significantly. More options have been made available to juvenile offenders across the spectrum of residential and treatment services. In general within physical juvenile facilities, there are year by year fewer locks and practices of solitary confinement along with more mental health professionals and extracurricular activities. The focus has increasingly been placed on school accreditation and oversight in transitioning from incarceration back into the school system following release. Throughout the American juvenile justice landscape, mattresses have become a little softer, libraries a little more stocked, food a little more nourishing, time served a little less dreadful on the edges. Yoga classes and restorative justice seminars have been a burgeoning trend in juvie.

The overarching goal of all changes in treatment and accommodation has been to reduce the recidivism rate among incarcerated American youth. In any era or year, this one statistic has always been absolutely paramount, signifying the effectiveness of a given system in a given place and time.

Judging by this simple metric, the systems that had never worked well were still not working well in this increasingly progressive era. Though no comprehensive national recidivism database existed, the aggregate local numbers suggested that despite improving conditions and programs, children were still far more likely than adults to be re-incarcerated within three years of release—up to 84 percent by some estimates. The figure was harrowing, especially in contrast with the far rosier outcome numbers for juvenile arrestees who were put directly on probation or sent to drug treatment facilities or diverted by other routes from the full weight of the justice system. The disparity in these numbers spoke to some near-universal breakage of spirit that occurred within young people the moment they were confined in *residence*, which was one of the myriad terms used in juvenile courts to leaven the term's actual meaning: prison. Whatever resilience that children inherently possessed seemed to vanish the moment a dead bolt fastened loudly behind them. Whatever national ethos championing the notion of self-determination that still presided over the country's educational systems became irrelevant.

Entering a juvenile hall was statistically dooming. While juvenile records legally expired at age eighteen (or a certain number of years after one's last offense, depending on the state), the unlikelihood of a juvie resident ever fully unshackling him- or herself from the justice system was writ in the grim outcomes of nearly all who'd been incarcerated before, predating the nation's founding. These outcomes had little to do with food quality or exercise. They were a testament to the way that life-affirming essences such as hope and perseverance didn't just retreat within young souls in small rooms behind locked doors, but ceased to operate entirely.

For many, this loss had begun long before any police officers or judges had made decisions regarding the rest of their various lives. Every kid in juvenile hall had a story to tell, and most of these stories involved deep histories of neglect, trauma, hunger, abuse, addiction, loss, isolation. Few kids told these stories willingly because there was no point in trying to untangle the mechanisms of cause and effect, in relating the challenges they'd experienced to the laws they'd decided to break. Drawing those lines was too complicated and didn't change that they'd officially been deemed dangerous to a society that had long since grown numb to blanket terms such as *poverty*, *drugs*, and *gangs*. Self-analysis also made them look weak and whiny in an environment where posturing was vital. Looking inward was depressing on its face and mattered little within the mechanics of jail sentences.

The kids' only collective choice, which wasn't a choice at all—which was the opposite of choice—was to serve the time assigned to them. Whether they did so passively or rebelliously, the time itself was unyielding. They served this time within a system in which black youths were represented fivefold more than their percentage of the overall population—tenfold in some cities—and in which two-thirds of inmates had not actually received a formal judgment from the court of guilt, and in which countless other absurdities abounded. The system had been redesigned dozens of times over hundreds of years and always produced the same, relentless results.

In that system, all the chaotic chemistries of adolescence were exacerbated. Unexpended physical energy was pent up and roiling. Stress levels were always, always high. The oppositional forces that perpetually stood between adults and children—between one group of people telling another group of people what to do—were at a constant point of combustion. Tempers flared, reason dissolved, mistakes were made—on all sides, all the time. Most minutes inside were objectively hard minutes.

An average American driving past a juvenile hall en route to work most likely saw an intentionally featureless, low-rise concrete structure with tinted windows set a ways back from the road, adjacent to some outdoor space surrounded by tall fencing, maybe topped with barbed wire, maybe not. If such a person registered this place at all, he or she might simply think, *That's the place where bad kids go*, and drive on.

*   *   *

THE WEATHER WASN'T great for a football game: humid and sticky, the sunlight glaring from directly overhead, gnats swarming eyes and nostrils. And the game itself wasn't much fun to watch with its wobbly passes, dropped balls, and poor tackling. Yet the players who'd gathered on their knees for a halftime huddle in their bright red jerseys watched their gesticulating coach with a rigid intensity. Their coach was a large man flinging sweat beads from his dark-skinned bald head as he swatted his arms and uttered the hallmarks of most any high school football huddle: remember technique, take it one play at a time, don't look at the scoreboard. The ultimate command was essential, as Ferris School was losing by twenty-four points at the half.

From the perspective of onlookers watching from a distance outside the fifteen-foot-tall fence that fully enclosed the field, the score differential didn't seem as if it should matter much to the Ferris School players, who were fortunate that other schools were willing to play a team of juvenile delinquents in a game such as football. (Ferris School teams were only permitted to compete against the JV teams of other schools, who had to volunteer to come, gather liability forms from parents, pass through metal detectors, et cetera.) For Josiah Wright, standing on the fringe of the huddle, the game was high stakes and fairly terrifying, even though he'd spent most of the first half watching on the sidelines because he was both new to the team and lousy at football.

The collisions did not frighten him; contact in this level of play was not all that violent, and he'd gotten his head smashed many times in harder, meaner ways throughout childhood. What scared him was the prospect of making mistakes. This game contained two kinds of mistakes, as Josiah saw it. There were the hidden variety, such as missed blocks or poor reads, which those spectating and even those playing in the game wouldn't necessarily notice. And there were the mistakes that totally exposed you, such as fumbling the ball or whiffing on an open-field tackle. People saw those plays and remembered them. The errors trailed you for days or weeks or potentially the entire length of an incarceration. If egregious enough, they could come to define you. He'd joined the team mainly to gain a few extra hours outside per week. But he'd never before played organized football, had yet to learn the scheme, and was quite content on the sideline.

As the halftime break ended, the coach told him to be ready to enter the game during the second half, but Josiah didn't believe him. So Josiah was startled when, just a few seconds into resumed play, Coach hollered his name and frantically gestured toward the field. Josiah didn't even hear what position he was supposed to fill. He lined up at wide receiver, as far away from the ball as he could while still remaining in bounds.

When he heard the shout "Hike!" he ran about ten steps straight ahead and stopped in time to see a pass land in the vicinity of no one. He trotted back to the huddle looking confused.

Bosley suddenly lunged in front of him, vised Josiah's helmet between his hands, and screamed, "Man! You were supposed to break toward the middle of the field!"

"How was I supposed to know that?" Josiah said defensively.

"You listen to the fucking play calls!"

"I couldn't hear anything! I was all the way over there!"

"Holy shit, are you stupid?" Bosley's eyes were shocked wide within his helmet. One cheek was caked with dirt. Spit sprayed from his mouth when he exhaled. He clenched his fingers around his face mask and groaned the way Josiah's mother did when she considered him a hopeless case. Others on the team were now yelling at both of them because they were delaying the huddle. Josiah felt his fists clench involuntarily, and his teeth bit hard into the rubber mouth guard. He was a few inches taller than Bosley but weighed probably fifty pounds less. Regardless of size differentials, he did not like anyone being this close or using a certain tone with him. He did not like the feeling of others staring at him expectantly for a reaction. He felt rage. Coach promptly pulled Bosley from the game. The next few plays were runs for other players, and Josiah was able to take deep breaths and calm himself from his place away from the action.

He watched Coach lecturing Bosley on the sideline, Bosley pleading his case, Coach hearing none of it. Bosley moved behind the bench and began stomping in circles and shadowboxing the air around him. Teammates gave him ample space, leaving the boy alone to his furious antics. Gradually, his energy seemed to fade, and soon he was just standing there, slumped, staring at the ground.

The ball came Josiah's way once more, but this time the quarterback told him beforehand where he should be. He almost got his hands around it, but he was a step slow and the ball plunked on the ground, a turnover on downs. As mistakes went, Josiah figured that this one wouldn't count as mortifying, just a matter of a few inches. The problem was that he was unaccustomed to pads, and his arms were long relative to the rest of him. When sprinting, they tended to flail sidewise and throw him off-balance. Even though he was athletic looking, he was slow when running in a straight line. Jogging back to the huddle, Josiah slapped his hands against his helmet a few times in a show of disappointment.

Bosley had been permitted to return, having finally emerged from his tantrum. Although Josiah steeled himself for some derisive comment, Bosley had suddenly become—in a jagged behavioral swing that would grow familiar over time—the most encouraging and positive teammate imaginable. He grabbed Josiah by the shoulder pads, stared directly into his eyes, said, "You got the next one, boy!" and crashed their helmets together.

Josiah was confused, but nodded seriously. "We got this, bro."

By the end of the third quarter, Ferris was losing by three touchdowns to a team composed mostly of high school freshmen. Bosley continued to act as a paradigm of positivity, but rebounding from adversity on the field was an emotional skill that Ferris School students collectively lacked. The more lopsided the score became, the more disrespectful and lazy the team as a whole acted. Coach called a time-out and exhorted them all to value their own dignity and—more important—the game's. They gave some slight effort in response. But the effort seemed to cost them.

These boys were playing football in the context of hard, unforgiving American lives. So the fate of a leather obloid in a football game against a JV opponent did not intuitively seem that it should carry much in the way of physical or emotional investment. Losing by many points to a more polished team who practiced every day (Ferris practiced maybe three times during a good week, but sports were the first privilege taken away as a consequence of disciplinary infractions, which were constant) didn't seem as if it should or would matter much in the great scheme of their lives. A missed call by the sideline referee didn't appear, from a reasoned perspective, like a matter worthy of deep passion—not when the boys were outside in the grass playing a game instead of inside their concrete living space serving real time. But in reality, being crushed by a visiting team in some way magnified how crushing their lives were, and the Ferris players crumbled easily. Sports were in some ways meant to be an equalizer, a venue in which kids such as those locked in Ferris could assert themselves as talented, capable, worthy people. But sometimes, as today, the prevailing feeling was despondency.

Josiah had a chance late in the game to show a glimpse of something special. He was tired, sodden with sweat, and itchy with dirt, but somehow a play found him sprinting down the sideline beneath a well-thrown ball. The other team had begun rotating second-string players in, and Josiah had left the young kid guarding him far behind. The pure power of his body had seized him, and his heart was bounding as the air fled past. He felt the way he always had when running away from a minor crime, such as stealing from a convenience store or defacing a wall or fighting someone outside school, and the entire meaning of existence and of freedom was reduced to the work of bone and tissue and nerves. The physics of the football play had aligned for him to make an easy, spectacular-looking score. Unfortunately for him, he was all too aware that this was the case, and during those elegant instants while the floating ball and his running body converged, his brain preoccupied itself with all the various disasters that could occur. On the other side of the field, someone shouted, "Wriiiiiiiiight!" The worst version of such a disaster followed: the ball hit him right in the hands and bounced upward, then was easily intercepted by the other team's safety. Discombobulated, Josiah tripped and fell out of bounds while the other player began running in the other direction toward Ferris's end zone. On the ground, surrounded by the other team's players along the sideline, he weakly raised his head and peered over his shoulder.

The ballcarrier zigged and zagged and seemed to have a clear path to score. Then a red Ferris jersey closed some distance. It was Bosley, with his waddling run and his fixed, serious scowl behind his face mask.

Bosley managed to tackle the smaller, fleeter kid a few ya
goal line. There was no collision; Bosley swatted the r
just hard enough to trip him. But still he stood and took
ated, stomping steps, celebrating himself and eliciting hig.. ..ves. josiah
slowly arose and jogged in that direction. His hands were planted on the
sides of his helmet and his head was shaking in shame. Teammates murmured, "It's all good" and "He just got lucky." Josiah continued staring
at the ground. He barely put forth any effort on the next play, and Coach
pulled him from the game.

For the last few minutes, Josiah stood alone and moped and watched
Bosley play ferociously. He wondered how Bosley could do that: ex-
pend so much effort at the end of such a lopsided contest. Josiah quickly
guessed that Bosley was no longer thinking about wins and losses. For
the rest of the day, wherever Bosley was, he was a prisoner of the state
of Delaware and subject to the rules and wills of others. In this hour, in
the circle of torn grass about a yard in diameter around his body, he was
a football player capable of asserting his own rules and his own will. A
shimmer seemed to surround his body across the field, something like
pride or maybe even joy. Josiah felt envy pressing in at the edges.

Ferris lost by a lot. But the field was nice. The sound of helmets col-
liding was satisfying. Bursts of exciting play brought the few spectators—
the other team's parents, Ferris teachers, a couple employees at the
Department of Services for Children, Youth & Their Families building
up the hill—to applaud for both sides. The dirt streaks across jerseys
and clumps of earth wedged in helmets and faintly crimson abrasions
across elbows and shins were all valuable, hard-earned marks that the
boys briefly carried, at least until they cleaned up the field and replaced
divots in the grass and streamed inside at the juncture where the door-
less metal fencing structure met the cinder-block walls on either side of
the school's side entrance.

Someone's supportive mom stood outside this section of the fence.
She called, "You played great, guys." She clearly knew little about football or what constituted great play.

"We got killed, man," a student muttered through his face mask.

"Well, that was a pretty good team," she persisted.

"They sucked! That was their JV!"

"They looked pretty good to me." She seemed to run out of white lies and stepped away from the fence.

The team filed inside. After leaving their pads and helmets in a gigantic crate in the hallway, the boys returned to their cluster units. They were given a limited number of minutes to shower and change back into their monotone T-shirts. State law required that they bandage even minor cuts and scrapes, but most kids attempted to hide their freshly forming scabs beneath their clothes untreated, maybe as a signal of masculinity. The YRS counselors knew this ruse and conducted a surprise "elbow/knee check," handing out Band-Aids down the line.

Afterward, another dull evening unfolded in the cluster with some card games, some PG-rated freestyle rapping, and some staring out of windows until the sky darkened and Josiah couldn't see anything. He'd anticipated a stream of negativity about his dropped pass, but no one seemed to be dwelling on the game—no one except Bosley, who walked around with a pronounced limp that had not been at all evident on the field. He made a few laps around the cluster to ensure that security staff and friends saw him hobbling. When any of them asked how he'd hurt himself, Bosley shrugged and shook his head, as if he were far too tough to be bothered with describing his injury to people. Then he launched into an acutely detailed, heroic narrative.

"There were two of them blocking me after that pick, but I knew if I didn't get the tackle, they were going to score because no one else was around, so I did a spin move around one, and then I threw the other one down—that was when his whole body weight landed on my ankle. I might of heard something snap in there, but I got my arm wrapped around the runner and got him down anyway. Coach wanted me to see a doctor about this, but, whatever, I just ignored how bad it was hurting. . . ." He shrugged again and motioned down at his gimpy leg, taking a ginger step toward the stairway to his room.

"That didn't even happen, Bosley!" a teammate said, calling him out with near glee. "Like, *no part* of what you just said actually happened."

Bosley scowled. He had highly expressive eyebrows: when raised, he could project layers of empathy; when lowered, no one he looked at seemed to possess any more value than lint. Now he kept his eyebrows low. "You didn't see it because you were probably on the sideline bitching to Coach about your asthma or some shit!"

Josiah blurted, "I saw that play, it was pretty much how he said."

"I believe you was watching the play—because you definitely weren't watching the ball!" The kid walked away, shaking his head and cackling.

Bosley nodded toward Josiah with an expression faintly resembling gratitude, possibly approaching respect. Then Bosley declared that he needed to take weight off his ankle, and he slowly pulled himself up the stairs to his room. Josiah went to his room as well and paged through comic books for a time until the warning for lights out sounded. He steeled himself for the long, lonely, dreadful hours ahead. He lay there and did some rough math and figured that he had 346 more nights' worth of them remaining, or upward of three thousand more total night hours in jail. Then he fell into a pattern of envisioning that football spiraling down just ahead of him and plucking it effortlessly from the air and coasting ahead, trailed by celebrating teammates. He wasn't sure when the vision segued into an actual dream, but in the dream he didn't stop running at the end of the field. With the football firmly tucked, he kept going, easily hurdling the fence and making it down the hill in a few loping strides, hurdling again across the busy street, over the rooftops, bounding into the expanse in his bright red uniform, not even heading toward home but simply vanishing free into the dusky light.

* * *

HIS MOTHER WAS a fantastic baker. The pans and trays she pulled from the oven on her days off from work filled most of his earliest memories. Crumbles, tarts, all kinds of cupcakes and loaves: her repertoire was vast, and she seemed to derive immense, earnest joy from watching her confections please others. The feeling might have been greater than joy; Josiah had always thought that whenever she was serving guests, she appeared unencumbered in her soul. Their kitchen was small, just a slit in the wall of the hallway, and between her many jobs and many boyfriends, which both consumed chaotic hours both night and day, she didn't have too much time for her hobby. Josiah had never learned to bake himself because she had neither space for him to apprentice nor patience for the errors and messes that teaching a child this craft entailed. That time belonged to her.

His vague understanding was that his mother had become estranged from her parents due to her relationship with his father. He'd met his grandparents many times at family events, and they'd always been warm to him, but with an edginess. His younger siblings had a different father, who had been nice enough while he was around, and who still visited and took them out frequently. Josiah had no part in their connection aside from envying it. Otherwise, his mother's many other boyfriends had varying degrees of involvement with Josiah's life. Some just treated him with head nods and grunts in passing. Others had attempted to play basketball with him or take him to a minor league baseball game with the Wilmington Blue Rocks at the nearby riverside stadium. None were too interested in him. All disappeared eventually and left his mother angry.

She was always working, and for the most part he was thankful for that. He'd only had to move homes once in his life, when his father left. Otherwise, he'd grown up in the same row house in a neighborhood southwest of downtown Wilmington called Browntown, named after a humanitarian doctor who had resided in the area during the mid-1800s. The home had two narrow floors and felt too small most of the time. I-95, the roaring mid-Atlantic corridor and an ugly hulk of infrastructure, was two blocks away. But the street itself was pleasant, with shade trees and not much traffic. Compared to the streets just a few blocks north and east, where front doors opened directly onto sidewalks crowded with loiterers, his was a relatively peaceful place to live. The home was the only stability he had. Though his mother was constantly employed, she was always changing jobs and shifts: restaurants, salons, warehouses, retail stores. Sometimes she was fired, but usually she quit. He'd asked her a few times why she changed jobs so often and so randomly. She'd always replied with some superficial metaphor for how easily she grew bored. Yet he always had a feeling that she possessed some deeper unrest, or perhaps discontent, that rendered her unable to do the same task or be around the same people for long. The same felt true of the men in and out of her life, though he understood how that was complicated. The feeling had always made Josiah insecure, as if her flightiness might also apply to her home and children, and he might wake up one morning to find that she'd simply tired of him and left on a whim. Even though she never had, he wasn't confident that she never would. She wasn't physically present much, regardless.

He was quiet and school suited him well. For eight hours a day, he could sit and listen and do what he was told. The subjects were not always interesting, and the people teaching those subjects were not always skilled at explaining them clearly. The classrooms were typically louder than they should have been, and kids razzed him regularly because he was shy.

Josiah's daydreaming mind was incredibly active. The sounds and images it cast on the projector screen of his imagination carried him through a decade of school. He would hear the lesson about partial quotients or the American Civil War, and he was present enough to take notes, but behind those motions he was often enacting epic dramas in which he and his friends would have to defend their homes or mothers or (imaginary) girlfriends against some assaulting force—corrupt police, maybe, or local gangs or fast-moving zombies. In these mental set pieces, the character "Josiah" typically began as the sullen and obedient follower of his more gregarious friends. As the action intensified, he proved himself decisive and powerful. Sometimes his father would be there. The young, handsome, bearded face he knew from his earliest memories was personified not as someone who'd left but someone who'd been forcibly taken—by the cops, the gangs, the zombies—and returned at great risk to help his son in conflict. By the end, Josiah and his father were either the last survivors of their crew or else had both died saving loved ones, or else one of them, usually but not always Josiah, had sacrificed himself so that the other could carry on. These sequences played on repeat within Josiah, more or less all day.

Historically, the fantasies had often ended with him breaking his father or a friend out of jail, where he'd unjustly been placed. They'd never ended with Josiah in jail. And he could never have fathomed how thoroughly uncinematic jail was.

In his therapy sessions at Ferris, Josiah did not mention his active interior life, because it made him feel like a child. If he had, the school psychologists might have asked him what purpose that interior life served, what insecurity it ministered, what pain it helped him avoid. They also might have reminded him that he was a child—that despite growing up black, male, poor, and fatherless in a rough city, he was very much still a child—and that generating rich, grand fictions was not unhealthy or a reason to feel self-conscious. They might have assured him that dreaming of a different life in a different place was a completely normal component of growing up.

Chapter 3

◆

November 2019

A 2014 NEWSWEEK profile dubbed the city of Wilmington, Delaware, where Ferris was located, "Murder Town USA" and the nickname stuck.

The city lay between Philadelphia and Baltimore and was home to roughly 75,000 people. Its history was tightly entwined with gunpowder and debt, which were also often the two operative factors in violent crime. The DuPont Company was founded in the early 1800s, in a row of mills along the Brandywine River, and supplied fully half of the Union's powder during the Civil War (Delaware, a slave-owning state, sided with the North during the conflict, though the sympathies of many residing in its rural southern counties lay with the Confederacy, a cultural split that has somewhat persisted through present-day politics). Over the following era, those mills along the riverbank became a sprawling chemical station rising up the steep sides of the river valley. The company invented Teflon, Kevlar, pigments and dyes, pharmaceuticals. For generations, DuPont was the second-largest employer in the state of Delaware, behind the state of Delaware. The DuPont family became one of the richest in the world.

A DuPont was the governor of Delaware when the state passed the Financial Center Development Act in 1981. Drafted by banking lobbyists and then passed in a famously secretive statehouse debate, the law essentially cemented low taxes while removing limits to the interest rates banks could charge and export nationwide. The Wilmington economy had failed to recover from the recession of the mid-1970s, its population was rapidly declining, and the new law was an attempt to reinvent the city's economic engine by drawing financial companies, their office towers, their employees, and their expendable cash. The gambit was tremendously successful: within a few years Chase, JPMorgan, Discover, Barclays, Citibank, Bank of America, and fully half of the nation's credit card issuers had filed their charters in Delaware, home to less than a million American residents. The era of mass-mailed credit card offers with Delaware return addresses began in earnest.

New residents came: middle-, upper-middle-, and upper-class people who worked in these buildings or catered to those who did. The city boomed economically in the eighties and thereafter. And in keeping with the machinations of modern American free markets, disparity became entrenched. The broad story resembles that of many American cities: suburbs sprawled outward into the surrounding townships while established urban districts—in Wilmington's case, the east side of downtown—suffered stagnation and neglect plus division by freeways; the generational wealth passed on through property ownership remained a commodity of the established upper class; school-funding structures tied to local property taxes generated deep educational imbalances between public schools often less than a mile apart, demarcated by district boundaries that were drawn during the blatantly discriminatory past and thrown into upheaval by busing and, more recently, charter schools. The complexity of the history is evident in the simplicity of numbers: between 1980 and 2020, the city's median income, adjusted for inflation, tripled. During that same time, the percentage of residents living below the poverty line remained constant at 25 percent. Concurrently, while violent crime and particularly murder rates fell by half nationwide, the numbers in Wilmington were also unmoving at over four times the national average. The high school dropout rate was usually around 60 percent.

Of the city's population under the age of eighteen, almost half lived in poverty, mostly in a handful of neighborhoods. A certain number of this half—including Josiah Wright of Browntown—added to these crime rates and became subject to legal judgments not only of their unique decisions but also of the vast sweep of the small city in which, by chance of birth or tides of commerce, they lived. These kids were enlisted in community service, they went on probation, they went to group homes, or they went to Ferris School.

At Ferris School, students hailing from Wilmington had their own nickname for their hometown: Killmington, Hellaware.

* * *

MIDWAY THROUGH AUTUMN, the students as a whole were on edge: a little louder and a little quicker to react angrily when chided for it. Their collective short fuse caused the adults tasked with watching and teaching them to be anxious as well, because they knew that any seemingly innocuous interaction could escalate toward conflict. Conflict was bad for everyone; it meant not only punishments for the children but administrative reviews for the adults. The source of unrest was clear: eleven students, or just over a third of the total number at the facility, had been released on the same day in the beginning of November. (Release dates often overlapped because the juvenile court system scheduled hearings in batches and most sentences to Ferris School were cast in three-month increments.) Ten years earlier, when Ferris had been at capacity with over seventy students incarcerated, the simultaneous departure of eleven of them would not have registered significantly. Now, with twenty-nine students, the loss of eleven promised to alter most every dynamic in the school.

The exodus had been looming for a few weeks, first as the subject of some light comedy—"This school's gonna go to hell without us here to manage the place"—and then as a spark for whimsical talk of the dichotomy between life inside and life outside, with references to girls the soon-to-be-released would call, food they would eat, money they would make, business empires they would found. Envy stirred in Josiah and others like him who were still more or less at the outset of their terms. Observing the bright anticipation on his classmates' faces, the way kids who had been acting fully depressed suddenly became prancing comedians, he felt somehow even more strictly confined. And he felt angry, as if the departing group had somehow rigged the system even as he knew that they'd simply committed their crimes months before he had.

In the days immediately before the emptying, kids referenced the change less often but seemed to experience its imminent effects more deeply. The football quarterback was leaving. A couple classroom jokers were leaving. An entertainingly spazzy kid was leaving. The overweight kid who spoke only of food was leaving (chili days made him moody; chicken-nugget days made him dance). The clingy fourteen-year-old with the squeaky voice who was everyone's annoying little brother was leaving. Many different personalities carrying many different forms of energy were leaving. Most of them had irked Josiah multiple times since his arrival, and he'd silently wished them gone. How absolutely strange it was, then, for him to realize that he would miss them—not just their dispositions and peanut-gallery comments, but their physical bodies, the space they displaced in the hallways, the occupied desks in class. Ferris was a sad place to live, and it became sadder the hollower it was. With fewer students, the illusion that they were just kids in school—which was already a shoddy construction— thinned in direct proportion.

That realization held a contradiction. As a teacher or YRS counselor or peer, one wanted kids to leave state care—to leave and thrive and not come back. Few would actually thrive, and a certain number would most definitely return. A latent, shared understanding pooled around beneath the surface of all these comings and goings: that while kids were here, as miserable as here could sometimes be, they were safe from others and from themselves. They were taught and coached and tested and looked after, even if they acidly resented most all of those doing the teaching and coaching and testing and looking after. Outside, the majority of them were on their own, and the worlds they returned to were threatening, the opportunities sparse.

In a way, the departure of those eleven boys emphasized everyone's vulnerability. At Ferris School, vulnerability tended to manifest not as a form of therapeutic catharsis but as a taut, complicated tension permeating every interaction—hence the general unease.

When the day arrived and they all left, some of that unease departed with them, but some also remained fixed in the less populated hallways and classrooms. The remaining students contended with how, despite all the anticipation, nothing had changed. There had been twenty-nine boys in school, and now there were eighteen. The number would rise again as new intakes arrived over the coming weeks. The toil and boredom and inanity would be the same as ever.

Which was why Josiah watched with rapt attention as a boy they called Little Axell began losing his shit in life skills class.

Life skills came mostly from the mind of Mr. Michels, a teacher with a trim beard whom most students considered to be the zaniest character in school, young or old. He was not in fact a zany person—he approached his job quite seriously and thoughtfully—but he felt that many of his students rarely encountered adult men in their outside lives who were self-deprecating and lighthearted. So, while teaching lessons about the behaviors required to hold a stable job and lead a fulfilling existence, Mr. Michels gesticulated constantly and used weird voices and was passionately, sometimes rashly honest. Today, in light of the recent student turnover, he was talking about time and the ways it could be either utilized or wasted, referring to his own past life as an alcoholic for context.

"That was me," Mr. Michels said while he mimed slamming back a shot of hard liquor. "Every night, for many years. Sleeping very happily through my days and then getting ripped in the basement. Didn't care that my boss hated me and wanted to fire me, which she eventually did. Didn't care that my wife wanted to leave, which thankfully she never did. I was just wasting time, wasting opportunity. But of course

I didn't see it that way. This"—he held the imaginary glass of booze up high—"felt like it *was* opportunity. The whole day was just a lead-up to *this*." Again he slugged it back and then, in an exaggerated motion, wiped his forearm across his muzzle. "Man, I thought I was free! But I was locked up just like you are. And I was just wasting time—years and years of it."

Mr. Michels was hurling a fair amount of raw candor into the classroom of four boys, and for the moment he was successfully ignoring Little Axell, who during the soliloquy had spontaneously begun pacing around the back of the room, futzing with knickknacks on a desk, tilting his shoulders oddly from side to side. Little Axell was fifteen, tall and skinny with long arms. His narrow eyes always appeared accusatory. The *Little* had been given to him because his older brother, called Big Axell (though he was about half a foot shorter), was also at Ferris. Josiah had been playing football alongside Big Axell, who was nice enough, but Josiah didn't know Little Axell well and didn't particularly like what he did know.

"Sit down, son, before you get points off," the YRS counselor in the room said, holding up Little Axell's sheet as a threat. The boy completely ignored him and continued stalking the room. Mr. Michels motioned to the counselor that it was okay for now.

"You're all here," the teacher proceeded. "Some for a few months. Some only for a few weeks. That's just time, and yet it's absolutely your most valuable asset. And I know it sucks here. I've been working here for twelve years, and it's always sucked here. But a month is still a month. A week is still a week. The question is, While you're here, are you just serving time? Or is time serving you?"

Mr. Michels had a precise segue planned out into discussions, exercises, and lessons. But Little Axell suddenly plopped down audibly behind a table and began pushing against the top so that the whole piece tilted away from him on its two rear legs.

"Uh, Mr. Axell?" Mr. Michels called gently. "That's not going to end well."

The boy shrugged and angled the table a few more degrees toward its tipping point.

Mr. Michels drew a simple chart on the whiteboard to explain the difference between optional skills and earned skills. "Optional skills are skills that you already have, that you can choose to use for your own benefit and the people around you, or not. So, for example, not cursing. You never hear me curse in this class. Do I know some curse words? Yes. Do I say them out loud if I'm at home doing a wood project and I hammer my thumb? Yes. But here in school, where I work, I choose not to curse, because it's not professional." He jotted *No cursing* in the left column.

Little Axell's table fell over.

Bosley, who was also in this class, cracked, "You look like you might be about to curse right now!"

"Thanks, Mr. Bosley," Mr. Michels said dryly. Then, to Axell: "I told you that was going to happen."

"Hoorah for you," Little Axell replied with some venom, pronouncing the word *who-ra*. He made a laborious display of picking the table up, as if it were a chore arbitrarily assigned to him, then began pacing again. He leaned over the trash can and let a thick globule of spit fall slowly from his mouth.

"Be polite," Cassio, the remaining student in the class, said.

Mr. Michels, still fixed on Little Axell, responded, "Pardon?"

Totally ignoring the sideshow, Cassio pointed to the chart on the board. "Being polite is an optional skill."

"Good one. I think there are examples both ways happening now."

Mr. Michels wrote *Polite* under the *Optional Skills* heading, and then in quick succession Cassio added *Clean, Good listener, Asks questions, Smiles.* The other boys just stared at him, marveling as they usually did at his unflappable classroom focus. Everything about Cassio was difficult to square. He was an unathletic, heavyset kid with close-cropped hair and an almost perfectly round face. He constantly raised his hand to speak in class and without fail behaved respectfully toward adults. Yet Cassio was from North Philadelphia and was at Ferris because he'd come to Delaware to shoot someone in a long-running gang back-and-forth. Josiah considered him a major kiss-ass, yet secretly feared whatever anger might lurk behind Cassio's soft demeanor and impeccable manners.

The teacher tapped along the fresh list and summated, "These are all skills you possess right now, that have nothing to do with high school diplomas or any paper certificate, that you can use to get a job. Even if you don't feel them, even if you have to fake them, you can use them. It's very, very important to remember that you don't have to be authentic all the time."

"What's *authentic*?" Bosley asked.

"You know what the word means," Mr. Michels asserted. Despite the rampant posturing at Ferris, the idea of personal authenticity was preciously and loudly guarded. "It means to be *you*, to be real."

"So how can I not be me? Because, you know, I'm real."

"I know you are, Mr. Bosley. Trust me, everyone here knows you're real." Mr. Michels laughed, then entered into the nuances of a philosophy to which the students here ascribed almost indescribable depth and importance. "I have an old friend. He works for an investment bank. Does anyone know what investment banking is?"

Cassio raised his hand, but Bosley superseded him by miming inserting a key into a keyhole. He closed one eye and squinted the other as if peering into a hidden space. "They unlock the *money*."

"Sort of, yes, that's basically right. And so my friend does pretty well for himself, he actually has his own company. And I think he's going to visit this class later on in the year." Mr. Michels paused so that this news had a moment to land. He didn't seem to notice—or he didn't let on that he had noticed—how Little Axell had stopped pacing and now stood oddly in the center of the room, regarding the teacher with intense seriousness. Josiah had an ominous feeling as Mr. Michels continued, "So, Mr. Bosley, again, I know you, I know you're real. I know that being real is important to you. I know that when some white guy in a suit and tie strolls in here to babble about his lucrative business endeavors, you are not impressed by that, and there's no reason you should be. That guy, my friend, hasn't been through what you've been through; that guy couldn't *survive* what you've been through. Yes or no?"

Bosley smiled almost sheepishly and shook his head. "Probably not."

"And yet I've also watched you act in very different ways in this classroom, day to day, sometimes on the same day. A couple weeks ago you were tearing this place up. You tore a poster off the wall, you got a bunch of points taken off, you were stomping mad—remember that?" Bosley nodded, now with some pride. "But on weeks when you have a football game, you're perfectly behaved. Sure, you're faking it to get something that matters to you, and we teachers all know that. But, whatever: you listen, you ask a lot of questions, you set an example for the students around you. This week, everyone in school's been acting out. It's been nuts. A bunch of kids left and it's the Wild West—and you've been like a model citizen. Can you explain to me what's going on with that? Can you explain to me who is the *real* Bosley?"

Josiah was beginning to tune out because the teacher was being wordy and also because he was striving to make a simple behavior seem complicated and illustrative. Bosley shrugged.

"It's *all* the real you," Mr. Michels said. "It's all your experience and the skills you have. What we're doing in this class is separating the parts of you that can help you make a good impression and get a good job— like not cursing, like making eye contact—from the parts that won't, like tearing posters from walls or hocking loogies in garbage cans. We're not talking about selling out here. I would never ask you to do that. I'm just saying that when my investment banker friend comes to visit, and he meets you all and of course is *stunned* by your brilliant minds and scholarly attitudes"—Mr. Michels's eyes radiated positive energy as he paused briefly in case anyone wanted to laugh, but no one did—"and he decides he's going to offer one of you an internship at his company when you get out of here—*which has happened in my class before*—I know who he's going to talk to. It's not the tough guys. It's the guys listening and caring—"

"You ain't shit," Little Axell suddenly muttered. He'd been visibly roiling this whole time, and now a rootless animosity gripped his whole long body. "You talk and talk and you ain't shit."

"Thanks, Mr. Axell." Mr. Michels looked away to resume his speech.

"Out there I make more in a day than you make here in a year. This is bullshit. You're bullshit."

"That's your choice to think like that," the teacher replied.

"You are really bothering me right now," Little Axell said lowly, coldly. "I'm about to have to get physical."

The performance was tiresome, but Josiah watched closely because he didn't know how it would end, and that was rare. But after a few seconds during which some wildness threatened to overtake the classroom, this situation ended in the usual way, with Little Axell talking and threatening and not doing anything, then being given a thirty-minute time-out amid many ridiculous protestations—"I haven't done shit!"—and a protracted fuss over his points sheet. Josiah sighed and used the disruption to lower his head to the desktop and close his eyes, because even sequences that seemed extraordinary ended up being rote and ultimately pointless. Moments later, with Little Axell glaring scornfully, harmlessly through the glass window during his long time-out in the hallway, Mr. Michels moved on from optional skills into the realm of learned skills, the ones that allowed you not just to be hired for a job but to keep a job, the next-level attributes that couldn't be faked, such as *Patience, Persistence, Humility* . . .

Josiah thought that this set of characteristics would take more than a single class for this group to grasp.

*   *   *

"YOU CAN GRADUATE high school this year," Ms. Martin informed Josiah. On her laptop screen was an Excel spreadsheet that listed his high school credits in different courses, a vital resource prepared by the Education Transition Specialist for each student. Compared to most, Josiah was not all that far behind. "You would have to do some extra work," she prodded, "but you really could graduate, whether you were planning on it or not."

He grew increasingly squirmy as she explained that his year in the Cottages followed by his quick return to Ferris School had actually helped him in the numbers and figures by which school districts tracked student progress. Before his first arrest, Josiah's school attendance records had been spotty but at least consistently so: he'd ditched school now and again through tenth grade but had avoided truancy flags; he'd received a few D's and F's but had mostly passed core classes. Josiah didn't know how school would have gone had he not been booked into the system after his sophomore year. He might have met enough requirements to graduate, or he might increasingly have disengaged and dropped out. He hadn't planned that far ahead.

While under state care, however, he'd had no choice but to go to class every day. He'd had no choice but to turn in the day's assignments. He'd had no homework or exams to ditch out on. So the attendance rate and credits he'd earned as a ward of Delaware had kept him above the threshold required to earn a diploma on time. None of this information affected him emotionally. He kept shrugging and repeating, "Okay."

Ms. Martin had held this job for a little under a year, having come to Ferris from the Red Lion Christian Academy in the small satellite town of Bear, Delaware, thirty minutes south (before that job, she'd spent her early thirties working at a Marshalls department store for minimum wage while pursuing her master's degree). At Red Lion, she'd served as the school counselor for the small parochial school that mostly drew mon-eyed families along with some scholarship students. Her responsibilities had primarily encompassed college counseling and responsive services to students in distress. A devout Christian herself, she had for the most part helped steer teenagers who'd been on the college path since preschool.

Here, she rarely came across a student who could actively, independently contemplate higher education. Her Ferris charges lived exclusively in the past and present, specifically in past decisions that had engendered their present situation. The linkages between the two could be so intense as to leave little emotional space with which to extrapolate even a vague course toward the completion of high school and life beyond. Trying to could trigger depression, mania, and rage—but for the most part, her students hid their uncertainties behind lots and lots of jokes; her meetings were often hilarious and belied the stress of mapping futures. She began that mapping process for each individual with a "Student Success Plan." Each student's SSP involved a goal, such as to graduate high school, pursue a vocational training program, make the Ferris School honor roll, or even all three. Over many hours spent with each student as well as gathering information herself, Ms. Martin compiled an overview that included academic preparedness, family support, current standing in the home school district, placement in alternative schools, job skills, mental health, and the influence of friends outside. Then, hour by hour, she worked with each boy at Ferris School to meet his goal.

These hours could be alternately inspiring and vexing, depending on the mood fluctuations that were part of the rhythm here. External challenges were also unpredictable and sometimes cruel, including the unreliable landscape of employers and institutions willing to accept applicants with juvenile records, as well as the bureaucratic reality that could make receiving a textbook necessary for a correspondence college course take four months, by which time the student who'd ordered it was already gone. Even in instances when personalities and systems aligned such that a student met his goals and transitioned from secure placement into a positive situation, an event could quickly dismantle that balance: a family member's death, a girlfriend's pregnancy, a sudden drain of motivation, a cell phone number canceled for lack of payment, the sheer shock of having every minute accounted for here and then leaving and being held wholly accountable for those minutes and their consequences.

Some days felt pitiless in this regard, particularly the days when she learned that a former student had dropped out of school or been arrested again. The worst days occurred when former students who had been in regular contact suddenly ceased returning calls or emails. But most days contained some levity and some hope in the form of boys engaging with school here and beginning to look ahead. There was really no predicting who would follow through on these habits once released from residence, because the depth of external factors was profound. But every so often she encountered a boy like Josiah, who seemed to possess some internal motivation—some ability to part himself from the general noise and masculine pomposity here—that might lend itself to a more ambitious Student Success Plan.

At the moment, he was just sitting there in the library, refusing to see himself as exceptional or deserving in any way. "What kind of extra work are you talking about?" he finally asked, with the wariness of a feral prey animal.

"In math you're doing pretty well—you're basically at a tenth-grade level according to assessments. Reading and composition you would have a little more catching up. Since we don't do standard testing here, you would need to do some coursework in order to prepare for state testing on your own, to show that you've passed grade level."

"But they don't teach grade level here. They teach, like, fourth-grade math here, fourth-grade English."

"No. It's higher than that, but what they can teach here depends on the individuals in each class, and that's why we try to group your schedules according to your levels."

"Then why am I in English with kids who can barely read?"

"I know who you're in English with, and they can all read just fine," she said evenly. Josiah was contradicting anything she said. Most of her boys possessed this mode and weaponized it whenever she was trying to coax them out of a comfort zone. They relied on hyperbole, and she made a point to always countercheck it while also commiserating. "It's hard to have everyone at the same level in the same room because of space and different assessments, students coming and going. We do our best."

Josiah based much of his resentment on exactly this admission: that in some way he existed here as an assessment on a piece of paper, being shuffled around the education wing to accommodate the capacity and budget. Ms. Martin, in trying to be understanding, had entered some precarious psychic terrain.

In the hallway, kids moved between their classes; YRS staff loudly reminded them to do so without talking or loafing; kids talked and loafed in defiance. Some peered snoopily through the glass walls or made heart symbols at Ms. Martin with their hands. The electric bell in each classroom was staggered by two minutes so as to prevent clogging in the hallways, but clogged hallways were more interesting for the students, so they devised methods by which to stall and overlap.

From this crowd, Sargent's face suddenly pressed against the window, looking flushed and fleshy. Sargent was one of two white kids currently in residence at Ferris. He was older, almost nineteen. Short and thick, with a close-shaved head and a ridiculous brown lumberjack's beard, Sargent was a loud but genial knucklehead. He liked to steal cars. In particular, he liked to steal police cars, which was what had landed him at Ferris.

"Ms. Martin, Ms. Martin!" he pleaded insistently through the glass, pounding his palm on it. "I got to talk to you! I got to show you something!" His face was turning red with urgency.

She waved him away. "I'll find you later, Mr. Sargent. Get going before you get in trouble."

"You better find me!" he shouted. "It's so important what I have to show you!"

Sargent disappeared as YRS counselors threatened him with timeouts. Classroom doors began to close. The hallway quieted. "I have class, too," Josiah said. "I don't want any out-of-area points."

"It's really important to be thinking about this. If you can graduate while you're here, then when you leave, instead of looking at alternative schools or getting back into your old high school, you can be looking at college or trade school."

"*College?*" Josiah sort of mumbled while scrunching half his face. The word wasn't alien to him—he'd heard it in school and at home throughout his life—but as a concept it remained somewhat abstract, particularly since he hadn't been in a real high school in over a year. The counselor's temperate tone and expression confused him.

"I just want you to be thinking about it. We can do research together about specifics. But the materials can take a while to get here, so we need to begin deciding *if*. If this is an idea that appeals to you, we can start figuring out what extra stuff we need to get for you."

"How much extra?"

"Nothing you can't do."

As the day progressed from English to math to social studies, his head was a temporal confusion, zigging and zagging forward and backward through time, through memories bent by negative feelings and visions of various futures. In group therapy sessions they often discussed radical acceptance, a mental method by which to inhabit one's present circumstances unencumbered by what-ifs and what-could-bes. Josiah took to it fairly easily. He'd had a long time to come to terms with what most of his peers here seemed to struggle with the most: that he wasn't here by mistake, that he wasn't "too good" for this place or its other inhabitants. Yet Ms. Martin had just indirectly told him that he was better than most of his peers by certain standards—if only because he'd racked up more school days in attendance, if only because he'd spent more time in residence here.

This new notion of pride catapulted him forward months and years into a world in which he, Josiah Wright, was college educated. In this world, the light in the sky was a little brighter, the colors a little more vivid, the air a little more filled with oxygen. He had some money. He had a home and a car and a pretty girl. He had stability. He had a framed certificate on the wall. He had choices.

Beside the library door, a row of Walgreens photo prints was Scotch-taped to the wall. The faces beaming out held the prideful grins of boys wearing tasseled graduation caps and clutching rolled-up diplomas, flashing peace signs. There were seven photos at the moment, all recent Ferris students who had graduated from high school while contained in this building. Clearly, Ms. Martin and the other specialists hung them here in the nexus of the education wing, right where the hallways met, as highly visible motivators. Today the ploy worked; Josiah passed the pictures four or five times, and in each instance his gaze lingered ever so briefly on their exultant expressions.

At the end of that afternoon, in the RTI period that concluded each school day, Josiah sat with his chin propped on crossed forearms, gazing out the wide window that looked over the parking lot, the highway just beyond it, the DuPont Company office park on the other side of that. RTI stood for Response to Intervention and was devoted to filling in the various gaps in math and reading skills. Since it didn't count for any grade, it was also a period of hanging out and talking lowly and window gazing. Bosley sat a few seats down. He was excited about a squirrel. "Check that out!" he gasped, as children do upon seeing some astonishing fauna at the zoo. In the median strip of the parking lot, the critter was scuttling in a spiral up the trunk of a dogwood tree. Bosley observed its movements intently, weirdly awed by the wildlife. "He's got an acorn in his mouth, yo! He's about to have a feast!"

Other kids began crowding the window. "I've got some in my yard at home," someone said.

"He be storing his shit for winter," informed another.

Josiah was annoyed by the loudness. Yet, as he himself focused on the animal before it disappeared into the tree's canopy with its bounty, there was pleasure to be had in simply observing a living thing that didn't devote a single thought to this building or the gawkers inside it or what absurd systems had sentenced them there, that was just living, surviving in accordance with instinct. What captivated the boys was its blithe freedom.

Ms. Martin entered the classroom. She made passing, meaningful eye contact with Josiah, but she'd actually come looking for Sargent, who was playing a simplistic video game on the Smart Board, jumping a crudely pixelated dinosaur figure over a series of desert cacti.

"Yo, Ms. M!" Sargent shouted. He was from the rural, southern half of the state, known as Slower Delaware (an unclever riff on Lower Delaware), and had a mushy drawl. He spit a lot when he talked. "I've been looking for you all day!"

"What was so important?"

Sargent stood in front of her. He tipped his head forward slightly and formed his mouth into a long O shape. With a closed fist, he began rapping his knuckles hard against the crown of his head. A loud, hollow noise reverberated from his cranium through the room. Everyone watching was perplexed as Sargent looked up with intense pride. "I wanted you to hear this! It sounds like a coconut!"

*   *   *

THE ATMOSPHERE OUTSIDE the windows grew grayer and colder. The eleven boys who had left such a vacuum upon leaving in early November were for the most part forgotten as the school population climbed back into the thirties. Three of the boys were promptly rearrested and returned to Ferris, sheepishly. The weekends in the cluster were monotonous; the weekdays in school twenty yards down the hall were more so. Then basketball season began.

Josiah watched from the edge of the court as kids took turns swooping toward the hoop with leaping strides, mouths open and contorted, the whole choreography appearing to lead toward a slam dunk. But none of them could actually dunk. Ferris School did not often have true athletes among its student body. Josiah figured the dearth had to do with such kids being busy playing sports on the outside, not stealing cars or aiming guns at other people. Regardless of the talent on display, the shift from football to basketball went beyond the physics of the sports themselves. Football at Ferris was an exhilarating life force for its athletes during the fall. They were trusted to apply their bodies to the purpose of controlled violence, and to perform difficult individual tasks in sync with ten other teammates on the field. They could grunt and holler and body-slam another person against the earth without teachers reprimanding them by name and YRS counselors taking away their points. Football empowered them. But it wasn't "fun" per se; football was dirty, bloody, painful—and also embarrassing, since they'd lost every game.

Basketball, in contrast, was elemental, kinetic joy. Nearly all of the students had watched and played the game on some level from a young age. Its rhythms were rooted in improvisation and the ability to foretell the motions of others. The game was layered and depthless and lent itself to role-play fantasies; any kid of any shape or size could pretend to be LeBron or Steph or Embiid, no matter how ungainly his actual play was.

A boy named Crews appeared in the midst of just such a fantasy while he pinned the ball against his right hip and used his free hand to direct the positioning of teammates. He was tall, a little north of six feet. For rec time, he pulled his white socks up as high as they would go and seemed to be intentionally trying to look like a white guy playing hoops in the 1950s. Crews was a little crazy in general; Josiah found that a one-on-one conversation with him over a meal could pivot from quietly earnest to frivolously threatening in half a sentence. Josiah knew that Crews's older brother and the brother's girlfriend had been murdered a few months earlier, in the late summer, in some kind of murky, gang-related home invasion. Crews had been starting this term at Ferris at the time. Josiah credited Crews's manic mood swings to the awful trauma and felt for his classmate deeply—but kept his distance just the same.

Bosley was on the wing howling for the ball. Crews happily ignored him and drove toward the basket. But, as always, his dribbles were too high—nearly shoulder height—and Sargent, lurking in the paint, easily stole the ball. To be stripped by Sargent—who was short, overweight, white, with his silly beard and waddling gait—was an ultimate indignity, and Bosley let Crews know that loudly. In the meantime, neither player bothered to pursue Sargent, who broke down the court, missed his first layup but, being undefended, easily sank his follow-up. Grinning, red-faced, shiny with sweat, Sargent ran back up the court with his arms spread wide, gloating. "Y'all never hooped with us boys in Smyrna?!" Smyrna was known as a backwoods town in Slower Delaware. "What? *What?*"

Bosley said, "Shut up, you cowpoke," but without any menacing effect. He continued bickering with Crews for a moment, annoying their teammates. Then Bosley made a point to dribble the ball up the court himself, dismissing Crews to the wing. Bosley had the same squat body type as Sargent, but he was quicker and kept the ball lower to the ground. He voiced the play-by-play aloud as he drove in—"Bringing it on you, taking it to the hole . . ."—but was swarmed by defenders while attempting an ill-planned, over-the-shoulder, almost hook shot. Sargent stuffed the ball and, once more, took it to the other end for a layup while Crews and Bosley argued.

"That was sick!" Sargent shouted, arcing down the sideline with his arms spread wide. "That was so dang sick!"

Crews took the ball out again. He pointed and hissed at Bosley and the rest of his squad to sequester themselves in the corner away from the lane. He dribbled the ball hard against the floor. His frustration gave him even less control over his movements than he normally had. He edged inward past the three-point line. Intent on the basket, he didn't seem to see Sargent—with that gigantic grin now permanently set within the beard on his face—sneak up on his left side. Crews's teammates were too annoyed with him to give a warning. So when Crews stepped back to attempt a three-pointer, Sargent stripped him before he could set his feet. Once more, Sargent was off down the court. Crews dropped to his knees and watched masochistically. Sargent made his layup and then fell onto his back, spread-eagled. "Oh my God!" he howled. "Oh my God oh my God oh my God!" He began wiggling his arms and legs as if he were making a snow angel.

The sequence had everyone in the gym, both YRS counselors and students, unanimously cheering for Sargent while playfully jeering Bosley and Crews. For pure entertainment, these two minutes had been about as memorable as any two minutes could be at Ferris. All around the court, people danced and stomped and slapped the floor. The acoustics amplified all the sounds into thunder. The principal of the school, a typically serious woman, hurried in the side door looking alarmed and suspicious. She had the authority to shut the whole scene down, and the boys watched her raptly. She peered around, her gaze finally landing on Sargent, who was now prancing around center court performing a hideous shoulder-shimmy dance. She appeared confused. Then she just smiled, shook her head, and left. The roaring grew louder: pure and unchecked delight.

Josiah sat on the bleachers a bit apart from the ado. He was grinning and enjoying himself, but he wasn't making any noise, so as not to irk Bosley or Crews. Cassio, the star student of their life skills class, sat with him for a time. Cassio wore his shirt tucked in and his socks pulled up like Crews and had patiently been waiting for a rotation in which he could join the game. Josiah had watched him play before and been stunned by his court intensity in comparison with his placid classroom demeanor.

Cassio was going to receive his high school diploma from Ferris this year. He didn't advertise this, but everyone took it for granted and also assumed he would eventually go to college. So Josiah had been paying extra attention to Cassio of late. What he'd seen had surprised him: no one seemed to resent Cassio's intelligence or prospects. Aside from throwaway put-downs regarding Cassio's pencil mustache and nerdy mannerisms, the other kids in school acted genuinely supportive and even admiring of his goals. The observation felt incredibly important.

"What a punk ass," Cassio said.

Josiah wasn't sure if he was referring to Bosley, Crews, Sargent, or—maybe most likely—collectively to all three. Josiah laughed softly and nodded.

"You getting in next with me?" Cassio asked.

"Nah. Not feeling it today."

"Come on."

"It's not really my game, to be real."

Cassio grinned and motioned to the court. "Apparently, it's Sargent's game."

Sargent was still gloating around center court, stomping with his feet wide apart, scissoring his arms, shaking his head with his mouth open and tongue lolling side to side.

"You graduating soon?" Josiah asked.

"It looks like it. Just got to take a few tests, which sucks."

"Ms. Martin ever make you do, like, extra work for those?"

Cassio shrugged. "I guess."

"Is it hard?"

"Not really. And she brings food from Wendy's sometimes when I finish books."

Josiah had seen Ms. Martin distributing her Wendy's bags to Cassio and a couple others in the cafeteria. She did this for students whenever they improved on their standardized test scores. Some kids purposefully tanked their first-round tests to earn the perk.

"After you graduate and get out, are you thinking, like, college?"

Cassio turned his head to look directly at Josiah, without much expression on his face. "Did she have the talk with you about graduating or what?"

"Nah," Josiah blurted quickly. "I was just asking."

"All right." With an all-wise expression Cassio added, "If she ever does, or if you just have questions about it, just holler at me, all right?"

"Maybe I will get in the game."

Later, inserted onto Bosley and Crews's team, Josiah was hustling from corner to corner without touching the ball often. He mostly watched those two try to compensate for their earlier embarrassment by launching three-pointers, with little success. Cassio was on Sargent's team and was running doggedly at both ends. His body was soft but weighty, and he dove around with such force that others cleared space for him. Thus Cassio ended up with easy layups time and again, and he racked up points. On the other end, Bosley and Crews continued alternately to brick shots, bicker between themselves, and bark orders at everyone else. Josiah, relegated to spectating, began to feel that he was witnessing in real time his choices for what kind of path he was on, and what kind of person he wanted to be.

During his next meeting with Ms. Martin in the third week of November, Josiah told her that he wanted her to order those extra books
for him. She was pleased in a way that Josiah had never before in his
life witnessed an educator respond to something he'd said or done.

"It's going to be hard, though," she warned.

"Does this mean I get to order from Wendy's?"

"No Wendy's yet." She laughed. "You have to take some tests first."

*   *   *

ON THE FOURTH Wednesday of November, Josiah's mother came to
have some semblance of a turkey dinner along with any other parents
or guardians willing to spend part of their holiday in a state-care facility.
The school scheduled this gathering on the night before actual Thanksgiving, so as not to complicate holiday plans at home. The weather was
unseasonably warm. Of the thirty-two kids being held at the time, sixteen had adults who came to see them: exactly half.

The evening included a tour, a video presentation, and slightly above-
average food served directly to the tables in the cafeteria. The tour was
short and limited to the education wing, since the housing units could
be upsetting for parents to see. The adults poked their heads into the
ordinary classrooms and the library. They noticed the fish tank and its
two lonely goldfish in room 108 and the home economics equipment in
room 111, which still smelled of the Bolognese sauce made a few hours
earlier. School hallways and classrooms always felt strange without students noisily populating them, but at Ferris more than at most. The
dusky light fading outside intensified the eerie emptiness. Parents didn't
interact much with one another beyond murmuring, "Excuse me," in
the doorways. They were all part of a small and exclusive club that none
of them wanted to be in.

Whatever complicated individual narratives that had led to this
membership—whatever struggles, failings, opportunities missed and
opportunities never given by a society that both perpetuated and scorned
poverty—remained contained within the succession of somber faces as

the parents passed finally into the gym. There, they scooted into the bleachers and watched a video that the life skills class had made the previous term. In the film, the class was giving a presentation to a group of what looked to be businessmen, or maybe philanthropists or bureaucrats. Josiah had still been in the Cottages when this had occurred, but on-screen Cassio told the fable of the old man and the starfish, in which a toxic algae bloom left tens of thousands of starfish dying on the beach of a fishing village. The local people were revolted and sad and didn't want even to look at the creatures, just waited for them to die and wash away with their stench. An old man began walking the tide line, picking up starfish and hurling them back into the sea one by one. Adult villagers mocked him, then grew frustrated and angry with him. They told him he was being stupid, there were too many for him to make any difference. He replied, "But for this one, I can make a difference." Then the children of the village began to emulate him, and soon a herd of them were walking with the old man, gathering beached starfish and throwing them back to the sea. Their mothers joined, then the elderly, then all but the most stubborn in the village. Soon after that, the beach was clean.

Mr. Michels, who'd cut the video, stood before the bleachers and asked, "What part of the story do our students represent?"

The teacher and the exercise were both well-intentioned, but the parents were hungry and weary of being there. They wanted to see their sons for a time and then leave. As if to speed things along, a mother raised her hand and quickly posited, "They're the starfish."

Mr. Michels grinned, stretching the moment out. "Actually, no. The children here are actually the children in the story—the ones who first followed the old man. They just needed an example of what it looked like to save something before they could save themselves. Right?"

The parents offered a few nods. The metaphor didn't maybe entirely work, didn't go far in acknowledging the complicated human chemistry that had them all sitting on the uncomfortable bleachers in the empty gym at night. But they indulged the presentation, and soon they moved down the hallway to the cafeteria. Little yellow plastic flowers had been set on each of the four-tops. The boys with adults in attendance found seats with them. The other half of the boys sat in their usual groups but took care to be a few rows apart from the families, as if to keep their normal banter from intruding on the reunions, or maybe to protect themselves from overhearing the strained, distant yearning of them.

Josiah's mother was describing the menu she had planned for tomorrow, the usual fare of bird and sides. Since the weather was warm, she was trying something new by deep-frying the turkey outside.

"What are you frying it in out there? Like a pot?"

"Robert has a fryer. He's bringing it over." Robert was the man she'd recently been seeing. Josiah had never met him, just heard his name a few times when she'd visited. The mention of the name now threw him off a bit, and Josiah found himself oddly paying keen attention to the cafeteria din, the cracks of low-key laughter, the scuffing of shoe soles on the floor, the scratching of plastic fork tines against paper plates. His mother was rattling off her desserts for tomorrow: pumpkin pie, pecan pie, lemon meringue, chocolate soufflé on a Nilla wafer crust. Josiah hadn't participated in the last two Thanksgiving holidays at home. He grew sad and silent. In response, his mother did, too. They ate like that. The turkey slices were thin and dry; the gravy had a processed, starchy consistency that did little to improve on them.

The dinner was intended as a pleasant reprieve, a gentle assurance to parents that their sons were not living in perdition, an ephemeral reminder to students that their homes still existed outside these current confines. For Josiah, the event exacerbated his loneliness.

Sargent's deep, guffawing cackle swept the entire space at intervals. He was across the room, eating with others who didn't have family here. He was still wearing his apron; because Sargent was too old to be allowed to take classes here, he spent most of each day working in the cafeteria and had helped prepare this meal. Josiah knew that Sargent was regaling his tablemates with the story of his basketball domination of Bosley and Crews, a story he'd told about ten thousand times over the past week. Josiah found himself doing something he never expected he would ever do: he admired Sargent. The boy was just about everything Josiah resented: white, slovenly, loud, abrasive, and loaded with bad jokes. But Sargent, at least by all appearances, seemed able to experience joy more often and more fully than most of the others here. Josiah spent most of each day feeling incredibly complicated and torn—and even more so since he'd chosen to graduate from high school this year.

He didn't tell his mother about that. He knew exactly why: he didn't want to give his mother any extra hope for him, then bear that hope as expectation, then, later, as further disenchantment.

They managed to talk some over pumpkin pie. He asked about his siblings, and she told some cute anecdotes about how they tried her patience. She went on for a while about how bright his little sister was, how the teachers at her school just loved her. Josiah had been like that once: adored by elementary school teachers.

Later, they were given a five-minute warning to say goodbye.

"All right," he said. "Later, I guess."

The moment was awkward; both knew that they ought to try to make it meaningful, as some of the other families were doing. Crews, for instance, was squeezing his mother tight, rocking slightly, with his eyes tearing up. Josiah couldn't even fathom the emotions on the maternal side of the embrace. His knowledge of Crews's older brother's murder was pretty thin, mostly based on perennially unreliable gossip within the cluster, but Josiah knew for a fact that Crews's mother had one son in jail due to guns, and another son in the ground due to guns, and Josiah wondered how much endurance was required just to be here, just for her to bring food to her lips and chew and swallow.

Josiah's own mother pulled him in and they hugged for a moment.

"I hope you all have fun tomorrow night," Josiah said.

"We'll miss you. We'll pray that you will be with us at the next."

Then she left.

A mournful quality permeated the cluster during the time remaining before lights out. The muted facsimile of a family holiday had been pleasing in its break from routine, but in immediate retrospect had just emphasized the boys' isolation. More abstractly, the complicated dynamics of breaking bread with parents had made Josiah and the other kids realize that even the most elemental moments of childhood—such as sharing a meal with one's mom—would probably never again be simple. The boys' varied sadnesses manifested in a higher volume than usual. Kids shouted and moved hyperactively around the space and seemed incapable of the focus required to sustain a sensible exchange. Josiah sat near the stairs leading to the upper rooms and just observed, shaking his head and smirking now and again at just what a madhouse they lived in. He held his own feelings tonight tightly, silently, deep within his chest.

Chapter 4

◆

January–February 2020

THE DOZEN OR so boys ringing the library stood confused and silent when the young white woman in the room's center asked
them if anyone had ever seen or heard of the film *Animal House*.

"Really? *No one?!*" She raised her arms, then dropped them in mock
surrender. She was always theatrical like this; she was a classically
trained actress from Philadelphia who led a Shakespeare-themed acting
workshop at Ferris every Friday. "Have you ever at least heard the song
'Shout' by the Isley Brothers?" Most hands in the room tentatively rose.
"Phew." She wiped her wrist across her brow in mock relief.

She explained that they would go around the room singing, and they
would make their voices softer and softer and then louder and louder
in accordance with the chorus. As in the film that none of them had
seen, they would crouch lower and lower with the softening, then stand
higher and higher in the crescendo. When she finished explaining the
exercise, many confused faces stared at her. "Sorry, I made it make no
sense. It will make sense when we start—and you should all totally see
Animal House."

She began singing. Her voice was sublime. "'A little bit softer now . . .
A little bit softer now . . .'" The song took on a call-and-response aspect
as the words made their way around the circle, descending to the barest

65

whisper as the boys mimicked her and crouched down, rocking gently within their squats, until all of them were practically butt to floor. The chorus shifted: "'A little bit louder now . . . A little bit louder now . . .'" She led them gradually upward until she and all the boys were leaping from their feet, arms stretched in the air, belting the words. The group of juvenile delinquents performed as fictional, drunk, elated college kids. The Plexiglas windows visibly vibrated.

The order of the boys' days was fixed so much in stillness, with the freedom to raise their voices and move their bodies with any abandon relegated to an hour of daily rec time or hoops practice. Otherwise, their point sheets and privileges depended on their ability to restrain themselves from doing what their minds and limbs desired to do most of the time: run, dance, yell. Many of them were diagnosed with ADHD or other compulsive disorders, and so the urge to move was chemical, the body's actions sometimes seeming to veer independently from the brain's instructions. This woman's weekly class bestowed a release as valuable as it was mortifying. The icebreakers of the first fifteen minutes of each class tended to emphasize the latter—mortification—so as to countermand the powerful self-consciousness of a group of young males whose confidence depended largely on how imposing they presented themselves to be.

Every week found a small group who refused to participate in the embarrassment and instead sat hunched in corners muttering about what stupid shit this all was. To this point Josiah had reliably placed himself with the sitters. However, on this afternoon he'd joined the active circle, figuring perhaps that the mind shift he'd been undergoing with Ms. Martin should apply elsewhere, too. He felt ridiculous during the next exercise, in which the group composed a short story as each student ad libbed a single word in succession: "My—mom—mailed—her—underwear—to—Walmart—because—they—smelled—like—bananas—and—the—cashier—put—them—on—sale—in—the—video game—section. . . ." Josiah found that he somewhat enjoyed feeling ridiculous. He enjoyed being part of a circle. He enjoyed laughing.

During the second half of this class, the boys had to actually act, improvising famous Shakespeare scenes based on quick synopses. The class's coteacher was a black man, maybe in his thirties, with a baritone voice and a studious, contemplative aura enhanced by his tweed jacket. He called on Josiah to play King Claudius from *Hamlet*, Crews to play Hamlet himself, and another to play Queen Gertrude. As Josiah stepped tentatively into the center, keenly aware of all the eyes on him, the teacher explained the context: "So basically Prince Hamlet has figured out that his uncle Claudius killed his father and married his mother. His mother most likely has no idea that a murder occurred, but at the same time she jumped into Claudius's bed pretty fast. Right now, Hamlet's confronting them both about what he's learned. But the important thing is that Hamlet is pretty great at convincing himself that he's wrong, and his uncle is really good at acting innocent. So Hamlet is consumed by vengeance, but also by self-doubt." The boys were still processing this loaded scenario as the teacher grinned, stepped back, and said, *"Action!"*

It was not lost on many in the room that Crews, a young man whose brother had recently been murdered and who spent a lot of his time fantasizing revenge, was playing the part of a young man whose father had recently been murdered and who spent a lot of his time fantasizing revenge. In addition to typical stage fright, Josiah contended with anxiety over the unfortunate casting. Then Crews's face contorted into a genuine mask of confused hatred, and he hissed, "Why the hell'd you kill my father?"

Josiah stammered, then attempted to act surprised. "What are you talking about? I didn't kill nobody."

Crews's fists clenched. His brow rippled above his eyes. "You killed my father and you married my ma!" he shouted. "That is all kinds of messed up." He turned to the boy playing Gertrude and thrust his face close, such that the boy rocked backward. *"How could you marry the man who killed your husband?"*

Josiah wasn't thinking through his movements or tones; they were simply happening as he placed a hand gently on Crews's shoulder and said with serenity, "You are having an emotional moment right now, my son. You need to chill so that we can talk about this." For a brief instant, Josiah felt as if he were actually calming Crews—the person, not the assigned acting role.

Crews did appear to soften somewhat, and then the male acting teacher walked between them and said, "I have to stop you because: Wow. Just, wow."

"Wow what?" Josiah asked.

"What made you choose those words?"

"What words?"

"You called him 'my son.' And it was astonishing."

"It was?"

"Think about this." The teacher, with the grand, solemn physicality of a true stage actor, began gesticulating and opining. "You, Claudius, know that you've murdered this person's father, married his mother, and taken his throne. That's a lot to carry. And now he's telling you in no uncertain terms that *he* knows this. And he hates you and he's confronting you. And what do you do? You place a hand on him and call him *your son*." The teacher breathed out and shook his head. "It was so human and so stunning to watch."

Josiah didn't know what to say, so he just shrugged and took a mock bow. The teacher began clapping, and the rest of the room clapped as well. Usually when Josiah felt himself blushing, it was related to discomfort. Right now, the warm darkening of his skin had to do with pride.

*   *   *

OVER HER FIRST year of working at Ferris, Sarah Martin had reached out to dozens of community colleges, junior colleges, vocational-technical schools, and training programs as far north as Vermont, as far south as Florida, as far west as Texas. Most of those programs wanted nothing to do with juvenile delinquents from Delaware. A handful might be willing to entertain the notion of accepting one, but with a number of often disqualifying caveats. A small few, driven mainly by personalities in leadership, eagerly desired to participate in giving societal castaways an opportunity. For those schools, she bookmarked webpages with art-directed photos of young people half buried in the body of a car while learning to be auto mechanics, young people taking notes at a round table opposite a professor in mid-monologue, young people sitting in a circle on a grassy quad discussing lofty topics with wide smiles.

Any given student's reaction to the websites told her much about how her work with that student would proceed. Some faintly grinned and wanted to learn more. Some grew downcast and defeated. Some audibly gasped. Some remained utterly blank.

Josiah's response was blank-ish when she scrolled through his first glimpse of community colleges on her laptop. She had a few different links open to schools he'd never heard of in towns he didn't recognize in states he'd never visited. At a glance, they all looked like small office parks in the middle of nowhere.

"Pretty cool to think about, right?" she ventured.

"I guess."

"They have all sorts of programs, like business, teaching, nursing. They have places to live on campus. A lot of them have sports. This one in New York even has a lacrosse team."

Josiah didn't advertise it, but he was skilled at lacrosse. Ferris's team had begun two years earlier as an experiment, with a volunteer coach who was married to one of the facility's psychologists. No one had known if the boys would take to it, lacrosse being a niche sport mainly played by white kids in prep schools. But any opportunity to be outside with permission for physical contact was a draw, and most of the students had tried to play. Josiah's brand of athleticism had lent itself to the sport's movements: he wasn't fast running straight ahead, but was deft at moving side to side; he wasn't strong, but he was squirrelly; he wasn't quick with his hands, but his coordination was precise. While serving

time in the Cottages last spring, he'd stood out in practices and scrim-
mages. He'd been glad to be naturally talented at something, but he'd
never contemplated using those talents beyond Ferris. At Ms. Martin's
mention, he grew just slightly piqued.

"Are these places far away?" he asked warily.

"Some of them are." She'd learned that Delaware institutions were
not generally welcoming to juvie kids. Parallel to that local challenge,
she'd learned that, of all the many obstacles in motivating her students
to strive toward secondary education, the potential for homesickness
was among the most daunting. Her students tended to be hardened and
drawn to risks, but they collectively shared a deep fear of being far from
their neighborhoods and families—even more than a few miles, and
even from the most neglectful and toxic environments. That was the
reason she'd chosen to bring out the pamphlets now, still eight months
from his release: so that he could begin to contemplate separation while
it was still abstract.

Josiah had been adequately managing the added online work he'd
undertaken, but his progress was still too slow. School computers and
textbooks could be weaponized and so could only be used with supervision. In addition to his sessions with her, he was supposed to be working
during the Response to Intervention periods at the end of each school
day, but he didn't seem to be accomplishing much there. He blamed
this shortcoming on other kids in the classroom talking and screwing
around, but Ms. Martin felt that he was self-conscious about those others seeing him work and learning of his ambitions. It was January now,
and while Josiah's time still seemed endless to him, she knew that he
was already running out of it—that he was already using up the padding
needed to schedule the tests and officially graduate before his release. A
hard, cold rain was hammering the metal roof today. Josiah seemed particularly fidgety and panicky. The moment wasn't ideal for addressing
his time frame, but she chose to anyway.

"You really do need to get on top of your chapters, especially math.
You need to do it during RTI."

"I am," he mumbled.

She was silent.

"What?" he finally challenged.

"Just admit that you're embarrassed."

"Embarrassed around these people?" he scoffed, and shook his head. "Nah, nah."

"But you don't want anyone to know that you're interested in going to college?"

"Listen, I don't even know if I'm interested in college, all right? So chill."

"I'm hearing you." This turning against both her and the idea of higher learning was totally normal. The college webpages often spurred such outbursts. Josiah's was strange in how sudden and extreme it was. She'd learned from experience to eschew logic in these moments, abandon the assumption that she could or should convince anyone of what his best interests were, and simply assure kids that she heard them.

"I'm just doing this work so you'll quit messing with me. *Jesus.*"

"You're doing really well at this, Mr. Wright, but it is going to get harder. You're still reviewing tenth-grade stuff—stuff you've already done in school. In a month or two, you're going to be getting into eleventh-grade material, then twelfth: stuff you haven't done. You're going to need some extra time and help."

He veered into a more childlike, pleading tone. "But you're helping."

"I'll always be here to get material for you and oversee this, but I have a few dozen other students, and I'm also not a teacher. You'll be doing stuff that I don't even know. You're going to have to ask for help. And I know that's a really big ask for you. But there's going to come a time when you don't understand the math, or you don't understand the English, or you don't understand the history. And what will you do?"

"Read more," he mumbled. "Just learn it."

"You can try that way and see if it works. *Or* you can go to the math teacher, or the English teacher, or the history teacher, and ask for help."

"They don't know shit. That's why they're teaching kids in jail. Only jobs they could get."

She completely ignored his petulant nonsense. "And guess what? They are going to help you; they are going to be happy to help you."

"None of them give a shit about me."

"Mr. Wright," she said, though every part of her wanted to call him by his first name, which she was not allowed to do, "you're wrong about that."

* * *

SHE WAS RIGHT about the work: it grew harder and then unmanageable in three weeks. He thought he might do problem sets discreetly during RTI period, but his books and packets looked different from anyone else's, and anything different at Ferris drew massive attention. The first time he tried, instead of solving math equations, he spent the fifty-minute period evading ceaseless questions about why he was solving math equations. Ferris students had a tremendous aptitude for unearthing secrets and identifying lies.

"Stop bullshitting me and tell me *why—are—you—doing—this?*" Crews was poking his index finger against the paper stack with each syllable for emphasis. His face was taut with seriousness, as if wresting a confession of enduring consequence.

"It's just some math work, bruh."

"We do not none of us get math work that looks like this!" Crews shouted. He'd drawn everyone else in the room away from their window gazing and Smart Board games and toward Josiah's math workbook. Josiah closed the sheets and leaned his body over the cover, but not before Crews had glimpsed the words *University of Colorado* and *Algebra 2 Prep*. Crews's face scrunched up in confusion. "Colorado? What sort of shit is that? It's, like, forty states away from here!"

Josiah didn't bother explaining that Ms. Martin had found that the Colorado higher education system was the easiest and quickest from which to order standard mail-in materials. Now everyone in the room was murmuring urgently about Josiah and Colorado and advanced math. Josiah felt his physical body crossing thresholds between general annoyance and real anger. Attention, accusations, being called out for no reason, a crowd pressing in on him: these interferences disrupted reason and made him stuttery and defensive. He experienced the familiar electric burning that nearly always landed him in serious trouble. Crews was closest to him, and his wide-eyed face made a simple target at which Josiah felt a real urge to strike.

"You all shut the fuck up and back up!" Josiah screamed, rocketing out of his chair and standing with his arms stiff, fists clenched, chest heaving, eyes angled downward. He appeared willing to defend his math workbook to his last breath. The supervising teacher, a little confused by the sudden escalation, gave Josiah a five-minute time-out.

Josiah was grateful for the separation, but he couldn't help muttering on his way out, "How come Crews doesn't get one when he started the shit?"

"From what I saw, Crews was asking you about math and you flipped out. So just do the five and settle down and be done with it."

The time in the hallway with his head pressed against the wall and hands clasped behind his back served Josiah well. He breathed deeply and calmed somewhat. When the five minutes elapsed, no one in the classroom seemed to remember much about what had transpired.

But something important shifted after that day. In conjunction with his increasing workload, the kids around him paid more attention at all times to what he was doing. During his meetings with Ms. Martin, they squinted through the windows separating the library from the hallway. The double-teams he received during basketball games began to feel personal. In classes, even when he was trying to sleep, they made comments to the effect that he considered himself smarter than they were, more promising than they were, possessing a brighter future than they did. These alienating, exhausting dynamics were precisely what he had feared, and they seemed irreversible.

* * *

"WHAT YOU HAVE got to understand"—on another day of pouring rain Bosley was talking to the YRS counselor assigned to the math classroom—"is that this shit is not *practical*. It has no *usefulness* in the world we live in."

Josiah was playing a game on the Smart Board called 2048, in which he moved numbered tiles around a square board, combining like tiles in an effort to produce the sum 2,048 before space ran out. Josiah swiped fast left and right like a maestro even as he paid attention to Bosley.

"I'm not arguing with that, Mr. Bosley," the counselor said. A young woman fairly new in this job, she was not yet hardened by all the disciplining and arguing. She was generally friendly and nurturing with students. She'd also grown up in east Wilmington and had gone to school with a few of Bosley's older cousins. "Most of what you learn in school isn't *useful*, per se. But you still gotta learn it."

Bosley spread his arms as if one of the world's most vexing problems had just been solved. "There!" he said, breathless. "See? 'It isn't useful but you gotta learn it.' What you just said makes no sense! It's the *opposite* of sense! School makes the opposite of sense! We should just walk out. . . ."

"That's a really bad idea," she deadpanned.

"But why be here, doing this shit every day?"

The counselor refrained from mentioning that Bosley was here because he still had four months left on his nine-month term in state care.

The math teacher, an unexcitable middle-aged woman who was also training to take charge of the school's special education program, was sorting the cords that connected the computer with the Smart Board. "Because you have to if you want to graduate. Also watch the language, Mr. Bosley, please."

"I'm not going to graduate."

"That's a shame. You can if you want to." The teacher glanced at Josiah's arrangement of his game. "That's a nice board, by the way. Try working the bigger numbers down toward the bottom."

Bosley said, "I don't even want to. It's bullshit."

"Mr. Bosley, come on. You know I don't like giving time-outs, so please don't force it."

While they spoke, Josiah began discreetly following her game advice, moving his high numbers downward and thus creating space for the new tiles that constantly materialized in the grid.

The YRS counselor in the room added, "Stuff like math also just makes you smarter. It's good to be smarter. Good for jobs, good for hanging out with people, good for raising kids . . ."

"It's just good in general, in life," the math teacher said.

Bosley smirked and muttered something dismissive.

Josiah's brow furrowed in concentration. He had one tile valued at 1,024 and needed to build one more and merge them to win the game. He had never seen anyone win the game.

"Speak up," the counselor said to Bosley. "This is a good conversation to have."

"I said, y'all don't know nothing about life, or the kind of smart you need to survive where I'm from."

The YRS counselor immediately scoffed and raised a stiffened palm. "Mr. Bosley, I grew up about three blocks from you and we went to the same school. I hear you all talking a lot about smarts and all that you need to *be real* on the street and live the life and whatnot. But you all are in jail. So I'm not sure how well all this smartness is doing for you all."

"You're working in jail, though. Is that where being school smart is gonna get me? A job like yours?" Bosley gave her a pissy little smile, the way little siblings do as a last recourse when nothing is going their way. A new tension pervaded the room. Josiah's game board had only three empty spaces remaining with which to move tiles, and he was stuck with two 512 tiles that were in opposite corners. Three swipes later, he lost. Other students began filling the classroom.

"All right," the math teacher interjected. "Let's stop. Mr. Bosley, you took a productive conversation and made it unproductive. It feels like kind of a waste."

"Give me a five, then." He was referring to a time-out punishment. He'd pressed his chin against his chest and retreated into a mumbly, barely audible tone. He clocked Josiah moping toward his chair, bummed out because of the tile game. Bosley glared at him, for reasons Josiah could not fathom.

"Chill, man," Josiah said quietly.

"Or what?"

Josiah said nothing.

"You're being kind of extra," Bosley goaded.

"I'm not being anything."

"You think you going to go to college and be, like, better than me?"

The teacher said, "Mr. Bosley: last warning."

Josiah added perhaps unwisely, "You get that five and Coach might not let you play in the game tomorrow."

"I don't give a—" Bosley curtailed the concluding curse word, then broke into a rapping cadence: "Real niggers do real things, all day and tomorrow." Maybe it was a song lyric, or a bit of his own poetry. Bosley stopped talking and pouted throughout most of the ensuing class, which focused on the surface area of three-dimensional shapes and different methods of flattening them out.

"This is not math!" a boy shouted midway through the lesson.

"It's a kind of math," the teacher replied.

"No, this is art. This is drawing. I can't draw!"

"It's not really drawing," the teacher said. "It doesn't have to look good. I'm bad at drawing. It's just to help you visualize."

The boy emitted a gale-force sigh. Josiah echoed the sigh within his own soul. For a few days, he'd been amassing the confidence to ask the teacher for advice or extra help on his multivariable algebra independent assignments. He wasn't afraid, exactly. Rather, time here felt so absolutely unending that even the most minor of interactions, such as asking a math teacher for some help, were always easier to punt to tomorrow. From a young age, Josiah had always been timid around teachers. Some had found this trait cute. Others had equated it with apathy. Either way, he'd progressed through school by making little noise, being unseen. But he needed help now, and he spent most of class mentally rehearsing just how he was going to approach the teacher and say that he was aiming to earn a high school diploma and could he trouble her for some tutoring. He knew that she wouldn't laugh, she wouldn't turn him away, she wouldn't belittle him. But in his insecurity he couldn't help picturing her doing all of that.

The timer controlling the classroom bells had been screwed up lately, and the next math class abruptly began filtering into the room before Josiah's class had been given the go-ahead to leave. A logjam formed at the door: about a dozen boys moving in opposite directions through a narrow passage, exactly what the staggered bells were supposed to prevent. Josiah mucked it up further by deciding to leave and save his question for tomorrow, then changing his mind and jostling back into the classroom.

Around the doorway, some lighthearted, smiley bumping and shouldering began. Bosley made a sudden, strange full-body feinting motion toward another boy, who quickly recoiled in defense. Both relaxed and kept moving; most likely it was an inside joke carried over from a basketball game or something.

The math teacher blurted, "Mr. Bosley, that's a five."

Bosley stopped and turned, his face twisted in exaggerated confusion. "What?"

"I said that's a five. Do it in your next class." She motioned to the YRS counselor, who also looked a bit confused, to record the time-out and the subtraction of his points.

Bosley covered his face with his hands, and his carpal bones protruded with tension. His fingers dug into his hair coils. Josiah was puzzled, because he'd seen Bosley receive many time-outs over the prior months but never react beyond standard Bosley-ish griping.

Then Bosley raged: first at the teacher, then at the counselor, then at his point sheet, then at an unoccupied desk, which he violently kicked over. The other students in the room backed up against the walls, giving Bosley space to stomp around in circles. None could discern whether this was a performance for their benefit, or if he was having an actual fit. Josiah tried to make his way out the door because he'd been in the direct vicinity, and cameras were in the ceiling so that events like this could be reviewed. He was worried about getting in trouble by virtue of proximity. But the door was totally clogged with onlookers pushing in for a glimpse, so Josiah slid behind some bodies and made himself small.

Bosley picked up the desk he'd kicked over and hurled it against the window. The collision of hard materials made an oddly muted, unimpressive thunk. All the passing chatter subsided, except for a few blurted exclamations of "Whoa!" and "Aw *shit!*" Walkie-talkies blared from the belts of security staff spaced throughout the school, and they began to converge in the math room doorway to cordon the students, secure Bosley, and escort him from the education sector. Bosley marched ahead of them, arms straight and stiff, shouting over his shoulder a version of what he was often shouting, what everyone was often shouting: "I didn't do anything! You can't take my points for that!" Then the main door to the education sector banged shut, Bosley's protestations dissipated, Josiah dropped the idea of approaching his math teacher, and the day resumed.

*　　*　　*

THE MAN STANDING before them was in his early thirties. He wore thin-rimmed glasses and was tall, muscular, black, and genial. Earlier in the day the school's history teacher had played video clips for the students of this very man playing wide receiver for the University of Oklahoma and the Pittsburgh Steelers. He hadn't been able to find video online of when the man had played for Concord High School in Wilmington. Very few Delawareans went on to play Division I football at notable programs. Far, far fewer played in the National Football League. The boys who had earned the perk of spending a period with him included Josiah, Cassio, and Crews—but not Bosley—and they were in a peculiar behavioral state of striving to act casually unimpressed while leaning forward in hushed awe.

He spoke of growing up in a hard section of Wilmington and of many influences that pulled him toward weed and alcohol, small crime, and eventual jail. He had been fortunate to have a brother only a year older. The two of them became involved in weightlifting using some dusty, rusty equipment at a local church. They grew strong and fast together. They played football together at every level and eventually won a state championship at Concord before their trajectories diverged, and the speaker's talents took him to a big-time Division I college program while his brother played for Delaware Technical Community College and eventually dropped out.

The boys thought they could extrapolate the ending of this story and the talk's theme: that his brother fell back in with old friends, drugs, and bad influences and was now in prison somewhere or else killed. But his brother managed an auto parts store and was carrying on just fine. They were still best friends and played pickup games with their old high school teammates. Instead, he spoke of his own trials, namely that knee problems enabled him to play in only a handful of games over two seasons in the NFL before he was dropped from the infamously merciless league at a young age. He tried to hang on by playing on professional practice squads, but that job had been depressing and left him broke. The end of his prepared speech focused on the humility required to return home to Wilmington in his midtwenties, work regular jobs, and use free time to talk to high schoolers about his failures.

Even when he made self-deprecating jokes, the sadder parts of his story didn't matter here. This man had played football on national television. He had caught touchdowns in the NFL. The boys edged their chairs closer together as they peered at him with reverence.

After thirty minutes, he asked if anyone had questions. A hand shot up.

"How much money did you make?" a boy asked.

Those around him cringed and hissed. "Shut up with your dumb-ass questions!"

The visitor laughed and replied, "I did pretty well, but not as well as you think. I have to work every day. Now quit feeling around in my pocket."

The atmosphere eased. The Q&A session had a conversational quality. Everyone was respectful and everyone laughed. A sadness coursed through the room as well. Even though the speaker had probably told this story dozens or maybe hundreds of times, his experience with injury and washing out of the NFL—of achieving his childhood dream so ephemerally—still felt tender.

Near the end of their hour, Crews raised his hand. "Do you mind if I share some lyrics with you?"

The speaker shrugged and smiled. He was sitting down now. They were all in a close circle. "Sure, man."

Crews nodded solemnly and unfolded a crinkled sheet of paper that he'd brought. He leaned forward on his knees and his voice erupted, high-pitched and melodic. *"Little boy blast into the sky . . . Go back into the sky you'll see . . . Hear it all the time come back, rewind . . . Little boy blast into the galaxy . . . Little boy when you come around, little boy won't you stay . . . No one's gonna harm you, they all just want to play."*

Crews's eyes closed after the first line. His head and shoulders pulsed from side to side. Josiah hadn't known that he possessed such a voice. When he continued singing, everyone in the circle, including the visitor, began to lean forward, eyes closed, elbows on knees, rocking together. There was almost no space between anyone, joined in this low-grade rapture.

"I watch the birds of prey hunting in the canyon, looking for a lizard or mouse . . . I wonder if they appreciate the setting like me, to control your own direction choose to be free . . . And as for you and your crew I don't hate you, peace . . . Because what do you think I'm doing but crying after this?"

*   *   *

CASSIO STOOD IN front of the life skills class. He clasped his hands behind his back in a scholarly fashion and spoke in fluid sentences, each its own contained thought. Juvenile hall felt like a barrage of overlapping, stream-of-consciousness garble much of the time, so the soliloquy was stunning in its measured cadence alone.

"It's well understood that the wise man listens, the wise man steps back and tries to understand a situation, the wise man seeks advice. On the other hand, the fool doesn't listen at all, the fool acts impulsive, the fool doesn't think about his mistakes, the fool believes that he already knows all."

Josiah hadn't befriended Cassio in earnest. But he'd been paying close attention to the way Cassio carried himself, particularly in this classroom. Cassio seemed to do some things naturally—such as listen and ask questions—that Josiah needed to learn how to do. The other three boys in class slumped forward sleepily. Little Axell was particularly somnambulant. He'd gained considerable weight over the past two months and now had his arms folded atop a defined potbelly. Josiah assumed that whatever meds he was on caused lethargy and a slow metabolism.

"Can you learn from a fool?" Cassio asked rhetorically.

"Yes," Josiah said.

"Then is he really a fool if he's able to teach?"

"A fool isn't stupid, he just doesn't know any better."

"What would you call a person who doesn't know better?"

"Ignorant."

Cassio raised one finger. "Ahh," he said with a rehearsed smile. He was practicing for a presentation he was set to give at a conference for administrators and businesspeople in the realm of alternative education. "So maybe you would say that an ignorant man can become a wise man if he learns from his regrets."

Josiah shrugged. *"Maybe."*

"Then maybe you could say that you don't have to hold on to regrets if you learn from them. Maybe you could say that regrets are just teachable moments to help people grow."

Little Axell, who had looked to be sleeping, chuckled with his eyes still closed.

"You don't see many people learning much here," Josiah said. "Or thinking much, honestly."

"I see people learning and thinking every day," Mr. Michels interjected.

"Maybe you and I don't see the same thing, then," Josiah replied.

"What about yourself?"

"What about myself?"

"I've been with you for a year and a half, in the Cottages and now here. And I know for a fact that you've learned plenty since you've been here, particularly this year."

"And all you do sometimes is think," Cassio added. "Rec time, every night, all the kids are messing and talking trash, and you're just sitting somewhere, *thinking*."

"Not about anything much." Josiah was aware that he sounded defensive. He'd lost track of what point he was arguing, or why he was arguing at all.

"Back up a little," Cassio said. "You got here some months ago. You didn't talk for, like, two or three weeks. Your head was always on the desk. You seemed really mad most of the time. You wanted to keep everyone away from you. Do you think you were acting as a wise man or a fool?"

Josiah made a chortling sound and leaned back in his chair to suggest being finished with this conversation. Cassio just kept staring with gentle, inquisitive eyes.

"I guess I was mostly a fool," Josiah said, humoring the others to move the conversation along.

"Now I see you doing extra work in the library, never asleep in class. I hear you asking questions about random stuff and staying out of all the nonsense that happens. I see you avoiding conflicts and being on honor roll and trying to graduate. So . . . would you consider yourself a wise man now?"

Josiah nearly made a joke about the honor roll at Ferris School not signifying a particularly grand accomplishment, but he withheld it because the list was actually meaningful. His name had become a fixture on it. He didn't respond for a time. Both Cassio and Mr. Michels waited patiently. Finally, Josiah said, "I don't know. Maybe I could be."

Chapter 5

———————◆———————

March–July 2020

CURRENT EVENTS DID not infiltrate juvenile hall the way they did a typical school. The walls were intended to contain humans inside, but they also kept information out. The blockage wasn't physical or intentional; teachers, YRS counselors, and parents flowed in and out of the facility, interacting with kids and passing news along. Frequent phone calls and some closely supervised internet access were allowed. The history teacher began every class with a video segment from the world's happenings—maybe a report on President Trump's dealings with Ukraine, maybe some local sports highlights, maybe a bit about some random guy who built a jetpack and flew himself two hundred yards over a beach before crashing. The class would discuss for a few minutes—which mostly consisted of the boys marveling at the general stupidity of people, be they world leaders or DIY wackos— before segueing into the day's history lesson. In truth, the circuitry of the boys' brains had little bandwidth to process any happenings that didn't involve them directly. Even that one of the front-runners for the 2020 Democratic presidential nomination, Joe Biden, resided in a Wilmington neighborhood less than a mile from Ferris School and they sometimes saw his motorcade passing the campus held barely any relevance inside.

So the news that some respiratory virus had emerged in China during the fall and begun skipping into other countries in the months since was still a faint abstraction to the boys as late as February of 2020. Teachers would mention the numbers now and again: two dozen cases in Washington State, a new outbreak in San Francisco, hospitals in New York City calculating beds and oxygen tanks in the far-flung event of an actual pandemic. Some outlets were reporting that the mortality rate was a fraction of a percent, others that over a fifth of those who contracted the disease died. Young people were immune; young people were the worst super-spreaders; young people didn't really catch it, but if one did catch it, the case would be really, really bad. The noise quickly increased in volume but offered less and less clarity. The boys carried on, for the most part oblivious of COVID-19's progress and significance in the world.

Then, all of a sudden in mid-March, the coronavirus ceased to be a source of background angst and became a present, mortal threat within Delaware. The school system switched to remote learning for what was supposed to be two weeks. Then the shutdown extended through the end of May, then through the end of the school year in June.

At Ferris—a place where nobody was sick until one person got sick, at which point nearly everyone became sick; a place that was very safe until it was incredibly unsafe, with little room in-between—a few intuitive but extreme measures took hold immediately: classes were canceled, sports were canceled, and visitors were canceled. The bare-bones crew of security staff and administrators who physically came to work did their best to stay away from the kids and to keep the kids away from one another. Meanwhile, the kids were amused by the adults' general panic—rather, the kids strived to obscure their own panic by feigning amusement. That was the sense Josiah had as the cluster was divided up into smaller groups that could rotate between their rooms and the rec area in shifts while remaining six feet apart from one another. They learned that one could not play board games or do much of anything fun at that distance and so spent their rec time mostly sitting in the big chairs arranged in a wide ring and talking loudly to one another (scientists studying the virus's transmission had not yet concluded that talking loudly created superhighways of aerosolized spittle that COVID-19 hitched on with scary efficiency). Bosley and Crews were in the same rec group together and took to shouting across the floor space as if it were the length of the gymnasium.

"Yo, Bosley!"

"What you want?!"

"Nothing! Just, hey!"

"Man, you're on my nerves now!"

Their meaningless chatter reverberated through the entire living area and encompassed weeks of everyone else's lives. They talked of sports, girls, and what was irritating them at any given moment; they talked about anything except the coronavirus.

While they did, Josiah spent most of each day, every day, sitting in his own fear. The more details he overheard—the small state's fifteen new cases per day in mid-March climbed to over four hundred new cases per day by mid-April—the more helpless he felt. He wasn't worried about himself so much because he was a teen boy with a teen boy's sense of physical invulnerability. Rather, he worried about his family. The Ferris students had all been given extra time to call home, but every time he'd tried, one of his siblings had answered the phone and invariably told him that their mother was at work. Josiah couldn't help imagining her at one of the service jobs she relied on, where she couldn't skip days and where he doubted she would wear a mask voluntarily even while surrounded by a million little viral specks darting through the atmosphere with the aerial agility of dragonflies, which was how he pictured COVID-19. He admittedly knew little about the virus, and the reportage he did hear from YRS counselors was clearly thin and prone to hyperbole. But no matter who was talking and through whatever lens of anxiety and sensationalism, the coronavirus sounded bad to begin with, and much, much worse if you were poor, overweight, over forty, a cigarette smoker, and moving about freely in the world—all things his mother was.

They'd begun to hear stories about outbreaks in adult prisons: rapid transference, lack of medical care, lonely and agonizing death. A serious unnerving coursed through the passing days. Collectively, the boys responded with a manic energy that threatened to burst the round confines of the cluster: the same, ceaseless jokes over and over; the same, ceaseless fights over and over; the same, ceaseless questions over and over. There were few answers. Almost two months elapsed.

Then, at the end of April, the boys began hearing meaningful information that applied to them directly: in response to the virus, the court system was going to start releasing juvenile detainees early. They didn't yet know the parameters of the mandate. But the immediate grip of its promise made the pandemic suddenly seem like one of the best things to happen at Ferris during Josiah's long tenure.

*   *   *

"There are a ton of music producers in Los Angeles!"

"I know, I know. My uncle, I think, knows some of them."

"You can get them some of your lyrics!"

"Yeah." Crews shrugged coolly. "Maybe I'll do that."

"You driving there?"

"No—it's, like, a three-week drive. I'd be flying on a plane."

"Damn! A plane . . ." Crews's audience, including Josiah, looked at him, wide-eyed, as if he'd been touched by a divine entity.

"I've never been on one before," Crews said. The group was on the floor of the cluster. Crews was scheduled to be released in the spring, and the members of his extended family as well as his therapy team at Ferris were all concerned that he would immediately set out to kill the person who had killed his brother, whoever that person was. All the adults in his life knew that if his fixation on vengeance didn't result in his death or severe injury, which was likely, then it would lead to his being reincarcerated, which was certain. So his loved ones were sorting through the most daunting and heartrending decision that surrounded a child's release from jail. Rationally, they needed to distance Crews from Delaware and all the people he knew in Delaware. But that effort also meant removing him from the orbit of his mother and remaining siblings—as well as his deceased brother's surviving baby son, Crews's nephew, whom he had not yet met. The Crews family did not have the resources to relocate all together.

But Crews had an uncle in south Los Angeles who had volunteered to take his nephew into his home and figure out a school placement for him. This plan had seemed radical at first but had gradually been clarifying over the past weeks. Crews didn't know his uncle well at all—he'd only met him twice before—but understood that he was a reliable man with two sons in their twenties, who were also reliable, and all three earnestly desired to oversee Crews's remaining childhood. If his mother signed off on the relocation, then the State of Delaware could pay for transit and a stipend. On paper, the pros far outweighed the cons.

The coronavirus had turned Crews's future from a coalescing abstraction into a dire urgency—hence the gasping talk of record producers and human flight. The courts were processing and releasing virtually all kids who didn't have violence on their records. Every other day or so, the YRS staff seemed to pull one or two kids aside. A few hours later, those kids would be walking free outside. The number of students at Ferris dropped from twenty-nine to sixteen during the last two weeks of April, making the cluster eerie. As the population fell, the tensions and resentments in the space grew tauter, centered mostly on the question of who felt that he deserved to go right now versus who was actually permitted to leave. Every time someone left, those dwindling few remaining railed over being still here. Worry over the virus itself seemed to vanish, replaced by a constant, shrill chorus of *Why him and not me?*

Josiah spared himself this comparative torment. Virus or no virus, he had committed serious violence against another human being. No judge was going to let him walk before his sentence was served. He was not necessarily at peace with this reality, but he understood it enough not to doubt it or construct unfairness around it—and he also knew well that he would need every day of his term here to graduate from high school and earn a college placement, not that he'd been thinking much about either during these last few weeks. Among other effects, the virus relieved them all of any desire to accomplish schoolwork.

Since Josiah had little to look forward to and also no basis to resent others' getting out before him, he spent an inordinate amount of time thinking about Crews: the grief and rage he was still grappling with, the nephew he'd never held but desired above all other things to avenge, the sheer contrast between Delaware and Los Angeles. Crews's inner life seemed cosmic in scale at the moment, and Josiah listened raptly to the daily updates.

"Where in Los Angeles again?" some kid asked.

"South LA—like, Watts?"

"Is that, like, South Central? Is that, like, near Compton?"

"Yeah, I think it's all sort of, like, the same neighborhood."

"Dang . . ."

"What about your mom?" Josiah ventured to ask.

"What about my mom?"

"She's staying here, is that right?"

"Yeah, with my little brothers and sisters. And my nephew."

"So she's cool with it—with you being that far away?"

"I guess she is. She's the one, like, arranging it."

"Are you cool with it?"

Crews shrugged and thought for a long moment. "I'm cool with whatever. Except . . ." He trailed off and peered around to make sure no YRS counselors were listening.

"Except what?" Josiah asked.

"They'd be taking me, like, straight from here to the airport."

"So?"

"You know why, right?"

Josiah did, but he shook his head as if he didn't, because he wanted
to hear Crews say it.

"It's so I can't go smoke the motherfuckers who shot my brother.
Like, they want to make sure I don't even have one second to do that."

Josiah believed that "they" were pretty wise not to give Crews any
margin to act upon his revenge impulses, especially as Crews now
began ranting about what he wanted to do to those who had done him
this ultimate wrong. Josiah listened agreeably but also wondered if a
subtler part of Crews's complicated consciousness might actually be
relieved at being spared the mandate of trying to kill someone.

*   *   *

MS. MARTIN WAS coming to school twice a week, the max any staff was
allowed, and spent most of her time working with her colleagues, such
as the Education Transition Specialist and the Family Crisis Specialist,
to manage the slew of sudden releases. The process resembled triage:
an urgent diagnosis of the most pressing risks, followed by improvised,
imperfect solutions for school choice and living arrangements. With
the runway of a few months, and with the help of a constellation of
people—guardians, educators, transitional officers, security staff, sports
coaches—the counselors and coordinators at Ferris could set the table
for some creative, uplifting outcomes for her students. They could not
assure these outcomes, and Ms. Martin's year-plus of experience here
was already packed with dozens of valid hopes failed, but they could at
the least help lay the foundation of potential.

Potential was a tricky word in a place such as Ferris: at once a premo-
nition of what could be if everything went right, and a reminder that in
this world most things tended to go wrong.

During these COVID-19 times, they had neither options nor runway. Within a month, the juvenile court system had released over half
the students. The expressed reason was for safety. The actual reason
probably had to do with the loud PR disaster that was already envel-

oping outbreaks in the adult prison system. Ms. Martin understood that. But regardless of political persuasion one could question the safety that these boys were being granted by the courts, as they were being released with no well-considered plan into homes often unprepared to have them, into neighborhoods with no school to attend, where this virus was affecting minority communities at ghastly rates, where crime statistics were beginning to spike drastically, and where normal school aftercare support programs were being conducted remotely or not at all. The boys were elated upon receiving notice of release; Ms. Martin was scared and also knotted in the contradictions of the juvenile court system, which the pandemic seemed to magnify: jail was objectively a terrible place for a teenager to be; jail was a relatively safe place for some of these particular teenagers to be. Unlike most students in Delaware during the spring of 2020, the kids at Ferris still had school. Their teachers were on a twice-weekly in-school rotation. They connected via Zoom on the other three days. So the remaining students had a combination of live and remote learning. Either way, they were physically inhabiting their desks. Keeping them there was a taxing, risky job for Ms. Martin, the YRS staff, the medical staff, the teachers, and everyone else working in school. But it seemed important.

When Ms. Martin wasn't rushing from room to room to ensure that internet hookups were sufficiently stable for Zoom classes, she tried to carry on her typical work in tailoring Student Success Plans and methodically easing her students through the markers they set. The energy among the boys was more fretful than usual, the atmosphere obstreperous, but there was comfort in her work that fed both sides. The factors now dictating daily life in the facility were complicated, but the accomplishment expressed on a boy's face when he grasped a concept that had eluded him moments before held the same quintessential reward.

She was deeply prayerful, heavily involved in her church, conscientious about incorporating its doctrines into her daily life and work. Since starting her job at Ferris, she'd been challenged in her religion as she'd learned firsthand that changing the heart of a person was more complicated than biblical lessons tended to imply. A child's inner and outer well-being involved matters far more precarious than faith and often appeared unforgivingly random. However, she prayed more frequently and with greater concentration. Even though she was aware that clichés abounded regarding church and prison and the transformative power of prayer, she felt that if the tenets of forgiveness and change that she herself observed did not apply here, then they couldn't be of much use anywhere else in the world.

*   *   *

THE RECOGNITION OF Cassio's high school diploma in July felt like a ceremony that in some intangible way involved the spirit. The eleven students remaining at Ferris School wore pointy, polka-dotted cardboard hats in the cafeteria and hooted lowly as the principal transferred the leather casing into his arms. Cassio grinned in his shiny gown and tasseled cap.

Josiah thought Cassio looked even more childlike than usual, as if his face had grown rounder for the occasion, his eyes more airily bright. The moment was quiet and respectful. Many students seemed to find some solace in resenting Cassio generally, but no one could bear ill will toward him now. At the risk of great ridicule, he had embraced his Student Success Plan and done what the adults had told him to do, and now he was being rewarded in exactly the way they'd assured him he would be. Just what that reward signified in the greater world was unclear; the boys would have to wait for news of Cassio's exploits once he was released next week to learn whether this powerful moment would prove to be his journey's short-lived culmination or an entryway onto some more meaningful, sustained path. But still, the inscribed rectangle tucked in his arm looked pretty enviable. Josiah couldn't help being moved by it.

Bosley wasn't there to cast his caustic sarcasm; he'd been released the prior week. Crews, too, was now gone. Josiah didn't know the specifics, but they'd all heard that Crews's mother had canceled the Los Angeles plans at the last minute because she couldn't bear the distance after all, so he was back home in Dover, Delaware, about an hour's drive south of Wilmington. There had been no goodbyes between Josiah and either of these erstwhile sort-of friends. They'd been here and then some adults had summoned them and now they were not here. Life in the cluster resumed as usual minus the rhythm and volume of their talk.

"Do you feel different at all?" Josiah asked Cassio two evenings later during rec time. They were playing a rudimentary board game called Sorry! Cassio was scheduled to leave Ferris the next day.

Cassio shook his head definitively and, for the first time Josiah had ever registered, seemed disappointed in himself. "Nah."

"Don't you feel smart?"

"Nah, not all that much."

"What was the test like?"

Cassio rolled the dice and moved his game piece. "The test was a few hours long. It was pretty easy. I got sixty-three percent right. That's why I don't feel too smart."

"Hold on, hold on." Josiah was shaking his head in disbelief. "*What?* You're the smartest one in here by far."

"I passed a test—*barely*—that ten million other people pass every year. Graduating from high school is, like, a totally normal thing to do. I just did it in here, and so for everyone it's a big deal, get my picture by the library and all that."

Maybe the dullness that characterized the Bosley-less and Crews-less cluster these days generated a certain aura, but Cassio had appeared a little mournful over the last few days, ever since the diploma ceremony. He looked particularly so tonight. Josiah felt guilty for pressing him, as if he were responsible for Cassio's mood. Josiah knew that he wasn't, that elemental fears Cassio was experiencing on the precipice of his release had nothing to do with Josiah or his questions. The world outside was vast, difficult, and frightening. After nine months of being cared for and celebrated here, Cassio was apprehensive about reentering it. Josiah would be in the same position not too far in the future. That was all.

They continued playing the game a few more turns before growing bored. They drifted to different sides of the rec area and watched other kids play different games. Then came the warning for lights out. Cassio left the next morning.

Josiah had never been close with him, but had felt bonded through the quiet pursuit they shared. Every familiar face that disappeared—even those kids Josiah could hardly tolerate—made him feel a little lonelier. Bosley, Crews, Cassio, and Sargent were all gone. Big Axell and Little Axell were gone. The kid who danced constantly was gone. The kid who shot dozens of three-pointers every game and made zero of them was gone.

Almost all of the kids remaining were locked up due to real violence. Josiah found violent kids to be much quieter in general—either because they were embarrassed, had more on their minds, were given more drugs, or some combination. Life became incredibly boring as summer began. No one seemed to do or say anything interesting, ever. Josiah kept to himself and did his work and dwelled on the logic that if Cassio, by far the brightest kid Josiah had ever known here, had seen himself as unfit for the following passage, then Josiah had reason to be afraid.

He distracted himself by reengaging with his courses of study. With school life still on pause and most all the peers who had entertained and exasperated him released, he had plenty of time to grind through his lessons. For a couple hours per day, he worked in the library with a YRS counselor watching. On occasion, he Zoomed with teachers for extra help. When he grew frustrated with an essay or problem set, he stopped and resumed the next day. He was pretty sure that this progress would have been impossible without the onset of COVID-19, which was a strange intuition to hold. This work belonged to him alone and was a driver of time; none of the other kids asked him much about it, and he wasn't inclined to share. Josiah really, really liked it this way.

*   *   *

SARGENT WAS SHOT multiple times in some dispute outside. Amazingly, he was neither critically injured nor arrested, but his hospital stay was long. Sargent had turned nineteen while still at Ferris, so he was no longer a minor, and it had never sounded as if he had any adult support. Josiah imagined that those nights spent recovering in some Slower Delaware hospital room were even longer, more painful, and more despairing than the nights in Ferris could be.

Crews had been arrested by the Dover police within a week of his release from Ferris. He'd been walking with some friends late at night. A separate group began shooting at his group from across the street. Crews wasn't hit and had taken cover until a police car pulled up. Crews had tried to toss the gun he was carrying into some nearby bushes, but one of the officers saw the flick of his wrist and the glint of the metal in the street light. Though he'd apparently fired no shots during the altercation, Crews was back in jail six days after leaving jail. That was all Josiah had heard from the YRS counselors. With a probation violation attached to the weapons charge, the security staff didn't know if he would eventually be sent back to Ferris or be assigned some harsher penalty or maybe be taken out of state in light of the murder of his brother. They didn't know if Crews had been out that night, armed, because maybe he'd learned who had killed his brother. But, just as Josiah imagined Sargent in the hospital, he also used his mind's vivid inner film reel to see Crews in whatever cell he'd been assigned, turning his body over and over, stewing and hating and—maybe—picturing that alternative life in which he'd traveled straight to Los Angeles to live with his uncle.

Bosley was apparently doing fantastic so far. As the YRS counselor who'd gone to school with his cousins reported, Bosley's entire extended family—aunts, uncles, cousins, second cousins, a constellation of Bosleys stretching across the city of Wilmington—had rallied around his release. They had placed him in two different summer schools to catch up to his grade level and were indulging exactly none of his nonsense.

These ongoing sagas of the departed trickled back to Ferris School, mostly via the YRS counselors or new intakes who knew of them. The details were not necessarily accurate, but the general events were reliable. Josiah found himself rooting for kids he hadn't even known well, hadn't even wanted to know. He found himself heartbroken for them as well when their stories turned south.

However, no one, including Ms. Martin, seemed to know much about what was going on with Cassio. She explained that this was partly because he'd come here from North Philadelphia, far beyond her local contacts, and partly because he claimed to keep forgetting his email password and becoming too frustrated to follow the prompts by which to reset it. He replied to the simplest of emails—a casual check-in from her, or one forwarding news of a scholarship program tailored toward kids who'd earned diplomas in juvenile hall—weeks late, if at all. The few times she'd managed to connect with him via his cell phone, he'd been hurried and evasive. Then his number was disconnected, presumably for lack of payment.

Josiah worried more about Cassio than any of the others, because even though Sargent and Crews were in terrible straits, they were in the hospital and jail, respectively. They weren't going to be hurt worse. Cassio could still be.

All this concern for others seemed to energize Josiah's own work. He couldn't explain how or why. Time continued to pass at exactly the same rate as it always had, lumbering toward his release and all the uncertainty that spread beyond it. But something had changed inside him, in some as-yet-unseen part of him, because regardless of any negative thoughts orbiting his mind, he pressed on through his books, each day and on schedule. He began taking practice tests and then real tests. He also finally received his reward lunch from Wendy's.

*   *   *

THE COMMUNITY COLLEGE was in the exact center of New York State, in a small town about a six-hour drive from Delaware. A multipronged approach coordinated by Ms. Martin, Mr. Michels, and the volunteer lacrosse coach at Ferris secured Josiah a scholarship beginning in the second semester of the 2020–21 school year. The school didn't have any sort of special policy or procedure geared toward kids with juvenile records. The Ferris team—and Josiah's own work and test results—had simply convinced the admissions apparatus that Josiah was a student-athlete worth investing in.

Chapter 6

———◆———

September–November 2020

J OSIAH GAZED OUT the classroom window that looked upon the parking lot, which for nearly a year had been his most constant view of the world, his primary signifier of seasons changing. The scenery remained the same as ever, with the dogwood tree losing leaves beneath the gray sky, moderate traffic on the road beyond the lawn. A squirrel skittered around the base of the tree. He enjoyed thinking that it was the same squirrel as the one that had hyped up Bosley months earlier, but knew it probably wasn't.

A middle-aged white man, who taught one class on financial management and another on electric circuitry, was talking to a kid about the importance of résumés and building a record of employment, no matter what the jobs were. The kid kept pressing a reasoned case that selling opioids was a valid job by almost every metric except its illegality. The teacher was trying to convince him that learning how to lay broadband wires for a company such as Verizon was a much more useful skill long term, and that it paid better by the hour. The kid was laughing, and the teacher was growing flustered. The students mostly liked this teacher because he was easy to aggravate but also earnest and impassioned in his old-school belief in the merits of a hard day's manual labor.

"Man, what you're telling me just makes no sense when I'm talking about a thousand dollars a *day*," the kid said.

The older man made an indignant sputtering sound. "Listen, I promise you that you've never made a thousand dollars in a day, or even in six months, selling that crap. What I'm talking about, a decent job, is twenty-five dollars an hour, eight hours a day, year after year, with overtime, health insurance, a pension. This isn't even . . . it isn't even a conversation we're having."

"Of course it isn't, because it's like you're not speaking English. What is a pension?"

"Oh my Lord . . ." The teacher pressed his palm to his forehead and kneaded the skin in circles. "You're clearly not learning one useful thing here."

"Of course I'm not. This isn't a real school. This is, like, some bullshit imitation of a school."

"And if you don't hear me out, they're going to keep sending you back here, over and over and over, till you turn eighteen. Then it's on to Gander Hill." Gander Hill was the nearest state prison.

The kid avidly shook his head. "Nope, nope, nope. They got me on some bullshit this time. They'll never get me next time. I'm smarter than any police."

"Oh my goodness . . ."

This was often the rhythm of this teacher's RTI classes at the end of each day: decent intentions devolving into repeated incantations of "Oh my Lord" and "Oh my goodness."

Josiah realized that he would miss these conversations once he was gone.

Ms. Martin appeared in the doorway and flapped one hand to summon Josiah. Some shiny blue fabric draped from her other forearm, along with a tasseled square of cardboard: his graduation cap and gown.

He'd completed his work (most of it) and passed his tests (barely), and the time had come to take the photo that would adorn the library window for a time. In the hallway outside her office, while Mr. Michels waited to take a picture and a few of the YRS staff watched with some pride, he shimmied into the gown and fit the cap onto his head, then tilted it fashionably to one side. Ms. Martin took a moment to restraighten it and then unbunch the gown from his shoulders. She handed him the diploma she'd been holding for him. He did a spontaneous dance step in which his left and right feet alternately kicked out. He looked down at the fabric shimmering. He said, "Check me out, I'm a businessman!"

When Mr. Michels held up his phone to take the picture, Josiah did all he could to form a serious face toward the lens, but the expression captured on camera and later displayed in the busy hallway was one of deep self-satisfaction, with his head tipped downward, his grin crooked, and his eyes gazing up as if with some tantalizing secret.

"That one can be for the graduation wall in the hallway," Ms. Martin said. "Now let's do one for your mom."

She coached him to stand upright with his hands folded in front of him and a more symmetrical smile.

"We'll make a few copies of that to give out to family and whoever. Now one for my office." She posed with him and let him know that this image would inspire her during long days, months, and even years after he was gone, when he'd all but forgotten about this place. They both knew that such a time would never come—that Josiah would never forget about this place—but the benign ruse suited the moment and they shared it together.

"Can I take a walk?" Josiah asked.

"Not outside education."

"I know—but can I?"

The adults all looked at one another and nodded that a walk was fine. Josiah strutted about forty feet in one direction, where a hallway dead-ended at the locked gymnasium door. Then he came back to where they were by the library door, turned ninety degrees to his left, and walked about forty feet to the other dead end. A few kids were in a study group in the library, and Josiah preened for them, amusing some and irking others.

"I'm a businessman!" he repeated a few times. He came back and was able to project a hard, glowering expression for the camera, crossing his arms and pointing his fingers, for a few more shots. "Can you make some prints of these at Walgreens?" he asked.

"Who are these for?" Ms. Martin asked.

"These ones are for me."

The school bell sounded and Josiah passed the diploma back and squirmed reluctantly from his gown before other kids were released from the classrooms. Ferris had adopted a "village schoolhouse" model, in which students remained in the same classroom all day, so that they could have regular school while somewhat complying with social distancing. They were only in the hallway at the beginning and end of each day, plus lunch and bathroom breaks. This caused immense restlessness. By this hour in the afternoon, every kid was ready to burst through the doorways. Josiah filed in with his group.

The weather was cooling but still warm enough for outdoor time. They were not allowed to share contact, even that required to toss a ball back and forth, so he just milled around the grass of the enclosed football field. He found himself near the spot where he'd dropped that football pass last fall. He thought of his great shame in that moment. He thought of his shame while eating Thanksgiving dinner with his mother, and of his shame while asking teachers for help with his schoolwork, and of his shame while lying awake at night, and even of his shame while contemplating a future that seemed as if it would now find him in college. Then he thought of the photo just taken, and of his smile soon to be taped to the painted cinder blocks outside the library, and of his unbridled giddiness while wearing a gown and holding a diploma, and of kids jailed at Ferris School months or years in the future who wouldn't know Josiah Wright from anybody but would see his face beneath that cap. He was overwhelmed but glad in his heart.

He walked some laps around the field on this temperate fall day and pondered the weight he carried.

* * *

JOSIAH WAS RELEASED uneventfully in late September. He woke up in
the cluster after a terrible sleep, as he had almost 360 times in a row, and
by the afternoon he was standing outside in front of the school opposite
the classroom window through which he'd spent all those afternoons
gazing at the tree. He was with his mother and siblings and he was going
home. There were some exit forms to fill out, many warnings and instructions to process, and a series of probationary meetings scheduled,
but the day overall was unceremonious. His mother seemed rather tired
by the proceedings and eager to bring him home.

The city of Wilmington was an odd jigsaw of urban and subur-
ban pieces pressed hard against one another. Ferris School stood on
the corner of a woodsy area, not far removed from some large nature
preserves and historic home estates. Lancaster Pike headed southeast
toward downtown. Fields on either side of the road became strip malls
and apartment complexes within a few blocks, and those became tightly
packed row houses within a few more. Josiah had taken it for granted
that he would feel some excitement or nostalgia as his home neared
and he could tie specific memories to the various intersections they
passed. The memories were there: that was the sidewalk where he and
his friends had built a ramp out of scavenged plywood and taken turns
doing bike tricks off it, resulting in sprained wrists and scabbed elbows;
that was the block where he'd broken an old lady's window with a football and she'd made him walk with her all the way home so she could
tell his furious mother; that was the house where that girl he'd liked
in middle school lived and he would bend the routes of all his errands
to pass it in hopes of a chance encounter; that was the store he'd tried
to rob, which had resulted in his first incarceration; that was the park
where one of his oldest friends had been shot and also where Josiah had
once scored five straight baskets in a pickup hoops game. The memories were endless.

Yet he didn't feel attached to any of them, the good or the bad or the strange. He'd spent almost two years living just a few miles away, with other people who'd grown up close to where he had. He'd been reminded in some way of home most every day he'd been incarcerated at Ferris. But maybe the rules and structures had been so different as to disconnect him from his childhood, or maybe he'd done so much schoolwork as to feel that he'd outgrown home, or maybe he'd simply changed enough as a human being—not *grown*, necessarily, but changed—so as not to care much for the person he'd once been and the events that had formed that person.

The apartment seemed narrower. His room smelled musty and sad. His half-siblings were annoying. His day of release was going horribly, and within fifteen minutes of returning, he was ready to bolt out the door. What calmed his frenetic interior—what salvaged his day and possibly kept him from doing something that would send him back to jail—were the aromatic happenings in the kitchenette, where his mom had set to work. He'd been sitting on the stairs and contemplating the front door, but the baking drew him toward her and the tiny, claustrophobic space where she found her primary joy. She was cracking open the top of the oven with her face inches away. Four large cinnamon buns bubbled and swelled inside. He stood in the doorway between the cook space and the hallway and just watched her.

"Can you get me an oven mitt and tongs?" she asked him.

"I don't know where they are."

She made an irritated snort and then a laborious display of grabbing the items she needed from the hanging rack behind her. She'd gained some weight over the year. Her body almost filled the entire space.

"You didn't seem happy to get me," he said.

"I was overjoyed to bring you home."

"I didn't feel it."

"I didn't show it."

"How come?" The dialogue was taking the cadence of group therapy sessions at Ferris, in which boys trained by life to bury their feelings were exhorted to share them.

"Because Kayla and Demi were with me." Kayla and Demitrius were his younger half-siblings.

"So?"

"I can't have them thinking anything around jail is anything to celebrate."

"You know I graduated while I was in there?"

"Yeah, you told me."

"Is that anything to celebrate?"

From her crouch, she looked straight at him over her shoulder. She was exasperated. "What do you think these are for?" She opened the oven and poked at the rolls with a knife, emitted a deeply satisfied sighing sound, and used the tongs to coax them onto a plate. A moment later, the four of them sat around the table eating. The rolls his mother had made were as big as the children's heads. Josiah stared down at his. He'd dreamed of this, both sleeping and awake: sitting at this table with these people, eating some ludicrously rich confection. His sister, when prompted, said a rushed, clumsy grace. His mother said she was thankful that Josiah had his diploma. He added that he was glad to be with them and grateful for his mother's talents. Then they ate.

* * *

JOSIAH KEPT BLAMING the bus company, but everyone around him knew that the problems ran deeper than glitchy websites and confusing schedules. They were also thornier than Gmail system maintenance and forgotten passwords, which were the other main culprits Josiah cited when trying to explain why he wouldn't respond to urgent emails for days and why he didn't think he could get himself to central New York on time for the winter college term, maybe ever at all.

The work that had secured Josiah's spot at community college was voluminous, probably totaling in the hundreds of hours among educators on both sides of the shaky bridge between juvenile hall and higher learning. There were the layers of forms and money and legal permissions, but the bulk of this work was by a group of people at Ferris striving to convince and reassure a group of people at the college that Josiah Wright would be all right there—that he was not only capable of college work but of college life as well. These phone calls and emails consisted of refrains affirming that he was bright, he was eager, he was social, he was deserving of this chance to rise in a society that offered precious few chances for kids like him to do so. Ms. Martin and Mr. Michels in particular would invoke the narratives of students they'd had at Ferris who had gone on to thrive in college: the kid who had played lacrosse and majored in physical therapy at the University of Delaware, the kid who had gotten into Del Tech and was studying to be an electrician. These stories were powerful, and they'd helped greatly in Josiah's cause.

The community college admissions team had organized a special visit for him in mid-November—to introduce him to the rural New York campus and also, perhaps, to gauge for themselves his readiness. The lacrosse coach had cleared a full weekend to host Josiah. A few of the coach's best-hearted players had volunteered to show Josiah around the campus and facilities. The college was paying for his transit and had set aside a room for him. The weekend would include class visits and a lacrosse team reception, a chance for him to sit with teachers and deans to ask questions, some free time just to walk around.

And now Josiah was refusing to go.

He was sitting on the stoop of his home an hour before his bus was supposed to leave. He had a basketball and was trying to perform low, rapid dribbles around his feet and through his legs, but he wasn't quite deft enough. He was committed to making this trip but he hadn't yet packed or arranged a ride to the bus station or even told his mom that he would be gone. She wasn't home now. He thought that her boyfriend was inside, but sometimes the man would leave using the back alley. Josiah could walk the mile to the station or probably ask anyone passing by for a lift. But he sat there and kept not doing either. Nor did he answer his cell phone, which dinged with increasing frequency as the departure time drew closer: Ms. Martin, Mr. Michels, and other people who were fixated on his doing this thing that he suddenly had no desire to do.

He was harping on the COVID-19 test he would have to take upon his arrival—the rapid-response kind that necessitated a long, thin implement being crammed way, way up his nose. He'd suffered through dozens of those over the spring and summer at Ferris. Anytime there'd been a contact scare in the school, he'd have that wire scratching around within a few centimeters of his brain. The college lacrosse coach had sworn that Josiah would not be receiving that kind of test, but rather one in which a small vial was filled with saliva. Josiah didn't believe him. Josiah was aware that two crucial elements in transitioning into the world from jail were trust and flexibility. He'd probably heard those words more than any others since being released: he was all of a sudden supposed to trust his mother and trust his probation officer and trust the system and trust himself; he was supposed to be flexible in his schedule and flexible in his judgments and flexible in the guidance he received. But trust and flexibility were not switches that could be flicked on and off at will. Josiah had grown up in a world of broken promises, and those two mechanisms felt corroded.

The pale gray sky turned dark gray and soon rain began to fall lightly. Josiah remained on the step. The street was fully empty as he continued dribbling. The ball bounced off his toe and wedged itself under a car fender. He didn't retrieve it right away. His fingers were numb from the cold. After a time, he picked up the ball and went back inside to the couch in front of the TV. He spent much of his time these days moving back and forth between the stoop and the couch; anywhere else he felt like an unwelcome guest in the world. He saw that his bus had left about ten minutes earlier. He'd officially missed it. Somehow, he convinced himself that this was the bus company's fault, not his.

He watched TV until his mother came home in a fit because all of the people who'd been trying and failing to connect with him had been calling her: "First, it was Mr. Michels from jail. Then it was Ms. Banks from jail"—Ms. Banks was the superintendent of Ferris, the boss of the whole place—"then it was Mr. Michels again, then it was Ms., uh, Ms. . . . ."

"Ms. Martin."

"Yeah. They all wanted to make for damn sure that you got on your bus today. I didn't even know what bus, but as of yet you don't look on it."

"I think I might have missed it."

"You *think*?"

"Next time Ms. Martin calls, just tell her I lost her number, so I can't call her back."

"That doesn't make sense. If I say that, she'll just give me her number."

"Oh, right."

He turned away from his mother, toward the TV screen. She told him that she'd received one other call from someone looking for him, named Cassio.

Josiah suddenly sat up. "You talked to him?"

His mother had written down the number on a receipt. Josiah couldn't decide whether to call him back. He still felt gratitude toward Cassio and desired to know how he was faring outside Ferris. Josiah also understood that one of the teachers must have put him up to this call to convince Josiah to get himself to New York, so Cassio wasn't actually reaching out as a friend, but as a messenger.

"What's good?" Josiah asked, with more eagerness than intended, when Cassio picked up.

"Not much." Cassio sounded muted and resigned, as if he were watching his favorite sports team let a pivotal game slip away. "I called you because Ms. Martin *and* Mr. Michels called me. They want me to tell you to get your ass on a bus."

"I missed it already."

"Whatever. I'm not gonna tell you what to do with your ass."

The wordplay joke was weak and Ferris-like: vaguely homophobic, maybe, but not profane or cruel enough to lose points over. Josiah found himself often calibrating his language and humor to dance around the points-sheet parameters that were no longer relevant to his life.

Cassio's depleted tone disappointed Josiah. He'd expected some vestige of the energy of the kid he recalled from life skills class. Those classes had been months ago, but still Josiah remembered that avid curiousness that he'd resented at first before quietly desiring to emulate it. What he heard now was the voice of someone bored by his day.

"What'd they say about me?" Josiah asked.

"Just that you were having some trouble, maybe."

"Nah, I'm good. I just . . . The bus was going to a college in New York. It's cold as *fuck* in New York."

Cassio laughed a private sort of laugh. "They both told me you would probably blame the weather—that or say your internet was broke. I told them you wouldn't play it like that to me; you'd at least come up with something halfway believable."

"It *is* cold as fuck there."

"You got a coat." Cassio was still laughing.

"So you're just doing what those teachers say, then," Josiah replied, defensive and suddenly spiteful. "Just like you always did."

Cassio ignored the deep cut. "I'm just messing with you. If they call again, I'll tell them what I'm about to tell you."

Josiah waited a moment, then prodded, "What's that?"

"I don't give a fuck if you get on that bus or not. I don't give a fuck if you go to college or not. I think you're cool. I hope you do all right at whatever it is you do. But I got my own shit to deal with. I got about zero space in my life to worry about yours. I'll say something like that."

"So what did you even call for?"

"Because I told them I would, so that they would all quit blowing up my phone." Cassio sounded impatient now, ready to hang up and forget about Josiah. "Because I'm going to have to change this number if they keep on being in my shit."

Josiah wanted to ask Cassio what his own shit actually was. Around six months had passed since Cassio had graduated from high school and then been released from Ferris School, and Josiah wanted to hear the story of those months. Mainly, he wanted to know why Cassio's voice contained so much desolation. But he couldn't ask any of those questions outright because he didn't know Cassio well enough to venture crossing such lines. They'd orbited each other because they'd both spent time in the same jail and they'd both been a little more academically minded than others there. The connection had to do with proximity and some shared intellectual traits, perhaps an illusion of elitism, of having been tapped for something greater. It had nothing to do with experience, true loyalty, or blood. Despite Josiah's excitement at having heard Cassio's name and his voice, this exchange made him realize that a conditional friendship such as theirs would not endure in the outside world. So Josiah didn't have any business asking about Cassio's personal life. This would probably be the last time they ever spoke.

"It was cool of you to call me up," Josiah said. "I'll call those teachers back and tell them to get out of your face."

"That would be good of you. So—you gonna go?"

"Where?"

"To the New York college?"

"I don't know. Maybe, if they don't cancel my scholarship for missing this whole weekend visit."

"They won't cancel your scholarship," Cassio said with conviction. "I mean, don't, like, fuck it up entirely or anything, but they don't make those offers just because they feel bad. They want you there, if you bother getting yourself there—and if you don't get yourself all shot up like Sargent."

They both laughed authentically because jail time had a way of warping humor to where someone's being shot was hilarious. Then Cassio said he'd driven all the way to southern Delaware to visit Sargent in the hospital following his severe bullet wounds. Cassio hadn't been out of Ferris for long at that point and had still been in the grip of a tremendous gratitude toward his world and all the people in it (a gratitude that had since waned, his tone inferred), and he'd figured that Sargent didn't have many people who loved him, and so Cassio had made that trip after hearing the news. Now, months later, Cassio reported that he and Sargent were about to be roommates; they'd found an apartment in

Chester, a working-class township on the Pennsylvania side of the corridor between Philadelphia and Wilmington.

Josiah marveled at the development and the particular image that formed of Sargent and Cassio—a black man and a white man, the former from the inner city and the latter from farm country, Cassio being one of the smartest guys Josiah had ever known and Sargent being one of the dimmest—sharing a space, forming grocery lists and cooking meals together, doing laundry, most likely bickering incessantly. Josiah could barely make sense of the concept, nor could he quite process the next bit of information Cassio gave him, which was that Cassio was about to be a father.

He gave few details regarding the situation. His voice carried competing tones of awe and terror and matter-of-factness. He didn't mention the mother's name or anything about their relationship. Josiah performed some rough math and figured that Cassio must have impregnated this girl within a couple weeks of leaving Ferris, and Josiah also speculated that this must have upended any and maybe all educational plans Cassio had made upon being released from jail. Across generations that included Josiah's mother and father and grandparents, having children young tended to do that. Then Cassio's general tired melancholy made sense.

Josiah was still processing all this information when Cassio suddenly became rushed to get off the phone. They promised to stay in touch, and Josiah said that maybe he would follow through with the whole college thing, even if it felt like kind of a mess, and they said goodbye.

Afterward, Josiah went back to sitting on the sidewalk stoop with the basketball in the darkness, not dribbling it anymore because the air was too cold for bare fingers. He sat with his hands in his pockets and the ball in his lap and his body hunched forward, quietly and sullenly marveling at where Cassio was and how his life appeared so vastly, vastly different from the blueprint Josiah had envisioned for it when he'd watched Cassio take that certificate from Ms. Martin in the cafeteria not long ago. The details were wild and funny and, yes, sad. Josiah saw no lessons to be learned in them. He saw no defined path ahead for any of them. He saw only the miraculous disarray that was human existence, and he saw how little import that even the greatest of promises held. Sargent, Crews, Cassio, Bosley, himself: he saw them all for the specks that they were, and for these minutes as dusk fell and his bus ticket lay crumpled up and obsolete on a dresser upstairs, he felt a strange but consoling sense of peace, and he enjoyed it.

Chapter 7

◆

January–April 2021

Josiah wandered with little purpose through the Port Authority of New York. Midday on a Tuesday in a city only tentatively recovering from COVID-19 closures probably wasn't the most hectic time at the world's busiest bus terminal, but Josiah was still overwhelmed upon stepping from the confines of the Greyhound from Delaware. He had over two hours before his connection to central New York. He was inexplicably famished, being that his mother had sent him with an entire marbled pound cake and he'd eaten almost half of it during the ride here. Maybe all the sugar had him craving something substantial, like a burger. But he found that the cost of lunch food was hyperinflated here—nearly $15 for a dismal little patty in a bun—and he could not bring himself to pay that much even though he had a $20 travel stipend.

He assumed this money would stretch further outside the station, so even though his duffel bag was heavy with winterwear, he followed overhead signs to an exit onto Fortieth Street. He ricocheted between hurried masked people and their luggage and stood on the sidewalk. A sheen of slushy wetness from a recent storm immediately began working its way over his shoe soles. The noise was oppressive: people hawking things, cars and trucks and cabs honking, the resounding whooshes made by buses sweeping along the overhead latticework of ramps. And

112

police were everywhere, in and out of their vehicles, as if completely ringing the massive building for a raid. He couldn't evade the ingrained belief that every single person in a uniform was intently focused on him, waiting for whatever he would do next.

Josiah immediately retreated back inside. He bought a glazed pretzel from an Auntie Anne's vendor for $5.95, found a spot against the wall that was close to his connection gate, and sat on his duffel bag. He ate, and the sugar laid upon all the sugar he'd already eaten caused a fidgety surge followed quickly by a crush of fatigue. People were asleep all across the station, both delayed travelers and homeless people and drunk people. Josiah badly wanted to be asleep. But he was responsible for his possessions and his money and couldn't do that; he really, really couldn't do that. . . .

He slept for a time on his duffel bag cushion while announcements streamed over the terminal speakers and travelers hurried past him without looking down, and he started awake just in time to catch his bus. The vehicle left the city and headed into the woodsy sameness of central New York State. Josiah felt farther and farther and farther away from home.

His eighteenth birthday had been two weeks earlier. The weather was cold but people still weren't supposed to gather inside, so some extended family and a few of his mother's colleagues from various jobs she'd held were invited to a cookout in the alley of grass between two blocks of row houses. The ten or so people had sat around in plastic chairs, wearing thick coats, hats, and gloves. An uncle scooted ribs and chicken around the grill with tongs. His mother's boyfriend, intimidated by the onrush of family and the too-personal questions being asked, drank four or five beers in quick succession and spent the afternoon in a pleasantly stupid state, nodding and grinning every time someone spoke to him but rarely opening his mouth. The younger kids had run around for a time and then begun complaining loudly about the cold until the adults finally gave up on the social restrictions and everyone congregated inside to eat.

Josiah had spent most of the time severely self-conscious. He hadn't
seen most of these people in two years. Dialogue that should have been
banal but easy was overlaid with tension as adults tiptoed around the
topic of jail. Even his mother, energized by vodka and overemphasiz-
ing the achievement of graduating from high school in a slurry speech,
sounded a bit embarrassed—or maybe she didn't sound embarrassed at
all, but Josiah projected that onto her. Regardless, he was unhappy all
day. The only authentic conversations he had were with young cousins, who had no compunctions with blurting questions about imprisonment.

"Did you fight a lot?" one asked, clearly anticipating war stories.

"Nah, not really."

"Oh." The cousin looked deeply disappointed.

"Was the food terrible?"

"It was pretty bad." Josiah shuddered at the memory, and his cousin
laughed. But even then, he thought he saw other adults glaring at him,
as if any lighthearted interaction meant that Josiah must be glorifying
gang life and prison life to the youngsters.

One of his uncles had served time in juvie, as well as a few years in
prison during his early twenties. During the party he pulled Josiah aside
to try to share in the mythology of difficulties: gigantic rats and evil
guards and lost childhood. Josiah nodded along. His uncle seemed so
fully wrapped up in these visions from twenty years earlier that Josiah
saw no purpose in saying that he had seen mice but not rats, that some of
the YRS counselors were surly but for the most part they were just tired
human beings who tried to embrace their titular roles and offer counsel, that the valid grief of losing half of high school was somewhat—
somewhat—assuaged by the knowledge that Josiah would probably not
have graduated from high school or been signed up for college otherwise.

The cake was not Josiah's mother's best work: a plain three-layer
yellow cake with a buttercream icing. It was a bit dry and not much to
look at, at least relative to what she was capable of. By the time dessert

was served, she was busy getting her boyfriend to the bedroom to nap off all the beer.

The following day, Josiah had taken two buses to the courthouse downtown to sort out the details of attending college while still on probation, since Delaware did not expunge juvenile records until five years after the last arrest. The Ferris School coordinators had done much of the paperwork for him, but he still had to sign a few papers now that he was eighteen. His PO had given him detailed instructions of exactly what rooms to visit and what names to ask for, but the process still took up half the day. Lines were long, offices were understaffed, forms were easy to confuse, clerics were cranky. He felt as though the process of clearing his path to college should have been more rewarding.

* * *

NOW JOSIAH WAS touring the community college campus with his new lacrosse coach, a broad, gentle-voiced man with thin hair and thick limbs. The campus did not have many acres or components to show: a classroom building, a dorm building, and a sports building, all nestled among the woods and fields. Between indoor spaces they rushed through frigid wind. The coach joked that it wasn't always like this. Josiah didn't tell him that he had spent some time on weather.com and seen that the weather had been like this for months and looked to be like this for months to come.

Yet the physical spaces, which were modest by college standards, were massive and intimidating to Josiah. He'd looked at pictures many times with Ms. Martin, and so no visuals actually surprised him. But a picture could not capture the feeling of a three-story atrium, or a classroom containing actual science equipment, or a bedroom that had enough space for a desk and a closet and a window that he could easily glide open and closed, even in the freezing weather, whenever he wanted.

The coach asked a few times if Josiah had been working out, and Josiah just mumbled, "Yeah," because he didn't feel comfortable enough with this man to admit that he hadn't picked up a lacrosse stick in almost two years, since the season before the season canceled by COVID. He didn't own his own stick, pads, or cleats. None of his friends played lacrosse. Josiah found it wholly bizarre that his matriculation in college was at all related to a game he'd picked up in juvenile hall only because it was offered and it was outside. The coach showed him the weight room, then a netted-off section of the gymnasium where the team could practice indoors, and then they walked a lap around the outdoor field. Their feet crunched on the frozen grass. The coach talked about the Mid-State Athletic Conference and how, with a bit of work, Josiah could dominate it. He seemed to Josiah like a good man, yet spending time with him and nodding along to the conversations he led caused an upwelling of homesickness.

The coach left him at the dorm entrance. The late afternoon was already darkening, rendering the campus even more austere. Lights glowed in the living spaces above. Coach told him that he would be checking in regularly, and that Josiah should absolutely reach out if he needed anything at all, such as guidance registering for classes or introductions to faculty or tutoring—anything. "This must seem like a pretty big place to you, but it's actually a really small place. We all know each other. We're all easy to find."

Josiah had been assigned a single room, which, judging from the double rooms up and down the hallway, was an anomaly. He could only speculate that they were giving him special treatment to limit the number of variables he had to adjust to, or maybe his entering the school a few weeks into the current semester made space tricky. Most likely, he couldn't help assuming, this arrangement had been made for the benefit of the students around him, so that the college wouldn't be fielding calls from parents concerned over their son's pairing with a juvenile delinquent.

Regardless, he was glad to be alone, even though he was vaguely aware that being alone was probably the worst thing for him right now. The walls were cinder block painted white, which was familiar. Glances inside other rooms in passing showed him how kids strung up lights and hung posters and corkboards and other art to cover the depressing surfaces. Sitting in his room that night, making slow revolutions in his swivel chair, he listened to these same kids chatting with one another up and down the hallways, pranking, playing unbearable pop music too loudly. Along this corridor of kids his age—kids who were blithely college-like—he kept his door locked and left his walls bare. He spent an awful lot of his time those first days and nights just staring at the locked door and the bare walls.

*   *   *

SARAH MARTIN TRIED to tell herself that texts consisting of a single word or a single acronym were simply the way that young people communicated these days. She tried to tell herself that when she wrote him a long and detailed text message to make sure that he'd asked his teammates for help logging in to virtual classes and he'd replied with a single, lowercase letter y, that he was simply in a rush. But Ms. Martin knew her students, and she knew human nature, and she knew something was wrong.

Generally, the students with whom she worked depicted themselves as functioning, mature adults; much of the chaos of the space they lived in came from boys trying to prove over and over the great delusion they subscribed to, which was that they didn't need help.

Josiah had stopped expressing those well-worn behaviors. By the end of his stay at Ferris, he'd been activated, and not frightened or threatened, by the prospect of accomplishing more than just finishing eleventh grade, or finishing high school, or applying to local tech schools. He hadn't minded receiving help or even asking for it at times. And so Ms. Martin and the many other specialists and coordinators buoying him had truly hoped that he'd been ready for college. Even after the ignored emails and the missed buses, the voice mails unreturned and the phone call she'd bidden Cassio to make, she'd been confident that if Josiah could just get himself to campus, he would be sufficiently inspired to make an earnest go of his opportunity there, just as he had at Ferris

School. When the community college lacrosse coach had texted to confirm that, yes, Josiah Wright had physically disembarked there from the bus, she'd taken a moment to silently thank her God.

Weeks later and amid a number of troubling signals, she still maintained some fraction of the hope she'd let bloom then. But it waned further each day, with each fragment of information or noninformation that reached her. Josiah had missed two introductory writing classes in a week; Josiah had missed a lacrosse team meeting; Josiah had missed a mandatory COVID test; Josiah was in his room but the door was locked and he wasn't answering; Josiah's phone was going straight to voice mail; Josiah's phone number was no longer working. She still felt that if he could remain at school through these initial trials, going through as many motions as he was able, then his mind would cross that threshold of *wanting* to go to writing class, *wanting* to be present at team meetings, *wanting* to unlock his door and engage with the community around him—and then lacrosse season would start in the spring and he would be all right.

But she began to realize, along with all the people she worked with who had helped Josiah in their own vital ways, that this theoretical threshold was far away, hard to reach, and mysterious. She pictured him staring out his window at night into a dark, icy New York State winter and grasped how much was being asked of him, what terrible company knee-deep snow and near-zero temperatures made with loneliness. She fretted and wondered whether he would be having a far easier time if she had connected him to a school in Georgia or Florida or one of the Carolinas (she'd tried hard in all four states). Such ruminations were pointless, she knew, as well as a diversion from the emerging recognition that she, in her small office at the end of the education wing at Ferris School, was just as starving for a heartwarming success narrative as anyone.

School remained chaotic and difficult. The number of students had begun to rise again since the COVID-19 flurry of releases—not as high as they'd been before, but she was still surrounded by nineteen youths who were in more difficult circumstances and needed more attention than Josiah. The students here now still couldn't receive personal visits, and they also had none of the guest speakers or activities that typically, if only slightly, alleviated the monotony of life in state care. Teachers were only permitted in-person instruction three days a week. The boys were immensely stir-crazy. Every day carried new tensions. Everyone remained uneasy and a little afraid. Ms. Martin relied heavily on her faith during these weeks while coming to terms with the real-world limitations of hoping for too much. She was more impatient than usual. She was tired. She was struggling to accept how little influence she had over Josiah Wright's decisions now that he was no longer incarcerated.

She was above all devastated that Crews, who had been rereleased the previous fall for his gun charge, had just been arrested in a major police operation. He was being indicted for two counts of first-degree murder, four counts of attempted first-degree murder, and half a dozen other charges. According to the newspaper, his bail was set at $3 million.

In some ways, her influence was strictly limited to this building, even to the few cubic feet of personal space she shared with students during their meetings. In that space, she focused on the notion of resilience. She didn't invoke the word aloud often because it carried a connotation of being an innate trait, rather than a hard skill earned through work in classrooms and therapy sessions. She used the words *grit* and *perseverance* instead, which felt more active. Whatever specific words were employed, this language usually referred to the behaviors they could nurture in containment and theoretically rely on to carry them forward. Ms. Martin thought of these terms in a broader time frame. She applied the notion of resilience not only to the stories that continued from here, but to the stories that had led here: the individual narratives belonging even to the angriest, most shuttered boys she encountered, narratives that had brought them to Ferris School and could easily pass them into adult prison. These stories sometimes involved near-fatal gunshot wounds, unbearable peer pressure that threatened their lives and their loved ones' lives, homelessness and hunger, being asked to function as an independent adult from near toddlerhood, caring for strung-out parents and younger siblings from the same age. Ms. Martin would hear these stories—even just brief, reluctantly mumbled fragments of them while going over a Student Success Plan—and she would marvel at the astonishing strength required of these boys to still be alive, existing, talking about experiences and feelings with her, even if they were stuck here in lockup.

Sometimes she found herself in true awe of that strength. Sometimes it was the substance of her hope to believe that if their humanity remained intact by the time they were sent here—if they could still experience joy and triumph here—then her students could overcome just about anything. That was how she chose to think of Josiah, hundreds of miles away, however much he struggled or disappointed, because he continued to survive.

*　　*　　*

"Are you all right, Josiah?"

"I don't feel good," he murmured to the communications class teacher. Fear of a COVID-19 contact still coursed through the small campus, which was at half capacity for that reason. He was scaring others in the class. He gathered his books.

"If you're having symptoms—"

"I know to get tested." He left.

He knew he didn't have the coronavirus. As he fled back to his room, he was thinking of a video Mr. Michels had made for life skills at Ferris, in which the teacher played the role of a doctor diagnosing a student who was complaining of chest pains, confusion, listlessness. The short was silly, and it ended with Mr. Michels pulling away his stethoscope and stating gravely, "You have a bad case of terminal incarceration."

He was also thinking of that afternoon, one day removed from his first adjudication in the Cottages, when he'd been high and drunk with friends and, goaded by them, he'd spontaneously assaulted and robbed an older man. Josiah could try to undermine those images of his violence, when they struck him, by blaming their unfolding on peer pressure, bad weed, parental neglect, depression, and a truly stupid series of events. He also knew that the man he'd attacked, though he'd gone to the hospital and had pressed the charges that landed Josiah at Ferris, hadn't been badly hurt. Yet no psychological reasoning lessened the otherness that made time pass so slowly in college, made simple tasks such as going to the dining hall two floors down feel paralyzing. He knew that he was intrinsically better than his worst decisions, yet he felt as if he would always be defined by them, even in this place where few had any idea where he'd come from or why.

Part of the lifelong damage of youth incarceration stemmed from the societal beliefs that because the offenders were children, they were not capable of regretting whatever they'd done; that they could endure punishment and maybe change behaviors to avoid further punishment, but kids were too narcissistic to feel authentic regret; that kids such as Josiah and his Ferris classmates would always be *bad*. This stigma latched itself deeper and more insidiously than probationary requirements and criminal records did. It commandeered everyday thoughts and pivoted them downward. It made walks down the hall to the stairway feel loaded with tension.

Josiah's dorm room was, unfortunately, near the center of a hallway that ran the length of the building. He spent much of his time dwelling on this positioning and blaming it for how difficult the first weeks of college were proving. He was pretty confident that he would have attended most of his classes if he'd only been assigned a room near the end of the hall, where he could have slipped in and out of the exit stairway without the threat of passing multiple people and the open doorways of occupied rooms where some kid leaning back in his or her desk chair might offer him a casual head nod and ask him, *What's up?* Even though most students stationary or walking seemed to spend most of their time staring at cell phone screens, the prospect of such an interaction made him feel perilously exposed. He tried to relegate his transits of the hall to times of the day when interpersonal encounters would be unlikely.

These windows also entailed hiding out between classes and being late to his seminars. But once he knew he would be late somewhere, he wasn't too bothered by not going at all.

He was making this trek one morning and thankfully not seeing any signals of human contact except for a single open doorway. He sped up to flit past it, then realized that the room was empty. Someone had left without closing the door, let alone locking it. A laptop computer with music coming out of it was plainly visible on the desk near the door. Even though its owner had probably only stepped out for a few minutes, maybe to visit the vending machine on the stairway landing, Josiah was stupefied by the carelessness. He imagined the returning resident catching Josiah staring into the room and assuming he'd just broken into it or was at least contemplating that. Josiah practically sprinted the rest of the way to the stairs. The panic of those seconds was valid—the situation he'd imagined could easily have come to be—and it reinforced his general apprehension.

*   *   *

"HI." HE'D SEEN the girl many times in passing. Maybe they'd made eye contact once or twice, but she'd never approached him. She was short, normal looking, black though of a much-lighter skin tone than his. All he knew about this girl was that she was almost always smiling and almost always wearing an evergreen school sweatshirt beneath her winter coat. They happened to be walking in the same direction across the parking lot.

He made a muted, grunted greeting back to her.

"You're funny," she said.

He felt defensive, even a little angry, but he managed to smile. "Why?"

"You just are."

"Okay."

He was en route to his intro composition class. He'd skipped the last three classes and ignored multiple emails about his attendance. The only email he'd replied to had been from the lacrosse coach gently asking why Josiah was missing so many classes and if the coach could help in any way. Now Josiah was thinking about the discomfort of having to answer to the professor once he reached the classroom. Since he didn't have a real explanation, he was thinking about turning around and returning to the dorm.

"So where are you from?"

"Delaware?" Like many Delawareans, he tended to reply to this question of hometown as if the reply were itself a question.

"What's in Delaware?"

"Nothing. It's just a state."

"So how did you end up all the way here?"

"I don't know. I got a scholarship so I came." About forty yards lay between them and the class building. He began walking a little slower, maybe to prolong the moment with this girl. "Where are you from?"

"Rochester."

"Where's that?"

"Upstate."

"Is it colder than this upstate?" He didn't know whether she was flirting with him—most likely not—but, regardless, he felt foolish for talking about the weather.

"It's about the same. Actually, it probably is colder because of the lake."

"You live on a lake?" He was picturing a cabin on the bank of placid water, surrounded by trees.

"The city's on Lake Ontario. I personally don't live on the lake. I live more in the hood."

"Must be a big lake to have a whole city and a hood on it."

She looked at him amusedly. He didn't know why. "Okay . . . Yeah, it's a pretty big lake."

They reached the door to the classroom building, and he stopped. She walked a few more steps before noticing that he wasn't with her. Other students had to alter course to slip past him.

"Don't you have class?"

"I remembered I forgot my books."

"You 'remembered you forgot.' You really are funny."

"I have to go back."

"All right. I'm going to dinner right after this class. Maybe I'll see you."

He turned around and traversed the parking lot again. He passed the dorm entrance and continued on, across another parking lot to the sports fields. The unbuffered wind struck his face like a solid object as he looked across the grass, which was dusted with snow from a flurry earlier that day.

That was when he knew that he was going to leave. The knowledge didn't feel like the result of a life-altering decision, but rather an existent, observable fact: the season was winter, the sky was gray, Josiah was leaving college. He felt glad to know this, even though letting others know would cause a far-ranging disappointment, would make many individuals believe that much time and effort had been wasted on him, would maybe affirm certain preconceptions about juvenile hall and the kids who passed through it, would maybe even ruin the prospects of some other Ferris kid weeks or months or years from now who'd overcome enough to consider applying to college and thought that this campus looked like a good place. The therapeutic tools he'd learned at Ferris allowed him to separate somewhat his experience, his understanding of where he felt that he belonged right now, from the expectations others had built for him. So he wasn't going to make absence excuses to any more professors, and he wasn't going to falsely assure the people overseeing his college experience that everything was great, and he wasn't going to google *Rochester, NY* and *Lake Ontario* so that he could appear less ignorant when he met that girl in the dining hall later. He was depleted, and he was going to gather up his clothes and devices and figure out how to get himself onto a bus, and then he was traveling home.

*   *   *

SOMETIMES WHEN HE was running an errand for himself or for his mom, or when he was walking to the bus stop to get to work or his probation meeting, he would hear his name called. He would look up and see some old acquaintance signaling from across the street. He would nod and smile and maybe raise an arm in acknowledgment. He might have gone to elementary school with the person or played pickup basketball at the park or caused some trouble. He might not recognize the person at all, or he might remember him with deep fondness. But as a rule, Josiah never paused to chat with people. He'd perfected the art of smiling and claiming lateness to something important, professing a genuine desire to catch up later, wishing the person's family well, and never slowing throughout.

The routine saddened him because in this neighborhood people stopped and talked all up and down every street—he'd passed entire days here throughout his childhood just stopping and talking and laughing, stopping and talking and laughing, sometimes not making it more than a couple blocks from his home. But now he consciously insulated himself from the neighborhood, partly because he didn't want to answer questions about Ferris School and what had come after, mostly because he believed that his being antisocial was his only successful strategy for staying out of adult jail. He carried on this way for months: two, then three, then six. This was the new rhythm of his life until it began to feel like an old rhythm.

He worked at the Boys & Girls Club of Wilmington. Upon his abrupt return from New York, the people in his orbit had moved past his dropping out with surprising directness and ease. No one had clung to the college plan or tried to convince him to resume it. The ground didn't shake when his foot hit the pavement at the Greyhound station, a pit didn't open up to swallow him, a crowd didn't gather to weep for him. The world just carried on. Some outreach calls had been made on his behalf, some testimony as to his character given, and the Boys & Girls Club had invited him as a part-time volunteer to help keep the small facility organized, play some games with younger kids in the gym, and every so often join an intervention with a teenager who'd had contact with the justice system. Josiah liked the job but didn't like not being paid. His PO told him to keep showing up, to strive to see himself as a counselor and not a babysitter or janitor, and never to view himself as above whatever he was doing. After a little less than two months, Josiah was put on the payroll for twenty hours a week.

A diverse set of Wilmingtonians ran the club: an older white man with a thick mustache who'd been there for decades; a younger black woman who yelled all the time and rarely smiled but seemed beloved by the kids who came every day after school; a middle-aged black man who was totally easygoing until he coached basketball practices in the afternoon, when he became loud and sharp; an Italian woman who presided over the front desk with an authority no one ever dared challenge. Josiah interacted with them all, quietly and strained at first and then, as time passed and COVID restrictions eased, more and more openly.

The atmosphere bore similarities to rec time in the cluster at Ferris: a bunch of young, predominantly black kids passing time playing games, pushing the rules as far as they could, while adults strived to keep order and also, in small moments, guide them. As at Ferris, Josiah felt stifled and bored all the time, yet experienced surprising moments of empowerment; he relied on the people around him while knowing that the relationships he was building were temporary; he dwelled on the notion of greater purpose while flailing to grasp what that purpose was. He didn't know what he wanted to do and whom he wanted to be, only what and whom he didn't. Maybe life was simply a prolonged process of elimination, he thought sometimes. Since he'd only eliminated a few possibilities—he didn't want to be in jail; he didn't want to go to a four-year college; he didn't necessarily want to be involved in community-based youth work forever—he figured he must be in the early stages of that process.

"Aw no, you stupid bitch!"

"Don't talk to me like that!"

One kid, maybe eight or nine years old, came to the Boys & Girls Club three times a week in the afternoons. He was physically large and pretty loud much of the time, but he had a softness about him. The expression he wore when he was doing schoolwork—his quiet focus when he didn't know anyone was looking—reminded Josiah a bit of Cassio. The kid's jagged swings and behavioral contradictions recalled Bosley and perhaps Josiah himself.

Right now the kid had started an altercation over a checkers game that was missing half a dozen pieces. The kid and another boy were both standing over a table midgame, glaring at each other. Their profane threats and counterthreats had frozen the rest of the lobby.

Josiah had been working at the club for more than three months now. The school year was almost over, and he wasn't sure if he'd be seeing many of these kids consistently over the summer. As the older staffers moved forward to intervene with yelling and time-outs, Josiah sent them an expression that asked if it was okay for him to handle this. He went and leaned on the table in between the two fuming boys, addressing the troublesome one first.

"Man, you're gonna be tired."

The kid scrunched his face up in absolute disdain. "What the fuck are you even *talking* about?"

"The battle—the work it takes to battle." Josiah picked up a paper checkers piece substitute and let it flutter to the floor. "Over this? It's gonna make you too tired for anything else."

"What do you even *know* about it?" The kid stepped forward as if he were aiming to fight Josiah, too.

Josiah could only smile, shake his head, make a dismissive *pshh* sound. In general during conflict resolution here, he tried to avoid speechifying about how he'd made mistakes and paid for them, and how the younger kids ought to learn from his experiences. At Ferris, he'd physically rolled his eyes at dozens of speeches like that and certainly hadn't learned from them. But sometimes they just couldn't be avoided, and he started speaking without thinking.

"You know about Ferris?"

The boys both nodded. "It's like jail."

"I was there for near two years."

The hard kid smirked and muttered, "You should have thought about that before you got caught." Then, under his breath: *"Dumbass."*

That Josiah didn't experience immediate, overwhelming anger was somewhat remarkable to him. He almost wished that he could rush down a hall, knock on Ms. Martin's door, and interrupt her work to explain how some punk had messed with him and he hadn't even let himself get mad. She would be proud of him. Instead, he tried to summon a levelheaded rejoinder, something that would educate the kid while also silencing him. But there were no such words, not for someone so young and so emotional.

"It's all right if you talk to me like that. Nothing's going to happen to you except maybe a time-out. But certain people out there, you talk like that to them . . ." Josiah shook his head again grimly. At Ferris, while performing his fortieth or fiftieth five-minute time-out in the hallway, he'd concluded that time-outs were the dumbest, most useless form of punishment in all the world. Now, he assigned one himself and headed back behind the front desk. He felt lousy about the interaction—as if, with all the experience he had and all the empathy he was capable of giving to that boy, he should have been able to accomplish more than some words that didn't land and a time-out. He fell into a bit of a funk while he watched the kid serve his time-out, grinning and mugging for others throughout. But the older staffers around the desk encouraged Josiah.

"You stopped the fight from happening, first and foremost," the basketball coach assured him. "You prevented violence—that's your main job. You didn't let him get a reaction out of you with his bullshit—that's your second job. You did great at both of those. Then you gave him some knowledge. Of course he's not going to do anything with it the first time, but you keep giving it to him, over and over, then down the road he might. He'll find you when he needs advice. It doesn't seem like it, but that stuff does eventually stick. He'll find you. It might not be until after he gets in bigger trouble, maybe after he serves time like you did, but he'll find you. You should feel good about what just happened."

Josiah didn't feel good at all, or confident. But he thought about small moments and repetition and the clumsiness that existed between two people in taut instants, and he figured that he had in fact handled this one with some maturity if not total aplomb.

Ms. Martin still emailed him now and again. Usually she just did so to check in. Sometimes she forwarded school or job opportunities that she'd received and might be of interest. She neither encouraged him nor offered aid; these days, she simply passed along information. He made an effort to reply every time, usually just to write one word, *Thanks*, whether or not he clicked on any links she'd sent.

Recently, she'd sent an online brochure about a two-year degree program at Delaware Technical Community College. The program entailed a couple of hours of classes a couple of nights a week and could be paid off over time. The degree options included Communications, Marketing, Sports Therapy, Automotive Technology, and a few others. Josiah wasn't inspired to sign up immediately, but he was piqued enough to re-read the information a few times and contemplate how such a program might work in his life, how he might pay for it, what it might be worth to his future. He had no certain equation by which to gauge the value of any of these options. But mulling it over online at least gave him something to do besides actively resist the urge to just walk out the front door and find people to hang out with.

He did this while his little half-siblings watched TV at night and they all waited for their mom to return from work, hopefully with groceries for dinner. It being spring, more people were on the street, their mostly pleasant voices sounding alongside the cartoon voices on-screen. Those voices amplified the feeling of being home, which was a good feeling. Josiah couldn't stay here forever or even for much longer—he would probably go stir-crazy before his mom began grumbling about the space and money he cost. But for now, he was all right here. He was able to think and to plan and to make daily choices—to strive to make sense of the world as it continued to unfold, to add some measure of order to the mess of things. That felt like enough for now.

Book II

———————◆———————

Education

WOODSIDE LEARNING CENTER
SAN FRANCISCO, CALIFORNIA

Chapter 1

◆

~1700–Present

THROUGHOUT THE EIGHTEENTH century in America, troubled children were subject only to the discipline of their own families—except when the children were either such terrors in their communities or were so blatantly being abused that surrounding residents removed the children from their homes by force. If the parents had the will, disposable income, and possibly a firearm, they could prevent this seizure. If they were too poor to fight or relocate, they couldn't. Usually, the child would then be placed with a volunteer family, typically to work on a farm or in a factory, a form of indefinite indentured servitude. Because some children were so challenging that no family would house and feed them even for their unpaid labor, an alternative arose called almshouses. Adopted from the British system of workhouses, and colloquially known as poorhouses, these were locked, one-room structures in which children of all ages, from all backgrounds, carrying all forms of trauma and mental health problems—whose lone commonality was that no one else wanted to deal with or even see them—were imprisoned. Virtually all of these children came from abjectly poor families.

The 1800s brought increased poverty across many regions of America, from urban growth in the Northeast, economic downturns, and immigrant influxes (from Ireland in particular). The country in its economic

engines and social changes was moving faster. With the country's increased density and pace, almshouses began to fill far past capacity, and
their brutality became impossible to hide or ignore. Authorities began
sending unclaimed children to adult jails simply for the space—until that
space, too, ran out. Less from humanitarianism than from a conservative
fear of an upset to the social order, local city governments created new
facilities called houses of refuge, and their expansion along with a rash
of legal decisions established the doctrine of *parens patriae*: that children
whose guardians were unable to serve their best interests would become
children of the state.

Houses of refuge were designed to look like fortresses both within
and without as a presumed deterrent: kids were not supposed to want
to live there. They housed up to two thousand young people—the delinquent, orphaned, neglected, impoverished, sick, starving, deaf or
blind or both, epileptic, autistic, bipolar, impulsive, and violent children of America. Houses of refuge were the first corrective institutions
to incorporate some education—basic literacy and evangelical religious
instruction—along with disciplinary efforts. This discipline included
caning, flogging, food and light deprivation, the withholding of medical treatment, and ubiquitous solitary confinement. For the most part,
the detained in these places spent their days producing goods such as
hardware supplies and shoes.

During the latter half of the nineteenth century, following the public
realization that house of refuge board members—who often were among
the richest men in their cities—were making thousands of dollars of personal profits per year from the forced labor of child prisoners, the child-
saving movement took root and focused on the urban poor with the aim
to establish nonpunitive community programs for wayward youth. In
the most progressive of these programs, minor delinquents were permitted to live and work outside state facilities but under strict state oversight:
the earliest official incarnation of youth probation.

In a corollary effort, which was also considered progressively humane, impoverished and troubled children (more than two hundred

thousand of them) from East Coast cities were sent westward on packed trains. At each stop along the way, the children would disembark to be inspected by local families for usefulness for labor. Often, the children would be herded into the local theater and placed onstage, a practice that originated the term *up for adoption*. The social experiment was useful and effective in clearing urban Eastern streets of their tens of thousands of homeless, parentless children—which in New York City in 1860 comprised roughly 5 percent of the entire population—but at the cost of the trauma of forced removal, the separation of siblings, the potential for child abuse, and the reality that once the trains reached their final destinations in Arizona or Kansas or Michigan, the mentally and physically handicapped, who invariably had not been chosen from the various stages, would again be left to homelessness on entirely new streets. This "placing out" practice continued until the Midwest's own native populations of homeless and delinquent children became overwhelming.

The words *reform school* were originally intended, in the late 1800s, to destigmatize youth rehabilitation systems. New advocates tended to be middle-class and often female. They decried the foreboding facades of current facilities, their total lack of oversight beyond private supervising boards, the money that the members of these boards pocketed from the long days of manual labor of the children within. Above all, the advocates argued against responding to all different forms of delinquency—from violence to truancy to being poor—with incarceration inside a huge structure without open space or natural light.

Under nonprofit supervision and the very beginnings of a federal acceptance of science that had determined adolescence to be its own stage of cognitive growth distinct from adulthood, reform schools were conceived as small, cottage-like units with a day-to-day structure resembling a rural household in their chores and schooling. Though adult civil courts remained the arbiters in delinquency, the new model—on paper—provided a form of punishment that was reflective of the evolving concepts of child development. Fifty-two such schools were established nationwide by 1896—primarily clustered in the Northeast corridor, operated by state or local governments, and featuring separate facilities for boys and girls.

The settings and basic amenities were nicer than they'd ever been for these children. The wide results were unchanged from prior incarnations. Various forms of indentured servitude persisted under the blanket doctrine of *parens patriae*, which stated that once children entered the purview of the states they lived in, then whatever life those states assigned to them was, legally, in their best interest. After over a century of activism and advances in developmental science, the building and dismantling of thousands of physical structures, and experimentation with both ambitious and myopic models, the meaning of the term *best interest* had held fast with remarkable consistency across governments: perform hard manual labor, with punishment for refusal or inability.

The first juvenile court, distinct from the adult justice system, was established in Chicago in 1899. Over the following two decades, these courts proliferated across forty-six of the forty-eight states and were a key component of the larger child-saving movement. The movement in general and the juvenile courts in particular were the result of largely female activism but were governed entirely by white men.

Foundational differences from the adult court system, as well as any prior court that had handled children's issues, were manifold. On the technical side, court proceedings were held in private, and the information revealed in those proceedings was kept confidential. There were no indictments or jury trials. Judges had the mandate to treat almost all juvenile cases as civil, not criminal. For the first time, state laws began to define delinquency with specific categories rather than simply conflating it with poverty. The courts employed social workers and psychologists to work with families through the legal process and actually inform the judges' ultimate decisions. Jurists ranging from judges to prosecutors to advocates (again, most all of them white men) were instructed by new laws to approach each case with the belief that people under a certain age (sixteen in some states, twelve or fourteen in others) could be reformed with proper oversight. In many courts the judge and the accused sat across a table from each other during their discussion so as to remove the psychologies of judgments passed downward from a high dais.

The human forces behind these laws (again, most of them progressive women) believed delinquency to be a social problem, not an innate pathology. The juvenile court system was intended as a gentler institution whereby individual judges well versed in the issues of delinquency and youth could determine the most direct route to self-sufficient adulthood for each offender. The judges' range of choices was relatively wide: the foster system (adapted from the orphan trains), the probation system (adapted from the concept of supervised release), work training programs (adapted from industrial schools), reform schools (adapted from houses of refuge), and, as a last resort for serious and repeat offenders, youth detention facilities (adapted from adult jails and usually retrofitted from older versions of those). So, whether the adolescent in question had been charged with arson or theft or just hanging out on the street with nowhere to go, there existed for the first time ever official channels designed not to remove and punish but to minister.

Yet, as ever, it was the seemingly small components that didn't change that doomed the potential for a lasting departure from the fairly recent era of locked fortresses. The supervision plans specifically designed to be reformative and informal became untenable due to massive caseloads; the bulk of these related to minor infractions that didn't reasonably merit state involvement to begin with. The majority of adolescents within the juvenile courts still came from poor families or being abandoned or being homeless, or some combination of the three. The majority were also immigrants, living in immigrant neighborhoods, where American versions of justice had not yet penetrated lingual and cultural barriers. These layers of bureaucratic challenges engendered more and more and more bureaucracy, such that the court's onus became simply to process the numbers cycling through it, thus undermining the core of the child-saving movement: the recognition of the individual child. The benevolent ideals of the court grew difficult to sustain when single judges were seeing dozens of kids and their families each day, most of them destitute people without any legal wherewithal, many non-English-speaking.

These situations, made relentless by the surging tides of immigration, industrialization, and urbanization that persisted in America through the turn of the twentieth century, overwhelmed the various rehabilitation systems as well as the courts themselves. The more individualist the system, the harder a time its managers had coping with the caseload laid upon it. No aggregate figures were recorded from that time—the juvenile court system was not obligated to report its numbers and outcomes, part of its intentionally informal structure—but observable patterns began to emerge. How a child looked and dressed in court, what language he spoke, and how much money the family standing behind him possessed (if a family stood there at all) seemed to influence sentencing in addition to what that child had allegedly done. Poor kids were much more likely to be sent to jail.

For the first time, America had a thoughtful, dignified system by which to manage the increasing numbers of children on its streets beyond simply locking them all in big, unsightly buildings without mental health treatment or medical care, and that was a societally pleasing notion. In the meantime, more and more and more of these children were locked in big, unsightly buildings without mental health treatment or medical care. The number and size of those buildings grew larger while the conditions within them grew worse. World War I, the Spanish influenza, and the Great Depression only strengthened the regression. Correctional-facility placement of delinquent youths in America numbered ten thousand in 1900. By 1940, the number had grown to one hundred thousand.

Increased youth-crime statistics in the 1950s, paired with a faster, more far-reaching, and sensationalist media landscape spawned something like a national panic over juvenile delinquents. The fear compelled the Kennedy administration to appoint a juvenile delinquency committee in 1961 (preceding and unrelated to the Moynihan Report in 1965). Recommendations from this committee included a preventive focus for those children and adolescents most at risk; an overarching confidence that delinquency was linked to urban decay, poverty, school failure, and family instability; and the mandate to establish diversion alternatives for adolescents. That same year, Congress passed the Juvenile Delinquency and Youth Offenses Control Act, which made federal funding available for delinquency prevention and diversion programs throughout the 1960s and was expanded upon in the Juvenile Justice and Delinquency Prevention Act of 1974. This law required youthful offenders to be separated from adults in local jails and the removal of adolescents from the adult criminal justice system (unless they were charged and transferred as adults, which remained commonplace). Some states also attempted to shift their large-scale and often poorly maintained correctional facilities toward smaller, home-type environments. Leading states such as Massachusetts, Missouri, Vermont, and Utah decreased their juvenile offender incarceration populations in some cases by 90 percent. The Missouri model, born in one of the most judicially conservative states in the union, set the national standard for trauma-based therapy, restorative justice, and group work fostering interpersonal connection.

Yet the juvenile system in many more jurisdictions, including in more progressive-seeming states such as New York and California, still tilted increasingly toward retribution as a means to address delinquency—the hallmark of the adult criminal justice system. Certain politicians found a powerful support bloc in the message of "nothing works" in rehabilitating youthful offenders. During the 1980s and '90s, these individuals and the political movements they fostered—which encompassed both parties—set the stage for the tsunami paradigm shift in interpreting crime and punishment of juveniles that became known by the ubiquitous brag "tough on crime." They also solidified a new word within the national consciousness—purportedly a moniker for dangerous people, but really a coded method to draw white votes by stoking fear of young black men—*superpredator*.

The five syllables encompassed nearly five hundred years of racism in America. The word also willfully ignored that, during all of those centuries, black juvenile offenders had for the most part been tried as adults and sentenced to either segregated facilities, brutal work camps, adult prisons, or—at rates exponentially higher than for whites and for crimes that should never have drawn capital punishment—death. An untold number that will never accurately be represented in the statistical telling were executed outside of any court setting, in fields and forests and city streets where police or just regular people took the ultimate administration of justice upon themselves.

Punitive legal reform during the last two decades of the twentieth century increased juvenile detainment and incarceration as well as the transfer of many youthful offenders into the adult criminal justice system. The concurrent rise of the crack epidemic in American cities provided an ongoing justification. At its peak, between 1992 and 1997, forty-seven of fifty states moved toward "get tough" and "adult crime, adult time" type policies and passed laws accordingly. Forty-five state legislatures increased transfers of youthful offenders to the criminal courts; thirty-one state legislatures expanded juvenile court mandatory minimum–sentencing options; forty-seven state legislatures made juvenile records and court proceedings less confidential; twenty-six states changed their juvenile justice codes to endorse and expand the use of punishment; and twenty-two state legislatures increased the role victims had in juvenile court proceedings, expanding prosecutions and lengthening conviction sentences.

Numerous reasons were cited to explain the sea change from rehabilitative back to a retributive philosophy in such a short time. Both liberal and conservative stakeholders and policy makers, along with the general public, asserted that juvenile crime was out of control; concern was expressed about a—largely fictional—new class of irredeemably violent juveniles; a belief was growing that juvenile courts of the civil rights era had been soft on crime and ineffective, and that preventive or intervention programs did not work; and the crack epidemic had emerged and handguns had proliferated.

As had been constant throughout history, the nuances were not politically useful. What was politically useful was rhetoric and a shift to the portrayal of youthful offenders from children in need of intervention and support toward sociopaths deserving of a reckoning and harsh accountability. In a crescendo of reactions to crime rates, media narratives often exaggerated violence, focusing only on serious crimes and minority offenders. Some errant academics estimated that a population of impulsive, violent, and remorseless adolescents was growing and numbered in the hundreds of thousands. This class and these numbers didn't exist, but the suggestion of them was successfully used by many legislatures to overhaul their juvenile justice systems. In 1994, one of the most sweeping crime bills of modern times—the Violent Crime Control and Law Enforcement Act—was passed by Congress and signed into law by President Bill Clinton. Its decrees lowered the age for adult prosecution from fifteen to thirteen for certain federal offenses; made the penalties for drug distribution near schools, playgrounds, and youth centers (covering almost all areas in most urban communities) three times harsher; and made firearm possession a federal offense. During 1998, roughly 1.8 million people under the age of eighteen spent time in a locked facility, which was commensurate with the adult prison population during that time.

In the twenty-plus years since, the juvenile courts and the human beings processed through them have faded significantly from the national consciousness. Wars, recessions, the housing market, tech behemoths, Wall Street regulation, health care, the environment, immigration, China, billionaires, the adult prison–industrial complex—these issues and others have dominated the electoral and twenty-first-century media cycles. The quietude around the topic of juvenile hall has probably been for the betterment of children inside juvenile halls: aside from recidivism, the most important metrics have fallen by 60 percent or more during the twenty-first century thus far, representing a prolonged correction within the Department of Corrections. Systemic changes to date have been the collective result of the sustained humane efforts of thousands of people working mostly on local levels and without fanfare. But the racial and class imbalance that continues to proliferate in existing structures carries the residue of a knotty, obdurate past.

Chapter 2

◆

August 2019

Tʜᴇʏ ʙᴇɢᴀɴ, ᴀs always, with silence. On outdoor wooden benches forming a crude circle, the eight teenaged boys sat and said nothing. Some leaned back, arms crossed and legs straightened, faces angled up toward the sun. Others hunched forward, elbows on knees, hands clasped, eyes fixed on the few inches of asphalt between their feet. Someone snickered for no apparent reason—maybe out of discomfort, maybe at some rare and elusive levity inside his head, maybe to intentionally disrupt the reflections of others—and the sound caused the boy beside him to snort laughter in turn, and a moment later half of those gathered were laughing lowly. After sixty seconds, their teacher tapped her ornate Tibetan singing bowl with a mallet. A low and resonant chime passed over them all, and the meditation ended. She gently asked how everyone was feeling this afternoon.

"Tired."

"Pissed."

"Tired."

"I'm angry, man."

"Need to sleep."

"Tired."

"I'm just mad."

Fatigue and anger were the common feelings of this day, and of most days at Woodside Learning Center, also called the Juvenile Justice Center, also called the JJC, also called jail. After a brief discussion regarding the various sources of their fatigue and anger—all some combination of family, court experiences, conflicts with classmates, and being imprisoned—the group moved to two adjacent picnic tables, themselves set within a U-shaped alignment of waist-high planter boxes overstuffed with rosemary, cilantro, lavender, sage, and other shade-tolerant edibles. On the tables were arranged a large bowl of rice vermicelli along with small plates of shredded carrots, diced chicken, cilantro, ground peanuts, soy sauce, and a stack of rice-paper wraps. The boys received a quick tutorial on how to assemble a traditional spring roll.

The boys all wore kelly-green sweatshirts, khaki slacks made of some odd, stretchy, rip-resistant material, and bright orange sandals over white socks. They were all between fourteen and seventeen. They were all black or Latino. They all seemed glad to be outside with some relative autonomy in crafting their own meals. They all completely mangled their first attempts at properly soaking the wraps in water.

"The fuck, man?" The liveliest boy of the group, named Torrance, peered up as if aghast over the mush now clinging to his fingers. He was tall, thin, dark-skinned, and generally loud with his thoughts.

"Language, come on, please," the teacher, Megan Mercurio, urged in an easy voice. She was in her late thirties and wore thick-rimmed glasses above a not-small silver hoop piercing the center of her lower lip. Her dark brown hair was streaked with purple dye and contrasted sharply with her pale skin, which itself was not helped by the windowless classroom in which she taught every day.

"But *look.* How am I supposed to eat this?" In cupped hands, Torrance thrust forward the translucent, waxy material that he'd now formed into a ball.

The day was bright, not hot but not quite cool, which was pleasing for San Francisco in late August. The schoolyard was large, about a full acre of mostly featureless blacktop. Basketball hoops on the far end stood beside a tiered garden that rose up into a tall wire fence. Beyond that demarcation, a wooded hillside from which the street and school aptly derived their names climbed toward a row of large homes built into one of San Francisco's eponymous Twin Peaks. The cantilevered balconies seemed to peer directly down at the incarcerated boys. Behind those, a massive white-and-orange radio antenna called Sutro Tower, shaped like a trident, rose hundreds more feet into the sky.

The boys crouched over their malformed concoctions in a pocket of shade cast by the rounded cinder-block structures on either side. One of these comprised their current home, Unit 6. In the other, Unit 7, the occasional hand or face pressed against a window and sometimes banged the glass. The Unit 7 kids were under max security and were not allowed in the garden or outside much at all. They did whatever they could to bait a reaction, some wisp of human contact between themselves and the world outside the unit.

"Yours is a mess, just a mess," observed one student of Torrance's spring roll, even as his own seemed to ooze between his splayed fingers like wet sand.

"Be positive, please," Megan kept pleading. "This is really hard." She was one of the two English language arts teachers at Woodside. The other was Constance Walker, who was also outside, bundled in a winter coat despite the temperate day. The women moved from student to student to keep them from overstuffing the wraps. This garden-group meal was the only one of the week in which the boys could portion themselves, so they tended always toward overindulgence. "You want thin layers. You want a lot of overlap so that the wrap can stick together. Don't worry—there's plenty."

Megan had been teaching at Woodside for twelve years. Constance, who was in her fifties, had been here for twenty-two. The garden group had taken nearly ten of those years for them to establish: a decade for the picnic tables, planters, one weekly meal's worth of fresh ingredients, and permission for the Unit 6 boys to be outside with access to real,

albeit plastic, cutlery. Though planters and tables were mandatory on
the city's public school campuses, and Woodside was part of the San
Francisco Unified School District, they'd repeatedly been informed for
years that the school district could not pay for anything in the yard because only the classrooms within the detention structure were SFUSD
property. The outdoor space belonged to the Juvenile Probation Department. The furnishings they'd eventually procured had been hand
built by juvenile detainees at a more camplike facility two counties east
of San Francisco. That facility, known as the Ranch, had since been shut
down as a cost-saving measure. Constance's daughter had been the first
volunteer cooking class instructor at Woodside.

"Man, quit stealing my food!" A small-statured Latino student named
Araceli stood at the far end of the far table, glowering now at Torrance,
who was nearly as tall sitting as Araceli was standing.

"I wasn't." Torrance laughed caustically, motioning toward the rice
bowl. "It's a shared table. It's *shared food*."

Araceli suddenly whirled and turned away from everyone, now facing the planters. He stalked a few paces and sat beneath a tall thicket
of rosemary. Megan sat beside him, careful to leave a good two feet of
space, and the two began talking.

Other teachers had wandered outside. On gardening days, most
teachers, counselors, and building staff visited the picnic area. They all
claimed the food and outdoor air were the draw, but the claim was disingenuous, as decent food and outdoor air were available to them at
any of the upscale shops at the commercial center half a block from the
school. They came to watch the students: watch them struggle to chop
cucumbers evenly and wrestle with obscure materials such as rice paper
and bulge their eyes while ingesting ethnic spices such as cumin that
they'd never before tasted. The school staff all saw these kids multiple
times every day. But rarely did they have the opportunity to see them
just being kids, as they were at the communal table.

Torrance was already defending himself to the remaining adults,
hands outstretched and eyes wide in self-righteous indignation. "I swear

I didn't steal his food. I was just getting more rice *from the bowl we all share* and there's tons of it left."

They placated him: "I know, I know, it's fine. He must have something going on."

Overall, the spring roll compositions were becoming prettier. The remaining boys focused on their craftsmanship and snuck only sidewise glances at Araceli on the bench. Araceli was now crouched over, his shoulders tense and quavering, his head shaking in negation now and again in reaction to whatever Megan was telling him—most likely that he was a good person, he would make it through this place, nobody was out to get him or take from him, he would be okay. She was constantly telling her students some variation of that message to temper their meltdowns. Such scenes occurred over and over among students every day and usually had something to do with the frequent court appointments that dictated their various futures. Araceli had an appointment that afternoon in which he would be sentenced for the theft charge that had landed him at Woodside. He was feeling stressed, uncertain, and helpless and was flailing for any sliver or illusion of control, any faint slight against him by which he might claim some dignity in battling.

"I don't know what he's crying about," Torrance said while spooning dipping sauce onto his plate. "He didn't hurt nobody. They're just going to send him on probation."

"There was a gun, fool," the boy beside Torrance amended casually.

"He wasn't holding it, though, I don't think. He said he wasn't."

"Guns is guns. Judges don't fuck with that." The boy plowed some lettuce-and-tomato salad onto his plate and dumped a fifth of a bottle of Thousand Island dressing over it.

"He's getting probation and he'll be at his home tonight. I been here *seven weeks*. I got to *go* from this place."

Who was here, why they were here, how long they would be here, and what would happen to them after they left here—these were the most talked about subjects during meals at Woodside, which was a court school serving young people who had been arrested but not yet adjudicated in court, and who were deemed unfit to stay at home during the interim. Some arrived and departed within a day or two. Others with more complicated cases, such as Torrance, lived at Woodside for much-longer, indeterminate stays. These dichotomies caused nearly endless uncertainty, conjecture, jealousy, and friction.

They were all given a ten-minute warning. Araceli rejoined the table. Still sulking, he crouched over and idly picked at the already mangled spring roll on his plate. Megan helped serve him another round of fixings and began coaching him in the art of the quick soak for rice paper. The table fell quiet for a time, mainly because the boys were focused on eating as much as possible in their waning moments outside.

Soon the boys were bidden to line up and file inside under the oversight of three counselors: large men in black uniforms responsible for order in the facility. The boys passed through two sets of heavy doors and into the jail's central hallway, which connected all the various sectors of the building. This hallway was massive, roughly eighty yards long and twenty feet wide, dim beneath sickly orangish fluorescent lights, with cinder-block walls painted dark yellow. Like the esophagus of a great beast of old myth, it gulped them all. Megan lingered behind. Colleagues who had wandered out for lunch asked if Araceli was okay, and she gave a broad overview of his court situation and confirmed that he was fine. Yet she herself appeared fragile, grasping her elbows with her forearms pressed crosswise against her abdomen, as if steeled against a nonexistent chill.

She was suffering, and not really over Araceli. Though garden group was her most buoying hour of the long workweek, she'd learned just before class that a former student who had spent a few months at Woodside over the span of five years and three different arrests had been murdered a few nights ago. She didn't have many details, just that he'd been in his car with his girlfriend and a car had driven past firing. Maybe the murder had been because of the girl, or because of the color of the hat he'd been wearing, or because of some slight he'd committed years earlier that he'd forgotten about, or because he'd been selling drugs in places claimed by others. Such questions didn't serve much purpose. She'd liked that student. He'd always been participatory in class, a little obnoxious but funny, quite sensitive in an abrasive way. His engagement with school had been contagious to others. He'd been a powerful writer. She'd heard that he'd been doing well over the year since he'd last been at Woodside. He was seventeen. He was dead. A lot of students she'd taught over the years were dead.

Her grief centered on this person she'd been fond of, on all the little innocuous interactions they'd had and the hilarious things he'd said, as well as on the hope she'd maintained for his future. But around her grief's edges there clung a separate pain, about the futility inherent to what teachers did here, their almost total ineffectuality over life and death on the outside, the absolute chaos of cars and bullets and vendettas. And lurking unchecked was the possibility that soon—maybe as soon as tomorrow—she might have his murderer in her classroom and be trying to teach him how to read critically and write clearly. The next time the garden group met, the shooter might be sitting at one of the outdoor tables asking someone to pass the salad dressing. He might be angry over his court date and she might be sitting beside him, telling him that he was a good person and would be all right. And, most likely, Megan wouldn't even know who he was.

She was the last person remaining outside, and she paused for a moment and gazed away from the building, over the verdant planter boxes and the asphalt yard beyond them, past the fence, up the forested hillside toward the afternoon's pristine sky. She breathed in deeply before passing through the cinder-block wall into the dark interior.

*   *   *

"MY LITTLE BROTHER was there for two months, for a robbery he didn't even do, he was just nearby for, and that made him easy to grab," a young black woman said through emerging tears. "They locked him in solitary for no reason. . . ."

The public-comment section of the San Francisco Probation Committee meeting had just begun, and a long line snaked from the microphone around the edges of the room at Sunset Youth Center, a modest community nonprofit hosting the meeting on Judah Street, in the Outer Sunset district, six blocks inland from the stunning expanse of Ocean Beach. The rows of foldout chairs were filled, as were the narrow aisles surrounding them. The corners were cluttered with beat-up drum sets, outdated computer hardware, and bookshelves half filled with spiritual guidebooks and "quit lit."

The woman at the microphone gathered a few breaths, choked up, gathered a few more. "He said they didn't ever turn the lights off in his room. They had him on meds so he was so tired he couldn't barely stand up, but with the lights it made it so he couldn't even sleep. And the rats running around . . . It was so horrible he couldn't even come here himself to talk about it. He's got PTSD."

The committee members, seated lengthwise across a table facing the audience, nodded gravely. There were eight of them, quite diverse in age, race, and professional experience. Throughout the public comments, they spoke little except to murmur here and there that they were sorry for the experiences described, usually in excruciating detail. Older ex–juvenile offenders spoke witheringly of their time at Woodside in the nineties and even as far back as the eighties. Legal advocates used pointillistic, argumentative oratory, as if in a courtroom, to decry the city's juvenile justice system. Employees and volunteers at Sunset Youth Center argued in succession that the work they did here held far, far more value in juvenile reform than whatever work was being done "up there"—pointing vaguely southeastward, toward Twin Peaks and juvenile hall. The public comments stretched on for nearly an hour, and north of thirty people spoke, every single one passionately exceeding the allotted time of two minutes per person. No official was going to interrupt someone talking about child abuse, which was what every speaker talked about.

Chris Lanier, the Woodside principal—who lived just a few blocks from here and surfed Ocean Beach almost daily, including during the hour before this meeting—was given eight minutes in which to speak. Wearing his typical uniform of dark jeans with the cuffs turned up and snug-fitting button-down shirt, Chris declined to use the microphone and stood genially in front of the committee. He held a palm-size Moleskine of notes he'd scribbled, which he didn't look at. The serenity stored from the time just spent on his surfboard in the water infused his conversational tone.

His role required that he present at events such as this often, but he still had little understanding of why the events occurred. The Juvenile Justice Center—Woodside, his school—would be closing on December 31, 2021, a little over two years from tonight. That decree had moved all the way up through the apex of city government and was now a San Francisco law, making this city the first ever in the country to shut down not just a facility, but its entire penal system for youth. This meeting felt engineered to build support for a proposition that had already been ratified.

As principal of the educational sector of the old system, Chris could habitually be seen as the "bad guy"—the warden of sorts—even though he worked for neither the San Francisco Juvenile Probation Department nor the California Department of Corrections. He worked for the Unified School District and had for most of his adult life, which was the first thing he said tonight in order to lessen his association with youth incarceration. Maybe the gambit worked for some. At a meeting such as this one, the majority of facial expressions ranged from outright hostile to simply vacant, so he had a hard time discerning.

Chris could have stood there and taken issue with the political motivations behind the law and the arbitrary deadline—he did take issue with both, loudly, when alone with his staff—but such an effort would have been fairly pointless. He could have stated that he as well as most all the educators at Woodside favored a reimagining of juvenile detention and education in San Francisco. He could have added that they, as the educators responsible for actually schooling the city's incarcerated youth every day, had deep wells of input to provide. He could have complained that, with only one teacher on his staff having been invited to participate actively in the system's redesign, and her only as a labor representative, they were being more or less shut out of the entire process, and that, thus far, the process itself contained little reimagining (the coalescing group was called Close Juvenile Hall Working Group, and he felt that the lack of reference to any forward thinking in the moniker itself was telling). He could have pointed out that meetings such as this one might be useful venues in which to rail against perceptions of what had been, but the people who conducted them seemed to take for granted the ease of the task of deciding what would be.

But Chris simply used his minutes to list a few of what he felt were important, rarely acknowledged nuances within that concrete structure on the hill. The teachers at Woodside were highly focused on providing high school credits to their students to smooth their reentry into society following release and to hopefully lower the recidivism rates. Fourteen classes added up to one credit. Students took six classes a day. They had three adults in every classroom: one general education teacher and one certified in special education, plus at least one counselor. The school didn't suspend credits for disciplinary reasons. It didn't deprive students of classes even in the event of violence. It made school IDs for the students. It held graduation ceremonies, with hats and gifts and a cake, for students who graduated while inside. He'd been the principal for eight years and had, during his tenure, experienced zero turnover among his teachers: everyone who was teaching there when he arrived was still teaching there. He saw his job, at its heart, as figuring out creative ways to say *yes* to these teachers and their ideas within a construct in which *no* was the easiest and most pervasive word.

He concluded with a story he told often, about a young man who'd come to the principal's office an hour before he was to be released. The kid had asked if there was any way he could continue attending school at Woodside. He offered to come each day and go through the metal detector and put on the green sweatshirt and orange sandals, just to stay in those classes with those teachers. He proclaimed that he would be doomed in regular public school. "It was a hard question to say no to," Chris told the room. "Obviously, I had to say no for a lot of reasons, most of them technical."

While his remarks were not warmly received, exactly, they were not met with rancor, either, and he considered the evening somewhat worthwhile. Since the Judah Street meeting would no doubt carry on for hours, he left early in his pickup truck for some pizza and a beer, reflecting on the interactions from his day and recharging for those to come tomorrow.

None of the other Woodside teachers had been there that evening. Chris sometimes gently pressured them to give the school its own presence at public functions that mattered. Since this one didn't really matter, he'd never mentioned it to anyone. He'd only come himself figuring that his constant presence on the periphery of the closure process might ultimately lend him some modicum of influence within it. But listening to all the layers of scorn laid over the school and what was purported to have happened inside over the years was bad for staff morale.

Morale at Woodside was fairly low anyway. If and when the Close Juvenile Hall Working Group generated a new model for juvenile rehabilitation, the teachers on his staff would keep their jobs thanks to the teachers' union, but they would most likely be dispersed into different spaces, such as alternative schools and diversion programs, in a process called *consolidation*. The counselors, who worked for the Probation Department and whose jobs were directly tied to the physical space of Woodside, might well lose their jobs. The students would hopefully be better off—everyone involved wanted that—but the chemistry of being young and in terrible trouble would always be thornier than a mission statement written by a group of adults in a boardroom, portending positive outcomes as if the ink on paper provided that assurance. The outcomes of young people would always hinge on more than words and intentions; the outcomes would always hinge on someone kneeling in front of them and looking into their eyes and listening to their words.

The world they inhabited—the world Chris was in charge of—was so very, very small: a few classrooms and around thirty to forty kids at any time. The policy issues and philosophical implications in play right now were so very, very great. Chris could go a little cross-eyed squaring the two. While he did so, twenty-eight teenagers were currently locked in their units at Woodside this evening. These were twenty-eight teenagers whom the other roughly 1 million residents of San Francisco, by and large, regarded not at all—even when driving directly past Woodside, since the juvenile hall was set back from the street and tucked behind the juvenile court building and was all but invisible to passersby.

Chris entered juvenile hall the following morning at eight fifteen, a half hour before classes began. He parked in the dirt staff lot in the rear and climbed a short, steep hill to the lobby. He nodded hello to a young man in a suit struggling to secure his wallet, phone, and keys in the bank of finicky lockers—most likely a youth legal advocate not long out of law school. Chris ducked beneath the half-raised steel gate by the first checkpoint and warmly chatted with the counselor on lobby duty. He climbed a stairway to the second checkpoint, a set of thick metal doors that could only be unlocked via a call button to the main security hub. Each door took a few seconds to click and required a careful push-pull combination to haul open. The first and then the second door clanged shut behind him. Then he made the long, long walk down the always chilly central hallway beneath its dim lights.

The hallway took him past the visiting room first, with its decent city and bay views, and then each of the living-unit doors: tall, wide, imposing doors bordered by opaque, wire-meshed windows. Each unit was its own isolated ecosystem of kitchen, common space, classroom, and two levels of small, lockable bedrooms designed to incarcerate twenty children total. There were eight units in all. When Chris had first started as principal here and the building was usually at or near or sometimes above its capacity of 160, this traversal of the school had always been loud. Even when the noise wasn't pleasant—kids screaming defiantly at counselors and one another—it had been energizing, each morning providing a unique salutation to a wild day. All but three of the units were empty now, and the hallway was usually silent except for the muted echoes of heavy doors opening and closing elsewhere in the building—that metallic banging was ever present.

Technically, Chris didn't arrive at work until he reached the school sector at the far end of the hallway and passed through another call-button door (this one was perennially jammed and required a full-body lurch to wrest free). This irritating threshold marked the division between the probation and education units—jail and school. While the jail was immense, the school was a cozy sector of five classrooms, two offices, a little library, and a gym encircling a hybrid security station and utility closet (plus a Spartan bathroom that wasn't lockable). Most of the teachers were here already in their rooms, dealing with emails and prepping for the school day. Chris offered a few waves and entered his own workspace: a bare desktop in a bare room that he shared with anyone on staff who needed a little space during the day. A rack of wrinkled button-down shirts occupied one corner beside a blank white poster board (new intakes were offered student IDs, which were just laminated bits of symbolism meant to make the kids feel not entirely imprisoned, and they wore these shirts for the headshots).

Prior to this job, Chris had been in charge of special education for the entire SFUSD. He'd spent his days racing between schools and connecting with dozens of students per week to identify and meet their needs. Now his domain was here in this mostly quiet corner, with eight teachers and a little over two dozen young people depending on him. He wrote schedules and designed curriculums and managed daily gripes and ensured that water and toilet paper were in stock. His primary job was to foster an environment in which his teachers could do good work, even if that work was mostly belied by the fact that the majority of the stories of the kids who passed through their school did not end well—and even while that work was being discredited and vilified by the liberal politics of the closure.

Chris was feeling scattered this morning. The gears in his mind turned to his high-school-aged son, who was figuring out if he desired to continue playing baseball in college, then to the surf report for the afternoon, then to the steep budget cuts Chris was facing, then to the solutions he'd concocted that would resolve the money issues but please no one who worked under him. In his Moleskine, he jotted a few notes regarding each of these subjects, as well as about larger questions he'd constantly been wrestling with of late.

What does juvenile hall accomplish for young people?

What does juvenile hall symbolize in our society?

He'd written these questions down on facing pages, with a chicken-scratch stream of consciousness running beneath each.

In over eight years as principal here, in passing instants, which often occurred during these calmer early mornings before the eight-hour triage of the typical school day began, he felt that he'd attained purchase on the precise answers to these questions. Juvenile hall gave vulnerable young people school, support, and safety during a traumatic passage; juvenile hall symbolized the worth of these kids. He would feel confident enough in these principles that whatever accusatory noise came from people outside the building aimed at those inside the building didn't matter. Then something would happen—news that a former student had just died violently, or the court's sending him a kid who hadn't done much of anything wrong while releasing into probation another kid who'd fired a gun in a public space, or yet another program cut that he needed to absorb, or the publication of more disheartening recidivism statistics that his school would be indirectly blamed for—and his entire professional purpose would be thrown into confusion. These oscillations were fine; they were part and parcel of the bipolar nature of youth rehabilitation. All the staff here experienced them, all formed their own methods of controlling them (meditations, martinis, et cetera), and all did their work regardless.

But the looming school closure and its date of December 31, 2021, were so fixed, its process so imperfectly in motion, that Chris could no longer afford to not know why exactly he and everyone else here did what they did every day, year after year. Because the small, good moments—the fleeting glimpses of connection any of them might carry in their hearts after an otherwise wearying day, where the true meaning of their work lived—were no longer enough to sustain this place.

Chapter 3

◆

October–November 2019

I LIKE MENDOZA," Megan said. "I think he's kind of sweet."

"Tell that to the families of his victims," replied David Malizia, who was the primary special ed teacher in Unit 7, the maximum-security area of Woodside. Together, the two teachers were planning to lead a writing lesson that morning.

He was joking, sort of, but Megan still stiffened slightly. "I wasn't talking about that—I never talk about that." She tried quite hard to not know what her students had allegedly done to become her students, so that she could focus exclusively on teaching each of them in an individualized way, whether they were in her classroom for three days or three months. But their crimes did unveil themselves, often in the braggadocian banter among the boys before and after class, or in the muttered talk of the counselors who performed the taxing work of overseeing the units during evenings and nights, when there was no school structure. Most often and most powerfully, the details of their arrests emerged in their writing.

The boys in Unit 7, where Megan and David's English language arts (ELA) class was about to begin, were generally placed there due to violent behavior, serious gang ties, firearms possession, or a demonstrated tendency to abuse any leniency. These students were not permitted into the education sector of the building (where the lower-offense boys in Unit 6 and the girls in Unit 5 went to school) and instead took all their classes in a single room adjacent to their small eating area, which was part of their small rec area, which spread beneath the two exposed corridors lined by their rooms. All day, they shuttled around the few yards separating these various spaces, except for two exercise sessions in the gym.

David was in the midst of the thoughtful ritual of laying an individual work folder on each desk as a means of assigning seats. In a quickly running dialogue with Megan and the counselor on duty, nicknamed Sarge, the three established who needed separation from whom due to some petty grievance, who was a regular class contributor, who had a court appointment later and might need to lean against the wall to settle nerves. The arrangement was made more complicated because these boys, being incarcerated, grasped desperately for even the slightest speck of control over their days, such as claiming their own seat, so the teachers needed to gather an idea of where each had been sitting during the day's previous classes. It was a complicated bit of artistry, and most of the boys would complain no matter what.

The Unit 7 students filed in ten minutes after class was supposed to start, which was about average. Each took a short stub of pencil from Sarge and scanned the desktop folders looking for their names. There were seven today, same as yesterday, but some faces were different as one student had been released on probation, another was watching a movie in Unit 8 because he'd been trying to instigate fights, and two new kids had arrived overnight.

A large boy with slicked hair and a warm, crooked grin fixed to his face, named Pastor, immediately took his folder from the middle row and moved to the back.

"Really?" David said to him, smiling, though a bit uneasily. David was a short but fit and wiry man of Italian descent. He'd once aspired to be a stage actor. He'd been teaching at Woodside for ten years, and he spent nearly all his time in the max unit. He felt at home in this room and connected to the people in it, despite the constant barrage of slights he absorbed regarding his stature.

"That's not my seat," Pastor replied. "This is my seat."

The teacher quickly gauged the possible outcomes of arguing. "All right. Take that one."

David had known Pastor since the boy had been in first grade; he'd been in David's first-grade class when he'd taught elementary school in Potrero Hill. A number of Pastor's siblings and cousins had been in David's classes, both in Potrero Hill and later here at Woodside. Pastor had spent three prior stints here. They knew each other well enough such that Pastor could pull a little bit, and David could give, and they both knew roughly where the edges were.

"You get me some contraband, yo?" Pastor called while others were slowly settling into their seats. "Get me some chips?"

David was now at the computer connected to the Smart Board, which never, ever worked without some finessing. "What? No."

"It's cool. I already got some."

"Why are you telling me this?"

"Just bragging, bro. But for real, can you buy me some chips before I get out tomorrow?"

"I don't buy people food, but when you get out of here, I'll take you out to lunch."

"Anywhere I want?"

David looked up, eyes shining with a certain wary fondness. He laughed as one who'd been had before and had learned from it. "No. I'm not gonna promise that. I'm thinking, like, pizza."

Megan stood in front of the board and initiated the class with her constitutional moment of silence, beginning with a plea for everyone to focus and try to find his center and let various stresses loosen a little. She dinged her mallet against the singing bowl. The bowl was bronze-colored and etched with an intricate pattern of interlacing vines. It had been a wedding gift.

The boys, wearing navy T-shirts with their stretchy khakis and orange sandals, were working on prose personal essays that they'd begun earlier in the week. On the Smart Board, Megan projected a video that featured a cartoon pencil singing about elementary essay structure: thesis, support, conclusion. As the bright animation bounced around the screen chirping rhymes—*"How to go and prove your point? Write your evidence! That's the joint!"*—Megan meandered from desk to desk, checking in with students as they engaged—or didn't engage—with possibly the most disdained of all their academic endeavors, writing.

"Always be asking yourself, 'What's the hook?' " she said generally to the room. "Why is this story important to me? Why is it important to the reader? What did I learn?" She stopped pacing and added earnestly, "You guys have some really important stories. I know it's hard to do these assignments sometimes, but your voices really are special, and they really do matter." Someone laughed derisively at this supposition. Even with just seven students, the windowless room with its pale fluorescent light and yellow walls grew stuffy and claustrophobic quickly.

The back wall of the classroom was nearly covered with rows of past student work: poems, analytical essays, personal narratives like those they were supposed to be composing now. A thought piece about the relationship between the media and incarceration was beside a scientific breakdown of the symptoms of the Ebola virus, which hung next to a first-person account of someone witnessing his little sister murdered by his father. Personal writing, in Megan's opinion, was the most valuable exercise in ELA. The portal of self-expression could provide a novel, if painful, catharsis. On the walls of her classroom in the education sector hung dozens more written works matted on green construction paper, some dating back over a decade: odes to mothers and fathers, essays on slavery, memories of witnessing friends and family being shot or of being shot oneself, reflections on the media landscape in America and its portrayal of young black men, descriptions of flowers and the gentle act of planting them, visions of various streetscapes as mortally dangerous places inhabited by all the people one cared about, limericks bursting with regret and violence and longing and childish play and powerful expressions of love.

Personal writing was also the most difficult form for her students—
a difficulty split into two layers. On the surface lay the pervasive frustration of format, organization, word choice, punctuation, the bland
intricacies that rendered writing fairly dreary for the majority of teenagers in America. Beneath that mundanity spread the trauma—the invisible, intractable, sometimes immeasurable childhood trauma—that
seemed to the teachers to be almost a prerequisite for matriculation at
Woodside. Nearly every boy in this class knew some form of it and kept
it tightly contained in his core self. Writing had a way of drawing these
spirits forth. Unit 7 students produced sublime work now and again.

(That an anthropomorphic, off-key, dancing pencil provided the
introduction to excavating some of the horrors that had plagued the
youths within this room was one of the absurdities that everyone carried as lightly as possible.)

Megan glanced over Pastor's shoulder to skim his work in progress.
She said gently, "We're not rhyming today. I'm sorry. This is a prose
essay. Not a poem, not a rap."

Pastor scrunched his face and then his paper, starting over. "Man . . .
why?"

"It's just not the assignment. I know you like poetry and it's easier
and more expressive for you. This is a different form that's also important." To the very last, the boys preferred poetry over prose, musicality
over frankness—particularly in personal assignments.

Megan knelt by the far back corner desk, where a boy named Perez
was squirming, yanking at his hair, his heavy acne and sloppy ponytail all part of a miserable kinetic whorl. Megan spent much of her day
kneeling, placing her eyes at the level of her students' during all the
many dialogues they had. She was thirty-nine years old and fit but had
the knees of an aging baseball catcher. Perez was making soft, weepy,
grunting sounds. She ventured to place her hand on his elbow and ask
what was wrong. After some urging, he told her in cracked sentence
fragments that he had court today, and the judge was no doubt going to
send him to a group home somewhere else in California, hundreds of

miles away, and he wouldn't get to see his son for six months at least. Perez was fifteen. As a child, he'd survived an illegal emigration on foot from Honduras. The small fragments of that journey that he'd shared sounded hellish.

Megan and David exchanged a look, each filled with feeling for the boy, and they engaged in a silent dialogue with each other that ended with nodding. Then Megan said to Perez, "What if, instead of the assignment, you use this time to write a letter to the judge. Would that feel helpful?"

He nodded, then looked around the room to gauge how others were reacting to this moment. Two were actually writing, alternately pressing hard with their pencil tips and abusing the paper with erasers. A few were staring vacantly at the walls and the ceiling. Only one seemed at all interested in Perez, glancing sidewise at him with neither sympathy nor mockery, just curiosity. "I need to sharpen my pencil," Perez murmured.

Near the end of class, Megan asked if anyone might be willing to read what he'd worked on. She smiled at the muted mutterings of "Mine's horrible" and "No way." Only Pastor raised his hand. He lumbered to the front of the room with an odd grin, his height and girth intimidatingly manlike, his face and expression boyish.

"This one is called 'A Moment's Delay.'" He began reading, sidestepping left and right in rhythm to the words, in a compacted foxtrot. "'Either I'm here for life or six / It don't matter at the end of the day / This time isn't like a remix / It's just a moment's delay.'"

"Pastor, man, we said no poetry." David couldn't help laughing.

"'I miss my Mama dearly / And my girl won't come to play. / My dad's in San Quentin yearly / But for me it's a moment's delay.'"

When Pastor finished, the class snapped fingers dutifully in applause. Most had heard his somewhat chronic poetry readings and were bored with them, but indulgent. His current stint here was for hospitalizing his mother's boyfriend with a single punch, which had embedded the man's head in a plaster wall and fractured his skull on the stud behind it.

As the boys filed from the room, surrendering the pencil stubs to the counselor at the door, Perez held up his half-finished letter to the judge he was to see in a few hours. "Can I take this with me to finish?"

"You can take the paper," Megan said. "You know pencils aren't allowed outside the classroom, though." Pencils could be—and had been—used as weapons against others and more often the self. Classes were not released until all of the pencils were accounted for in a plastic jar by the door. Perez appeared crestfallen. "I could maybe arrange some time during lunch," Megan offered. "I can come sit with you then if you want to finish it."

"I don't want to take up your lunch break."

"It's totally fine." Normally during lunch Megan walked up a winding residential street that ringed the woods behind the school, ending on a cul-de-sac near Sutro Tower, where she would stand for a few moments before the sweeping view, a kind of emotional reset from whatever she'd seen and heard that morning. "I don't mind at all."

"Not like it'll be worth a shit anyway." The boy stared derisively at the paper in his hand, which she'd spent much of the class helping him with. The document began, *I'm truly sorry for what I did. . . .*

"You never know," she said. "It just depends on the judge."

Switching modes suddenly from helplessness to scorn, he blurted, "I don't know why I have to apologize to the judge anyway. She should be apologizing to me. Because of me, she gets paid. This is, like, my fifth time in front of her. She should be *thanking* me for being her money-maker. . . ." His gripes trailed out into the unit as he stalked toward his bedroom. He crumpled the paper into a ball as he went.

David said, "I guess he's not turning that in to the judge later."

"I'll come by at lunch and see if he's up to working on it," Megan replied. "We can iron out the paper with a textbook or something. It was starting to be a nice letter."

The teachers began to gather the papers that the other boys had left on their desks. A few had written two or three sentences in a little less than thirty minutes. For the most part, the sheets remained blank except for names and sometimes dates in the top corner.

* * *

SAN FRANCISCO WAS recognized for its romance, but it was a hard place to live in without money. The city by the bay was also an easy place in which to find trouble. Its forty-six square miles placed it last among major American cities in land area, while its nearly 1 million residents made it the second-densest big city in the nation. This crowding was leavened somewhat by open water often being visible from within its bounds—including, on a clear day, from the family visitation room at Woodside—but the average rent for a two-bedroom apartment was $4,430. Landlords increasingly took advantage of Ellis Act provisions allowing them to evict rent-controlled tenants to sell properties.

In a city with the second-highest average salary in America, luxury grew more profitable than affordability, and little tenable space remained for those earning closer to the national average of $55,000 or, below that, the federal poverty line of $26,000 for a family of four. Hunters Point, Bayview, the Outer Mission, Lakeshore, Potrero Hill—on a few blocks in these few neighborhoods, plus in Section 8 housing spread throughout the city's contours, much of San Francisco's working poor lived. No tight stats were maintained in this regard, but the majority of kids who came to Woodside lived in these places, largely out of sight of the city's techcentric residents and their progressive conceits. (As if to perfectly capture these undercurrents, a 2014 viral cell phone video showed a group of preppy, white, young professionals who had purchased a permit to use a public soccer field trying to kick off the young black and brown kids who had been playing a pickup game there; while the local players spoke of the unwritten rules of field use, the permit holder paced around lamenting that the situation was "disastrously awkward and weird.")

As in most any American city, the public school system basically reflected the economic geography. Schools in wealthy neighborhoods, where a large proportion of kids went to private schools anyway, were decent places with manageable class sizes, high parent involvement, and an array of enriching extracurriculars. Schools in places such as Hunters Point, which received the same amount of funding, were overcrowded, grim, sometimes dangerous.

Yet the distance between these spaces was so negligible in San Francisco, sometimes less than an eighth of a mile, and travel within the city limits by bus and BART trains was so quick, cheap, and easy, that any young person could be anywhere at any time—maybe to pluck a cell phone from the hand of a non-English-speaking out-of-towner studying Google Maps at Fisherman's Wharf, or to scan the lines of BMWs and Teslas parked on the streets throughout Pacific Heights and Telegraph Hill for an unlocked door, or to start a fight in the Mission, or to settle some vendetta over a girl or a relative, or to just hang out so as not to be at school.

Roughly four thousand property crimes and five hundred violent crimes took place each month in San Francisco. A fraction of these were committed by young people. A fraction of these young people were deemed unfit to live freely during the time between their arrest and their adjudication before a judge. During this period of limbo—while the legal system processed their cases but before the youths were declared culpable of any crime—they resided at Woodside, the juvenile equivalent of a county jail.

Here, following an intake psychological assessment, each new resident was assigned to one of three living units: Unit 5 for girls, Unit 6 for low to medium-risk boys, and Unit 7 for high-risk boys. They were given a room about six feet wide and eight feet long, with a tall, narrow recessed window overlooking the blacktop yard. Two pairs of stretchy synthetic khaki pants, color-coded T-shirts and sweatshirts, white socks, and a pair of bright orange Crocs sandals awaited on the cot. A weekday began with breakfast at 6:30 a.m. and staggered showers with three minutes allotted per student. LMA (large muscle activity) began in the gym or outside in the yard, weather depending, at 7:30: calisthenics interspersed with yoga followed maybe by a game of dodgeball or basketball. Fifteen minutes of free time followed, during which students could shower again or be in their rooms. The school day began at 8:45. Units 5 and 6 filed in line down the hallway to the rotunda of classrooms for three fifty-minute blocks, their physical locations and movements between rooms carefully choreographed to ensure that the boys and the girls never even caught a passing sight of one another. The students in Unit 7 remained there throughout the day. Then lunch was prepared in their units and additional shower time was given, if desired, before the afternoon block of two more school classes. Each day, each student attended class for English language arts, social studies, science, math, cinema studies, and PE. The school day ended at 2:45, and then all students were required to stay in their rooms for thirty minutes while the daytime staff turned over to the evening staff, after which the students could shower again before two hours of rec time. Units 5 and 6 had opportunities to use the outdoor blacktop before sunset. Unit 7 students remained inside except for the twenty-by-twenty-foot slab of concrete surrounded by ten-foot walls just off the common area, where small groups sometimes gathered to rap or play handball.

Individuals were escorted in and out of the units for family visits, legal consultations, or therapeutic work. A TV show might play if one of the staff was willing to haul the cart from the closet and deal with untangling the cords to the various consoles. Students did not have internet access except for special, closely supervised instances. They could journal or write letters so long as the pencil was always within clear sight of staff. Old puzzles and board games were stacked on the two-top tables in the eating area, typically untouched. Students could read in the semicircle of cushioned chairs or just sit in them and stare vacantly at empty pockets of space. Dinner was prepared at 6:00, followed by showers and another ninety minutes of rec time, followed by more showers, and then the students had to be in their rooms at 8:30. The lights remained on for thirty more minutes, a bedtime announcement was made, and then the units went dark aside from the soft yellow glow of the security desk in the common area, where the monitors were connected to ceiling cameras within each room. Students at Woodside tended to be bored and clean—though a handful always, despite the many windows of opportunity, refused to bathe.

Some might be there for a day or two before walking, shackled, across the overpass connected directly to the juvenile court building and being diverted to probation or deemed innocent. Those with more complicated cases involving violence might call Woodside, this unsightly concrete structure on the top of a hill overlooking one of the most expensive zip codes in the country, their reluctant home for months—months of being told at points throughout the school day by invested teachers that the students alone controlled their destinies, while simultaneously having their court dates and living assignments and entire futures dictated by legal actors who knew them solely by the thing they'd done wrong. Their days were absolutely rigid in their composition, most every minute accounted for and closely supervised. Yet their interiors teemed with terrifying unknowns. The single known fact they all lived with, students and staff alike, was that most of the stories that passed through juvenile hall had sad endings. The result of these cosmic contradictions stewing within undeveloped brains, the governing state of being at Woodside, was entropy.

* 　 * 　 *

CHRIS LANIER, THE principal, sat atop the front table in the English language arts classroom, swinging his legs idly as the school's nine educators filed in and sat facing him in the students' chairs. The school day was over. The students were sequestered in their rooms in preparation for the staff shift change. The education sector seemed absolutely quiet in a way that it could only be relative to a particularly loud day. Chris was eager to discuss a learning idea he wanted to try during the second half of the year, something called a vertical model, in which each different classroom subject shared an underlying theme month to month. In his boyishly optimistic mind, the concept might help with what he'd been striving to resolve for almost a decade, what he considered the greatest academic challenge facing everyone at Woodside: the deep, imperious disparity of the kids here.

Despite the commonality of having been arrested in San Francisco, the students came from a range of experience: different neighborhoods and schools and kinds of schools, different ages and grade levels, different credit situations and educational aspirations, different mental health states, different histories of incarceration, different degrees of family support, different severities in their alleged crimes and court ramifications and lengths of stay. Any of these teachers could have in the same class a girl reading at a third-grade level and a girl reading at eleventh. They could have a boy who had cumulatively spent years in juvenile hall, who felt nearly at home, sitting beside a boy in the midst of real trouble for the first time and paralyzed with terror. They could have a child who had beaten another to near death and a child who'd maladroitly attempted to steal a car stereo. The only dependable constancies, for the most part, were that all the students were black or brown, all of them were poor, and they were all here learning in the same classrooms from the same teachers.

The career educator in Chris yearned for students passing through Woodside, even those who were here for just a few days, to have a comprehensive experience that they could carry away with them. In his imaginings of a perfect world that none of them lived in, he saw a fourteen-year-old boy leaving juvenile hall with his parents, cutting through all their stress by exclaiming, "Guess what I learned at school this week!?" then demonstrating a *body of knowledge* as opposed to a daily, arbitrary dose of crisis education.

Chris's voice was emphatic and quick. His shoulders swayed and his arms waved in all directions, as they had during his many years of classroom teaching, while he drew amorphous pictures in the air of a hypothetical schoolwide unit on the topic of, say, civil rights. "So maybe Megan and Constance are in here reading *The Autobiography of Malcolm X*, and then the kids go across the hall and in film studies they're watching *Selma* or even a documentary on the Black Panthers, and then after lunch they're in social studies learning about what actually happened politically in the sixties and how it all went down, and science class that day could be about how people manipulated science to propagate racism and how real scientists overturned that junk. . . ."

Ms. Rayikanti, an Indian woman in her sixties who taught science, appeared dubious, and Chris grinned while his eyebrows shot upward and his hands outward. "I don't know! Math and science—I have no idea! Maybe, like, the physics of the space race and the Cold War! But we could get really creative. And we could really give these kids something that's a little bigger than they're used to, instead of just whatever's in the book. I think, working together instead of each doing our own thing in our own rooms, we could make it really exciting for them, so that they're in here for the first time, like, 'Whaa?'" He did his best to impersonate a teenager flummoxed by wonder. "Like, 'School is actually friggin' interesting?'"

The teachers nodded along, some dutifully and a few with chuckling enthusiasm. All except one of them had been teaching here longer than Chris had been the principal. They were accustomed to his periodic grand ideas. Even the more fanciful notions were interesting to discuss in development meetings such as this one, and having leadership encouraging them to depart from prescribed curriculums felt energizing. But instituting new modules in the classroom could also be precarious, and for the same reason that novel strategies felt so necessary: the kids were in such a flux of different emotional states that there was no such thing as a uniform or remotely predictable reaction. Certainly, not every kid was primed to be drawn in by this vertical teaching model or to declare that it was "friggin' interesting" (and exactly zero kids would ever employ such a phrase).

Left unstated but perfectly understood was the greater, thornier motivation underlying the change: now that the Close Juvenile Hall Working Group had been more or less formed, and the Woodside staff had largely been excluded from its processes over the next two years before the city closed the school, the small group of teachers here had to project an openness to change if they aspired to remain relevant to whatever form of education ended up replacing Woodside.

Chris already knew that his teachers did hard work well. For most of his tenure, he'd used his position to give them a protected space to do that while running interference on any bureaucratic distractions that might inhibit their focus on the students. At the core of his work he had held this directive: let the teachers teach. But his work had now changed. For the next two years, everything they did in this building would filter through the Close Juvenile Hall Working Group in some way, and the working group had in part been formed via the conviction that what they did in this building should be eliminated. The reality was that the nine people convened in the classroom on this late afternoon in October, however disingenuously they had been framed in the politics of it all, needed to modify their work to continue it. And Chris, rather than guarding their privacy, needed to begin flaunting his teachers for the power structures surrounding the working group.

Even so, no flashy innovations they made in their program could alter the physical structure around them. The Close Juvenile Hall Working Group was a public committee composed largely of public servants. The humongous, blockish edifice of Woodside was the school's most public aspect. Photos of its sprawling, gray, fortresslike exterior as well as shots of its grim, sterile interior living units accompanied every *San Francisco Chronicle* piece regarding the closure—most of them excoriating op-eds (in keeping with modern trends in print media, even articles posed as informational read like op-eds). Anyone who worked in the building made for an easy target to associate with the system being dismantled, regardless of vertical teaching models or any other efforts they might make to demonstrate adaptability.

Constance Walker, who cotaught English language arts with Megan for Units 5 and 6, was the only one among the teachers who had been chosen to serve on the Close Juvenile Hall Working Group. Her role was the result of some always loaded interplay between the city Board of Supervisors and the teachers' union, and she hadn't actively sought or wanted it. But Constance had been teaching in juvenile hall for over two decades, and her strong union membership plus the sheer breadth of her experience was optically pleasing. For the last six weeks, she'd been attending the sporadic working group meetings while reporting on them to her rapt colleagues.

Constance did so now, as soon as Chris finished his presentation, and everyone swiveled toward her. They all wanted her updates on the process and the subcommittees being formed. Constance was most likely going to remain on the labor committee, even though the programs committee, tasked with designing the future of academic learning among the city's juveniles, would have been far better suited to her experience. ("You'd think that the only person in the working group who actually teaches kids would be able to weigh in on how to teach kids," Chris observed dryly.) She spoke briefly of the meetings they'd had thus far, how they were run, and what the content had been. But San Francisco was small, its politics smaller, and its educational politics smaller still; everyone knew everyone here, had grown up rotating through the same schools and forming deep, enduring networks of alliances and grudges, and Constance knew that the Woodside teachers mainly wanted gossip.

"It's a little intimidating," she offered diplomatically. "You have some people who are very high up in leadership positions in the government, and in corrections. You have some very, shall we say, high-volume people who do programs"—she was referring to activists, mostly in the nonprofit sector, whose work was noble but whose voices often demonized the Woodside educational program in the *Chronicle*—"and then people like me who don't really have experience with committees and that sort of thing, but we have some specific knowledge about different areas that need sorting out."

Megan said, "You'd think that for a task this big they would make an effort to put people together with the most experience and the best track records, not just the ones who get in the paper the most."

"It does feel very political, even for San Francisco," Constance said.

She was petite, in her late fifties, with a sandy-brown bob just touched by gray. A measured person, she constantly observed rooms and the people in them without saying much. At the head of a classroom, she'd never been charismatic, and she knew this about herself. She also knew from her multiple decades here, which stretched back to the late nineties in the old and even more prisonlike building that had preceded this one, that the kids who came through Woodside did not need entertainment. They didn't need to be laughing all the time or to be wowed by pedagogical fancy. Nor did they need to be treated gently and with pity for all the countless environmental factors that had helped precipitate their respective plights. Above all, they needed to be seen; even when hunched over in the back row and absolutely silent in their reckonings, even when being obnoxious and making a chaos of the class, they needed to look up once in a while and register the teacher's eyes looking back at them, maybe paired with a faint smile. Constance had a gift for that: knowing which moment to devote to which student. Her skill and empathy were most evident in one-on-one work, when no one else was overhearing and the armor thinned. Within that complicated space, she could make fragile young people feel bright.

Serving on a big political working group with thirty-two members and high stakes lay far beyond her comfort zone. And she was a bit of a totem anyway: someone whom higher powers could hold up to prove that all important stakeholders in juvenile justice had had a hand in re-making the system. Constance believed that her value lay in that she knew, over her twenty-two years, she'd made tens of thousands of mistakes. In a juvenile hall classroom it was easy to grow flustered or lazy or be drawn in by the loud kids at the expense of the quiet ones. Myriad ways existed to land the small moments—the most vital moments—wrongly, and Constance had probably found them all. She worked hard to recognize whenever she did and why.

In an assembly that assigned no value to admitting errors, but whose own errors would bear consequences on human lives, she saw the absolute necessity of having someone like her: someone who held no political aspirations, able to point out the ideas that sounded beautiful in a sound bite but were not viable in practice—particularly those ideas that presumed a blanket constancy in how this lot of students responded to the environment and teaching strategies around them. People philosophizing from the outside—even those with the best intentions—tended to regard these children as monolithic.

"Everyone is really nice," Constance told the staff meeting, keeping her descriptions vague on purpose. "Well, maybe not *everyone*. But they all want to do the right thing, and it's just a matter of agreeing on what the right thing is. Simple, right?" She laughed weakly.

"If you don't mind me asking, what models are they talking about for after 2021?" Megan asked. "Is the focus on group-home models, or restorative-justice models, or Montessori models, or what?" She was asking a basic, informational question. But Megan was actually asking about a much-greater, abstract topic that would in time become all too material and demand life-altering decisions from each person in the room. She was asking how they, here, might factor into the reimagining of juvenile justice in San Francisco; she was asking if they would have a legitimate place in the newly coalescing landscape.

Constance, who was nearly impossible to frustrate in school, replied, "Well, that's the frustrating thing. They really don't have a model. Each person thinks that the model they have experience in is the model that everyone else should use, so there's some arguing about that. But really what the focus is on, is money." She paused a moment to shake her head in what appeared to be an expression of pity. "The whole law, the whole working group, this whole thing, got its traction not because of the kids here and what they need, but because of what it costs to keep them here. A hundred thousand and whatever per kid, per year. Kids who keep coming back, you have million-dollar kids, however they calculate that. So the whole presumption behind what we're supposed to be doing on this big committee is that there is an obvious, morally decent way to get better outcomes for these kids for way, way less money. And I think what they're all going to find, which is something we here already know, is that we can get better outcomes for these kids—no concrete walls, more individualized learning, all of that important stuff. But it's going to cost money—*a lot* of money. And at some point before December thirty-first, 2021, these people are going to have to stop going on about these perfect solutions they have and come to terms with that and find that money. If they don't, then we and every single one of the kids here . . ." She trailed off, gesturing through the wall in the direction of the units, where the students were passing the time before dinner however they could in their tiny rooms. She shook her head gravely.

A little later in the meeting, they all turned to the big white poster boards that Chris had hung around the room. Each had a different heading: *These Are My Strengths, These Are My Areas for Improvement, This Is a Success I Had Today, If I Could Ask a Colleague One Question . . . , The Most Inspiring Thing That Happened This Week, What Our Students Need the Most*, et cetera. There were nine thought-prompts in all, one for each educator, so that as the teachers milled around the room adding entries to each, no bottlenecks formed and they had a measure of privacy. Chris led exercises like this now and again because he believed that earnestness was a waning commodity in the modern world and it was always amusing to put teachers in the same sorts of group-sharing positions that the students rolled their eyes at. Chris participated himself. Though the teachers all groaned and laughed, he could sense their thoughtfulness.

Some responses he scanned were simply stock: *I need to work on staying calm*; *Kids need individual attention.* Others could only have been written by those who taught at Woodside: *Resident Strickland called me a "fucking bitch-ass failure," and instead of throwing him out of class, I sat next to him and asked how I could make the class more interesting*; *I need to remember that every day I have to learn how to do this job all over again, because every day is totally different.*

The prompts were fairly basic, and he didn't expect anything too revelatory to come from them. But when they finished and he asked them all to step back and just look at the white spaces filled with reflections and anecdotes, Chris was pretty sure that they were looking at a relatively vast and rare body of knowledge, a common language and currency that they had developed in this isolated sphere. He hoped the rest of them were seeing the same thing, and that they felt some pride in the whole of it.

Chapter 4

◆

December 2019–January 2020

F OR SIX DAYS a week, the school library, sandwiched between the social studies and math classrooms, was locked and darkened inside. But on Thursdays, the room was open and filled with browsing bodies. The library was small, about twelve feet wide and twenty long. The space was fully stocked with books, the titles ranging from John Milton's *Paradise Lost* to Jeff Kinney's *Diary of a Wimpy Kid* (the latter was by far the most popular series in stock). The system was part of the San Francisco Public Library, which was why it was closed so much. Legally, the room could only operate in the presence of a certified librarian, and the Woodside librarian spent her workweeks cycling through the Bay Area's penal system: the San Francisco County Jail, the San Mateo County Women's Jail, the state prison in Solano, the state prison in San Quentin, Woodside. She'd been doing this for fifteen years, and so in those other facilities she often encountered people whom she'd first met in juvie.

"Do you remember a kid named Kishawn Madric?" she asked Megan while inputting a newly donated title into the computer.

Megan thought a moment, then smiled as the name aligned with a face among all the thousands of names and faces in her memory. "Sure. He was a great reader. His brother Kenyon was in that drama class I tried in Unit 7 when I first started teaching here."

"I ran into him. He mentioned you. He said that you were 'cool white people.'"

"Where'd you see him?" Megan knew that both brothers were in adult prison for murder now, probably for life, but she didn't know where.

"He was in my book club at San Quentin this week. He actually asked me if you still have one of his essays that he wrote here. Or poem, actually—that's what he asked for. It was a particular poem."

Megan immediately knew what the prisoner was asking for, a piece he'd written called "Letter to My Ancestors." "I'll look during prep period later. Probably not, though. I try not to keep them." Except in cases when students specifically asked her not to, or when she displayed a piece on the wall, Megan deleted student papers after they left, mostly due to a vague inkling that retaining them meant that she subconsciously expected to see her students again in her classroom. She never wanted any student to return to her classroom once he or she left.

Students were routed to their library time through ELA classes with Megan and Constance. Unit 5—the girls' unit—was the first class here that morning. Two girls passed old copies of *Gourmet* magazine back and forth, looking at pictures of rich desserts and fantasizing about how many servings each would be capable of eating in one sitting. Two sat at the table in the back with a stack of books, mostly hood lit. They were playing a singsongy hand-slap game: "Lem-o-nade"—*slap-slap-slap*—"Iced tea"—*slap-slap-slap*—"Co-ca-Co-la"—*slap-slap-slap*—"Pep-SEE"—*slap-slap-slap* . . .

"I finished all the James Pattersons," a tall girl said to the librarian, sounding a little desperate. "Now I don't know what to read."

The librarian recommended a few other crime authors. She wore a sleeveless shirt and had floral tattoos up and down both arms. "Michael Connelly's good. They're set in LA. There's not actually a lot of action. It's very *boy*."

The girl made a face and shook her head tightly. "No, for every one of those reasons."

"What about something besides detectives?" The librarian led the girl to a different corner and pulled out a few spines. "This one is about a girl with Tourette's syndrome. . . . This one is sort of a thriller about Biggie Smalls still being alive."

"There are a lot of books about Biggie Smalls still being alive."

"That's because he is!" called another student from the table where until now she'd been sulking. She was clutching a stuffed purple dragon to her chest with both arms. Megan kept an assorted heap of plush toys on her desk in the classroom for kids to hold on to during class. Almost everyone—boys as well as girls—used them.

Megan leaned on the table beside this girl, named Lexi. The library, while cramped in space and fleeting in time, was almost always a leavening place where kids could form ambitious stacks of literature they'd probably never read along with comic books that would spirit them outside these walls for an hour or two in the evening, and a place to gently bicker over this and that. This group of girls were particularly supportive and even nurturing of one another, which was not always the case in Unit 5, where a clash between two personalities could toxify the whole unit by splitting the girls into sides and pitting insecurities against one another—like a normal high school classroom, except locked. So Megan was concerned about Lexi's sour mood—particularly because earlier in the week, when she'd first arrived at Woodside on Monday morning, this girl had been almost buoyant, as if on a field trip of some kind from her actual school. Increasingly over Tuesday and Wednesday nights, her spirits had plummeted. Nights could do that to kids: darkness, loneliness, interminable hours, bad dreams while asleep, worse errant thoughts while awake.

Veteran teachers were generally skilled at discerning the sources of discontent based on the signals expressed: a sudden dip in grades usually meant stress at home, sullenness might suggest a bullying situation, high reactiveness denoted heartbreak. This skill was of little use at Woodside and juvenile facilities in general, where sources were myriad and signals were manic. Right now, for whatever reason, or most likely a complicated combination of many reasons, Lexi seemed fully depressed.

*   *   *

DEPRESSION WAS ONE of the most prevalent afflictions at Woodside, and maybe the hardest to witness and relieve. Young people thrived on connection yet were also quick to retreat inward to what perhaps felt like a protected space within their spirits: walled, hard, dark, much like their rooms in jail. Curled within them, time and emotion and reason could all easily warp into indecipherable shapes. Megan watched these shapes form and grip and make chaos most every workday. This was why she kept mounds of stuffed animals on her desk, why she'd worked quixotically for nearly a decade to procure a couple of planting boxes outside, why she knelt before students when talking with them, why she wept so often when she herself was alone. The purpose of her redundant singing-bowl ritual and minute of silence at the outset of each class was to instill calmness, but also to provide each student with that small measure of inwardness that they all seemed to need, even those who didn't know they needed it—even those who rebelled against it outright—so that they might be better able to look outward, if only in forty-five-minute increments of class time before they returned to their units and the flux of rec time and showering opportunities.

Megan had spent much of her life locating and refining some semblance of inward and outward balance—though being a teacher, wife, and parent living in a dense city meant that balance of any kind could be elusive. After growing up in the bright, lazy clime of San Diego and then attending college at UC Santa Cruz, she'd joined the Peace Corps and been assigned to work with at-risk youth in Ecuador. Three months into her training, she mentioned offhand to a nurse that she'd once been given a onetime prescription for Ativan due to a panic attack in college. She was then expelled from the Peace Corps for withholding information about her mental health. Devastated, Megan used the two years she would have spent in the Peace Corps traveling around Indonesia instead. She spent that time volunteering and learning about meditation—its meaning and its techniques—in different countries. She was particularly taken with the notion that a person could clarify her unique perception of the world, her translation of her personal history, her entire life force and future path, just by finding a peaceful place to sit and think. All the mania and noise that seemed to characterize civilized life could be shut out and prompted to dissipate entirely. She wished that for the kids at Woodside so much, every day.

After she'd spent her savings traveling, she returned to California to obtain a teaching credential at San Francisco State University. While student teaching at a massive area high school, she found that positive change—interior, exterior, any mode of change—was hard to bring about within huge classrooms governed by rigid procedures. The high school where she was placed felt like a factory of students, a giant box edged by withered state budgets and antiquated federal guidelines. A line of students filed in one side, spent a few years there, met a few academic and life markers, then filed out the other side toward goals manufactured by society or their parents or their peers, but rarely by their own hearts. Megan didn't fancy herself some kind of oracle or activist. She didn't aim to disrupt any lives or explode any systems. She didn't harbor grand ambitions. She modestly sought to have some positive impact within the small orbit she inhabited and on those whose paths she crossed. This prospect felt upsettingly faint in traditional high schools.

She pursued it instead within the San Francisco County Jail, where she began volunteering on the advice of a friend. Megan was in her mid-twenties, slight of stature, soft-spoken, and by all appearances fragile. In accordance with clichés regarding criminals, she expected to encounter deadened eyes set within leering faces set atop powerful "prison bodies" (muscular arms and chests, bird-thin legs). Instead, for the most part, she met small groups of sad and regretful humans earnestly taking part in meditation seminars, where she served as an assistant to a Buddhist monk from the San Francisco Zen Center. In the evenings she spent there, mostly sitting on the floor in silence except to offer the occasional breathing prompt, she wasn't sure if she saw transformations occurring in real time. For the most part, it was just people trying to escape for a fleeting few minutes from the uncertainties that pressed down on them like physical weights, people inured to their various plights, understanding that decisions could not be remade and consequences could not be altered, people trying to grasp the moment they were in and bend it into something useful. After long days spent in a teeming and hormone-fueled high school classroom, those evenings were simple and pleasant. She made friends with people there, and then the people left and the friendships vanished, and she could only hope that her own minor voice—echoes of her voice asking them to relax, breathe, probe their interiors for peaceful spaces—might hold some purchase amid the clamor that would always inhabit their lives. Megan continued volunteering at the jail for years, as well as with a reentry program to help convicts transitioning out of San Quentin. Through her midtwenties, this casual entwinement with the penal system gradually began to color much of her day-to-day life.

When she learned of the job teaching English language arts at Woodside, she applied assuming that she wouldn't be chosen due to her youth and soft demeanor—to say nothing of her limited experience in any classroom. But she figured that the effort might open volunteer opportunities with a young and neglected population who, unlike the adults living in a system all but designed to institutionalize them, might still have the time and malleability to do more than just survive the chain of events that had locked them in it—might still have time to form actual dreams and pursue them.

When she unexpectedly landed the job, she figured that a few years of intense learning would make her a better teacher and person while connecting her with channels by which to continue working with and for the incarcerated as an advocate of some kind. She did not believe that she was entering a career that would involve spending eight to twelve hours a day inside a jail, or that the human toll of her work would commute home with her each evening and inhabit every corner of her life. But she was, and it did.

Years passed, and she grew older, met a guy, fell in love, gave birth to a daughter, began weaving a whole universe with this tiny human at its center casting her own rules of physics and emotion. And still Megan spent each day at Woodside with kids subject to the rules of a bleaker universe. The pulls were unceasing, the severity of the contrasts surreal. Megan felt on the verge of a breakdown pretty much all the time. She struggled with the demands of being a working mother, of the bureaucracy beneath which she worked, and of sustaining a loving marriage, and she struggled with money (her husband was from Venezuela and had been trying to finish his engineering degree in the States but could not transfer his credits, and they rented out their living room via Airbnb for $40 per night). Bur her primary struggle was with the most elemental of all existential conflicts: life and death. She was raising a life—her daughter was now seven—while kids she taught and cared about were constantly dying. The weight on both sides was staggering.

In meditation practice with prisoners years ago, she'd always preached a vague, New Agey manner of thinking along the lines of resisting the natural impulse to battle, of forming a consciousness like water, and of smoothing a path of least resistance away from fear. Yet in her life, she battled daily. Resistance underlay almost every interaction, and she was constantly scared.

*　　*　　*

"Do you have court later or is something going on?" Megan asked Lexi, in the library. Court was usually a high-percentage guess as to what might be ailing someone.

"Out there I can do whatever the hell I want," Lexi replied in a murmur. "But in here, I have to do whatever the hell they tell me to do, or it goes back to the judge." She shifted the stuffed animal in her arms, rocking it like an infant. The girl had arranged her oversize, county-issued purple sweatshirt to look almost—*almost*—fashionable, but still the clothing was like a balloon inflated around her. Within the fabric, cradling the toy, she looked delicate and vulnerable.

"Yeah," Megan said. "That must be really hard."

"But at least in here I can frown, be mad, be pissed, be whatever I feel. Out there, when I do get out, I have to smile all the time or they probably send me back. Sucks in both places."

"No one's going to send you to jail for not smiling," a voice called forcefully from behind them. The voice belonged to Mama Rose, whose large body was tucked against the wall between two magazine racks. Mama Rose was sixty-eight years old. She'd worked as a counselor at Woodside since she was twenty-six. Her gray hair was pulled back in a tight bun over her light brown skin, and her breath wheezed with low-grade emphysema. Mama Rose spent most of each day sitting in the corner of whatever room the girls were in. She was not a heavy talker, but she heard and saw everything, tracked most every microdynamic that governed Unit 5. She'd learned the meaning of it all through sheer time: every inflection and sigh and flick of the eyes signifying precise feelings, like an emotional braille. When she did speak, she did so as a wise, nearly omniscient woman on a high spit of ground declaring exactly what was—sometimes with great empathy, other times with bladelike judgment. Even the roughest boys in jail virtually froze at the sound of her voice, and they listened.

"You've got to be yourself," she said to Lexi, who was not rough at all. "Smile, don't smile. But I've been seeing you and I know you're smart. And what foolish smart people do, particularly when running with other fools, is try to act like they ain't smart. So what you've got to realize is that being yourself also means being smart." Mama Rose chuckled lowly, almost pityingly. "Once you get on top of that, we won't be seeing you around here anymore."

Lexi was embarrassed because everyone in the library could hear. She made a bitter exhale and shook her head, as if dismissing the possibility that Megan or Mama Rose or anyone could understand a single feature of her interior.

Mama Rose stood slowly on her bad knees and navigated her way down a narrow aisle. One of the clapping girls immediately moved so that Mama Rose could plop down into the too-small chair beside Lexi. "You want me to apologize for being in your business, but that ain't gonna happen. While we're in here, all our business belongs to everyone else. That's just the nature of this place, you can fight it but you can't change it, so . . ." The old woman idly leafed through a few comic books splayed across the tabletop, then pushed them aside. "I love you. I love every single one of you. I might piss you off, but the love is real."

Lexi murmured, "It's like I just do some shit because I feel like it, and then one minute after it's like, 'Why the fuck did I just do that?'"

"That's called being young," Megan said.

"Well, when am I going to grow out of it?"

Mama Rose chuckled more. "How about I let you know if I ever grow out of it myself. Deal?"

Lexi peered up from her stack of magazines on the library table with such earnestness that Megan couldn't help smiling, and the girl smiled in return. Adjacent to them, the other girls giggled and the rhythms of the hand-slap game resumed: *"Turn around, touch the ground, kick your boyfriend outta town, and FREEZE!"* Megan let out her own light burst of laughter, then she and Lexi and Mama Rose were all laughing together. Megan wasn't sure what, exactly, they were laughing about from their respective vantage points of ages thirty-nine, fifteen, and sixty-eight. But few moments in any school day merited real laughter, and when one arose, it was always worth lingering in.

"I mean that," Mama Rose said. "I love you."

"You've only known me, like, three days."

"That's the whole point of the thing. I can't explain it, and I pray you won't be around long enough to understand it yourself. But that's the point of everything in this place."

Lexi clearly didn't understand the sentiment, and she was most likely rolling her mind's eye. But regardless, for this instant, the girl didn't seem so sad or scared. "That's cool," she said. "Now lemme find some books because there ain't shit else to do up in here and these magazines are, like, five years old."

*   *   *

THE UNIT 7 main door buzzed shrilly, clanked open, clanked shut. Megan looked a bit frazzled as she entered the space, a binder clutched in her arms. She was right on time for English class, which meant that she was about ten minutes ahead of everyone else. A boy outside the shower stall, dripping and with only a towel around his waist, appeared in no rush. She turned her head downward and hurried the five steps to the unit's classroom, muttering as she passed through the door, "I hate it when they're still in their towels. They really shouldn't buzz the door open when someone's not fully dressed. It's embarrassing for me and embarrassing for them."

"That dude hangs out by the showers in his drawers as long as they let him." A Unit 7 student named Darian Slay was in the classroom early, talking one-on-one with David Malizia, the special ed teacher. "He thinks he's ripped. He wants people to walk in and say how swole he is."

"He shouldn't be allowed to do that."

David filled her in on the discussion they'd been having: Darian had heard that if he could just gain entry to community college, then he would be guaranteed a transfer into any school he wanted within the UC system, including Berkeley or UCLA, so Darian had come to class early, eyes wide and body pumping up and down on the balls of his feet, to talk about the credits he needed to finish high school somewhat on time.

Even though Darian's idea regarding the California higher education system was false—either the result of misinterpreting something he'd heard from an adult or of another kid spouting fantasy—Megan and

David instinctively stoked any ember of motivation that arose in Unit 7. They did not refute or amend Darian's thinking as to what was possible for him.

"I can definitely do some independent work with you during rec time," Megan offered. "Depending on how long they keep you here, we can probably make up fourteen or even eighteen credits. How many do you need?"

Now Darian cast his eyes to the floor while David answered for him, speaking without a hint of the incongruity the numbers contained: "He needs two hundred and thirty credits to graduate, and right now Mr. Slay thinks he's at around thirty-six."

"I have to check with my PO for the exact number when I get out," Darian murmured. He was sixteen. That number—thirty-six—meant that he'd attended maybe two months' worth of full school days over the last two years. A decent portion of those days had occurred at Woodside, where Slay had been twice before for one- or two-week stints.

Without faltering Megan replied, "Okay, we can work with that. You don't have to wait to talk to your PO—we can get all your information here."

"How long are you here for?" David asked.

"Maybe a week. Depends on what judge I get."

"So we don't have much time. Let's make an appointment to sit down, maybe tomorrow, and go through it and see where you're the most short."

"The three of us can sit down," Megan said. "How about for lunch?"

Slay's fists began shaking at his sides, which was how he expressed happiness. "That sounds great."

While cuing up the Smart Board screen, Megan considered the stupefying math of this boy's education. By his own accounting (which wasn't necessarily accurate), Darian Slay needed to earn roughly two hundred high school credits over the next five semesters to graduate from high school. Every two weeks he spent at Woodside, he closed the gap by five credits. At his current rate of release and rearrest, he was on track to spend ten or so weeks at Woodside each year—or about fifty credits before his eighteenth birthday. If he could be prompted to actually attend school the rest of the time, then two hundred credits didn't seem like *such* a lofty number, and community college didn't seem like *such* a stretch. The irreconcilable variable of this equation was that his progress hinged on his continuing to be in jail here at the same rate that he had been. In reality, his repeated probation violations would at some point result in state detention rather than county, where the system and numbers worked differently. But right now, in Unit 7 English language arts class, as the teachers watched him fidget in the middle row and gaze at the writing samples taped to the walls, some distorted hope gestated between them all.

David was placing student folders on desks with the usual calculus regarding who needed to be separated from whom. He asked Darian casually, "What do you want to do after college?"

"My plan is to become a nurse."

"You will be a great nurse," Megan said. "You're a really compassionate person."

Darian suddenly paused, and his eyes pointed quizzically toward the ceiling. "Do they let you be a nurse if, you know, you've been in jail before?"

David told him something David told nearly all of the students in Unit 7, over and over: "Unless you're applying for government jobs like law enforcement or the fire department, juvenile records are totally private. They're legally not allowed to ask in an application."

"That doesn't mean they won't find out."

"They're not allowed to be influenced by that knowledge."

Megan said, "You're getting pretty far ahead now. Let's figure out that meeting, go over your credit situation, see what you need, see what we can do to help you in the short time you're here. And then we'll see how we can help you moving forward. You know there are *all kinds* of scholarships available for things like housing, laptops, if you can get to community college."

"What about UC Berkeley, after I graduate from community?"

David and Megan looked at each other, as close to expressionless as either could manage. Other students finally began filtering into the classroom, grabbing their stubby little pencils from the jar. "We'll get into all that," David said.

"Yeah, cool. I can do lunch."

"Pretty fancy," Megan added. "You're 'doing lunches' now."

After the opening minute of meditation, the class watched a five-minute video that featured a succession of famous people talking about how they'd been written off as teenagers, with some having dropped out of high school. Oprah Winfrey, Steven Spielberg, Steve Jobs, and others spoke amiably to the camera about how poorly they'd fared in school and how many people had assured them that they would never amount to much. Darian kept nodding emphatically throughout, and Megan led the ensuing discussion about negative talk, both external and internal, and how to overcome its insidious effects.

"What are some examples of negative talk?" she asked.

"'You ain't shit,' 'you're going to spend the rest of your life in jail,' 'you're going to die in jail,'" a student named Lawrence blurted right away. He was tall and outgoing, and he smiled almost sardonically while he shared these sentiments. He'd been at Woodside for a little over a week. The day after he'd arrived in Unit 7, Megan had made some inquiries with the transition staff about his background, because he immediately struck her as being bright and scholarly. She'd learned then that Lawrence was the murderer of the former student whom she'd spent much of the autumn mourning. Lawrence was here on that murder charge and would most likely be in jail and prison for the next decades of his life. At this point, she didn't know many of the details surrounding the killing. She didn't really want to learn them. "They say that shit to me all *day*."

"Who does?" Megan asked.

"Teachers at my old school. Counselors, doctors. Mom." Lawrence was tracking this list casually on his fingers with his eyes pointed at the ceiling in thought. "Uncles, cousins, friends."

"They don't sound like very good friends." Megan was growing visibly upset, arms tightly crossed over her chest, shoulders hunched forward as if guarding a precious object, pacing. She of course hadn't told Lawrence that she'd taught and cared about the boy he'd killed. She would never tell him, and he would hopefully never know.

"They're cool, they're just playing," Lawrence said.

"Don't listen to that," Darian Slay said forcefully. "You can go to college. I'm learning about how." He nodded toward David in a collegial way.

Lawrence appeared confused for a few seconds before releasing a high-pitched, boyish giggle. "All right, whatever you say."

Megan walked back and forth in front of the class three times, face tight and fixed downward, unable to speak with fluidity. "Okay, so . . . how do we . . . ? Let's sit with this and . . ." After a few more start-stops, she said, "Negative talk. That sounds horrible. That must feel horrible. How do you react to that?"

Lawrence continued, between bursts of that squeaky laugh that he frequently seemed to rely on to camouflage real pathos and hurt, "Just take it, I guess. Or, don't listen. People talk shit. Been doing it all our lives. Ain't no big thing. A lot of it's probably true anyway."

"None of it is true," Megan replied sharply. She met his eyes and the connection clearly made him uncomfortable. "And it *is* a big thing. It's a huge thing. It's terrible. It's abuse. And you're right not to listen. But you shouldn't have to just take it." Her arms had come unfolded and were now waving around on either side of her face. Her anger and sadness were bleeding from her. Megan had initially been hired at Woodside as a stopgap in a desperate situation, and others had assumed her tenure would be short precisely because of interactions like these. It was held as a general, intuitive truth that to work with incarcerated youth every day—traumatized youth, institutionalized youth, hopeless youth—one had to take measures to inoculate oneself against these kids' sufferings: stick to the surface of things, avoid internalizing their problems, have a drink or two after work. Teachers far more steely than Megan had left before due to the emotional weight.

When she'd arrived twelve years earlier, few had predicted that she would endure more than a semester or two. Aside from sporadic meditation, she had no defined strategy by which to slough off her students' burdens. She simply carried them every day, in school and out. She carried them right now. With a slight shudder, she did her best to resume with a more reasoned voice. "Does it ever happen to you that all these outside voices, these teachers you mentioned, these so-called friends, start to become like an inner voice? Does this horrible negative talk ever sound like it's coming from inside you, like you're talking to yourself, saying you're never going to accomplish anything important? Like when they're talking to you, it starts to sound like *you're* talking to you?"

"All the time, man," Darian said.

Lawrence pointed a thumb behind him through the classroom wall, toward the sleeping units. "What do you think is going through my head all night when I can't sleep?"

"None of us can sleep here, man," another classmate added.

Megan considered how in the span of a few minutes this conversation had veered quite sharply from Steven Spielberg talking smugly about being lousy at math in middle school. "So what do you do?" she asked. "At night when you can't sleep—do you ever, like, try to say anything positive to yourself in your own head? Just give yourself a compliment? I know it sounds dumb. But when you're locked in your rooms and it's dark and there are six or seven more hours of night ahead of you—what do you do?"

The room was silent for a moment. None of the seven students with their blank sheets of paper and tiny pencils seemed able to conjure an effective barrier against the negative cascade that trailed each of them inside and outside these walls, telling them what they weren't worth and what they couldn't do. Maceo Johnson, the counselor on duty today, was leaning forward intently by the door with his elbows on his knees. David stood by the computer console. Both men spent all their time in Unit 7, and both men now just watched and listened. According to their teaching guides, the "self-talk" section of today's lesson was supposed to be five minutes, and they should now be talking about the format of conclusion paragraphs in a persuasive essay.

"This is going to sound really dumb, okay?" Megan ventured. "It probably *is* really dumb, but it's something I try to do whenever I feel like I'm not doing a good job teaching, or I'm not doing a good job being a mom to my daughter, or I'm not taking good care of myself, or whatever."

"You seem like you always do a good job, Mercurio." Lawrence sounded earnest; less than a week into his incarceration for murder, which would take him from Woodside to a secure long-term juvenile facility and eventually to adult prison, he sounded as if his role were to give comfort, not hers.

"I appreciate that. I think you're kidding, but I appreciate it."

"I'm not kidding. I'm for real."

"I try to say things like that to myself sometimes. I know that's silly, but I really do. I tell myself, 'You know, you taught pretty well today.' Or, 'Your daughter really loves you.' Or, 'That's a nice sweater you're wearing.' Or, 'That former student of yours just graduated from high school, and you had something to do with that—good job!'"

Low-grade, amiable laughter coursed through the room. Someone mumbled, "None of us gonna graduate high school, that's for damn sure."

She ignored it.

Darian Slay said, "I know your daughter loves you, Mercurio."

"A lot of the time, it's hard to believe these things even if I keep repeating them. But it actually does help. Especially when the positive talk comes from someone else—like Lawrence and Slay just did for me. And this is exactly what I think we should try doing: let's just practice saying nice things to each other. Look around the room, look at people you know well and people you maybe don't talk to as much. And just say something positive."

The boys quickly grew uncomfortable, chuckling and squirmy, shaking their heads at the concept of unfiltered support. "C'mon, Mercurio, don't make us get all girly-like."

"I knew you were going to say that—which is very sexist by the way, but whatever—so just humor me. Practice saying nice things. There's no cameras, nothing leaves this room, it's not going to affect your cred, okay? I'll start." She moved in front of Lawrence's desk and squatted down and peered directly into his eyes, the eyes of a person who killed a person she grieved for. She waited for his eyes to stop darting around the room and land on hers. "Lawrence, you have a great sense of humor. Even on days when you're not feeling great, you always come into class and make people laugh. You always make the classroom a little brighter."

The students were all staring, somehow captivated. Blushing through his dark skin, Lawrence waved her off with a few wrist flicks.

She relieved him by moving to the adjacent desk. She descended to the eye level of an introverted boy who had yet to really engage with the class. "Montez, you are a great writer. Your thought progressions are very deep and very powerful, and you always choose just the right words to express them." Montez kept his face angled downward, but he glanced up at the end and she saw the faintest luster gleaming there.

She moved on to Arias's desk. Arias had been here for almost three months for an aggravated assault charge. He was always mopping the rec area before class. He always sat against the wall in the front row on the far left side. He understood a little English but spoke almost none, just a chopped-up sentence fragment here and there. "Arias, you are a great father. I know this because you are always thinking about your son. You're always writing him letters. When your son visits, I can tell how happy it makes you. I know that once you get out of here, your only goal is to make your son's life better. I know this because you write about him all the time. I really admire that."

Arias nodded solemnly. It was unclear how much of the sentiment he'd actually deciphered, but he mumbled, *"Gracias,"* and lightly thumped a fist against his chest.

Megan continued through the room, speaking directly to each student. David added a few of his own compliments. With some prodding, the boys began speaking to one another: "He's a cool person." "He always helps keep the puzzles and games organized so we don't lose pieces." "He's a really good reader." "He's fierce at basketball."

They passed the whole class period this way. Then the period began to run a few minutes over. The Unit 7 schedule was absurd in that classes often began twenty minutes late but ended with absolute rigidity, and they reluctantly had to adjourn before Megan could even think about how to emphasize the main point that she wanted them to hold on to when they returned to their rooms, where the terrible nocturnal hours later on would no doubt crush upon the goofy but meaningful time they'd just had: the practice of being able to turn these external compliments inward, of recognizing and emphasizing positive traits within themselves even when everyone in their orbit seemed intent on pointing out the opposite. Self-confidence generated from within truly felt like one of the hardest, deepest, most elusive efforts any of them could undertake.

Darian Slay made sure to linger such that he was the last student in the room. He nodded to David and called, "We still got that lunch in the books, right?"

"Absolutely," David replied. "I'll start pulling out the stuff we need right now and we'll sit down tomorrow. We'll go through all your options and everything you need to do to get to college. We'll set goals and make a list and make it happen."

"I'm looking forward to this meeting," Darian stated seriously, then left.

Once the teachers were alone, they both paused their cleanup and just inhabited the space for a time.

"That was good," David finally said. "More productive than writing conclusions, I'd say."

"I'm exhausted, though." Megan exhaled deeply with the words.

"Really? I got kind of jazzed listening to some of the stuff they were saying to each other. It was meaningful."

"It was. They were so kind to each other." She considered her own fatigue in relation to the class's content. "I guess the really good stuff and the really bad stuff, it all kind of tires me out the same. It's all just a lot of spent emotion." She suddenly became self-conscious regarding the share, the vulnerability of it, in the same way that her students did in general. And just as her students did in similar situations, she instinctively changed the subject. "Let me know if I can help with anything with Darian, okay?"

Darian never was able to have lunch with the teachers to review his high school information and strategize his future. That night, a new student arrived who was well known in Woodside, a young kid from a powerful gun-trafficking family who wielded considerable authority among the other boys. The staff knew him as Baby Ramsie. No one was clear on the exact sequence or causes of events, but Baby Ramsie ordered another kid to attack Darian, who was then jumped in the rec area, beaten up badly, and separated into Unit 8 for safety. He spent the next few days alone in the isolated unit watching action movies and rebuffing David's and Megan's repeated visits to look over his numbers. "I'm not feeling it today," Darian kept saying until his release early the following week.

*　*　*

WHEN SHE WASN'T working with individual students during lunch, Megan walked the same route every day. Behind the juvenile court building, a residential street bent off the main intersection and made a few switchbacks over a half mile to the top of a hill. The walk was short enough that she could easily complete it during her break, steep enough that her heartbeat quickened by the time she reached the peak.

The houses were large and architecturally interesting. The trees enclosed her for much of the walk, but at the top, where the road deadended, she sat on the guardrail and the view suddenly fell open to the west. She gazed out at the impossible folds of San Francisco stretching to the bay and the sea, the neighborhoods rising and falling with grace as if specifically designed to obfuscate how difficult living here actually was.

Then, as she always did after the first deep breath, she angled her head down. The hillside was steep, about two hundred feet of pines and scrub that dropped into the blacktop yard behind Woodside. The space was empty. The students were all in their half-cylinder units eating their lousy lunches. Up close, the building was situated against the hillside such that its true size was never quite discernible; each segment appeared as its own separate, modest structure. However, from above the place looked sprawling and massive, the living units like knuckles along a giant, closed fist. She marveled that on a typical day, such as today, fewer than thirty kids were being held inside the immense facility, yet those kids were allotted rooms smaller than the closets of the houses around her now. From this vantage, Woodside's existence was farcical—like a totem to some archaic interpretation of justice. If the building were as old as its fortlike design suggested, if it had been constructed during the "tough on crime" era, then its layout might have made some brand of sense, even of the unpleasant category. But Woodside Learning Center had opened just fifteen years ago, a relic even before its units held their first prisoners.

*   *   *

THE UNIT 6 class that Megan and Constance shared was down to three students following an altercation in the rec yard that had kept the rest of Unit 6 behind in order to parse through with staff what had happened. One of the kids present in the classroom was a new intake. He sat alone in the middle row, wide shoulders hunched over his folded hands, staring downward. He was both tall and overweight, and he looked incredibly sad, especially in contrast with the two other students, who knew each other well from being in and out of Woodside over the last few years and who were both energized by the fight that had happened. Since one of these boys had staked out the front row and the other sat in the back, their animated recounting volleyed over the new kid's head, causing him to retreat even further inward. He'd never been to juvenile hall before, and he was clearly afraid.

The desk that the teachers shared in the corner was heaped with stuffed animals of all shapes and patterns. The pile took up most of the surface area around a desktop computer. The boys picked which character they were going to spend their class time holding like a security blanket. One boy chose a frog. The other grabbed some sort of plush alien and held it close to his chest. Megan took a six-foot-long sequined serpent sold in zoo gift shops and wrapped it around her neck like a scarf from the disco era. When Constance asked the new kid if he'd like a stuffed animal, he winced and shook his head definitively, once.

The two talkative boys moved on from the fight and chatted a bit about the guest speaker who had spent the morning in their cinema studies class. The visitor's name was Matthew Cherry. He had written and codirected an animated short film that he'd shown them, entitled *Hair Love*, about a father struggling to style his daughter's hair in the exact right way. The boys had loved the film and loved meeting the creator behind it. They were flattered that he'd taken the time to share his stories of Hollywood absurdity and struggle with them in jail, and that he'd asked for their genuine opinions on his work before it was released. (A few months later, Cherry would win an Oscar for *Hair Love*.)

"This is so great to hear about," Megan said. "But we do have some work today."

During the minute of silence, the boy to whom Megan had entrusted the singing-bowl mallet kept lightly dinging the rim of the bowl and then sliding the mallet around the circumference. The notes lengthened and shortened in such a strange, pleasing way that Megan didn't ask him to stop.

The writing prompt that morning, what they called Do Now work, was to draw a vision chart detailing how the boys wanted their lives to look in five years, ten years, and forty years. Constance sat beside the new student. She'd introduced herself to many thousands of scared children during her twenty-two years here. She gently told him her name. When his reply was inaudible, she didn't ask him to speak louder. Her restraint and understanding immediately seemed to settle him, and they set to work.

"I know the number one thing you should all write down for your Do Now," Megan said from the front of the room. After no one responded, she said, "Don't get sent back here. Right?" The boys met her suggestion with cynical chuckles. She played music through her computer while they worked, a calm, lyricless hip-hop beat suitable for focused thought. Then she moved back and forth between the first and back rows while Constance remained with her charge in the middle. The front-row student stated dreamily that he wanted to live in Oregon, get married, have a couple kids.

"Maybe waiting until you're finished with school before thinking about having kids would make things easier." Then Megan asked, "Why Oregon? Have you ever been there?"

"No. I just heard that it's real chill there."

"I've heard that, too."

"So, yeah."

She told him that she thought he was brave to be thinking like this, as most of her students didn't like to contemplate leaving their neighborhoods, let alone their city or state.

He was a small kid, maybe five feet four inches, and frail, but coiled with energy such that he fidgeted and spoke fast. "I just want no drama. I come here and I go back and it's the same people, the drama gets you back in." He was talking about his home in Hunters Point. "And then I come back here and then I go back." He pointed to the space on his Do

Now sheet indicating the ten-year timeline. "It could be ten years later and it's still *boom-boom*. I could do a million positive things before then, and in one second, wrong place, wrong time, *bang*, and I'll be dead like everyone else. No one even remembers the good things. A place like Oregon, with lots of trees . . . maybe it won't be like that."

She nodded and gave him the silence in which to suspend his vivid thought. She found it both haunting and beautiful that he would associate the presence of foliage with the absence of violence.

They spoke for a few minutes about specific, realistic pathways to the Pacific Northwest. The timber industry was big in Oregon—Megan just blurted that out as a free association—and it required the maintenance of many large, sometimes dangerous machines. His five-year vision chart became a trade school degree that would qualify him for a union job in a field such as that.

He paused at one point and frowned. "I really like trees, though. I don't want to be cutting them all down."

Megan chided herself for walking into a bit of a trap there. "They cut down trees but I think they have to plant new ones in safer places. I'm sure there are sustainable companies that produce wood in Oregon"— she wasn't sure at all—"and I bet there are nonprofits you could get involved in that use that wood to build homes for people who can't afford homes but want to move out of rough neighborhoods. . . ." She trailed off because she was overreaching a bit.

But the words flicked the right switch somewhere inside his head. "That'd be dope." He finally ceased chatting to write feverishly.

When she checked with the back-row student, he expressed his desire to go to Georgetown University because he liked the basketball team.

"Does this feel attainable?" Megan asked. "Like, is your goal to actually play on the Georgetown basketball team?"

He shrugged and smiled. "I don't really play basketball. But I could probably learn and get good enough to."

"Let's think about some things besides basketball that you can write down. But keep that as maybe your second or third choice."

He banged the eraser of his pencil against his chin a few times, looking upward in deep contemplation. "Can we change the music?"

"We usually don't take requests, but you guys are being so great." She scanned her limited playlist and offered a few options—still nothing with any lyrics, because she'd learned long ago that any song lyrics, G-rated or not, caused problems—and he picked a track that sounded similar to the first one she'd played, but was more pleasing to the student because he'd chosen it.

The room's atmosphere—the music and thoughtful talk and pencils skittering on paper—was wonderfully calm. Then, with about twelve minutes left in the period, loud screams sounded from the social studies classroom directly through the wall, where the Unit 5 girls had class. It sounded as if all of them were shrieking, then stomping their feet and turning desks over. Megan and Constance looked at each other with great concern while the boys wondered loudly, in unison, "What the fuck?"

Constance volunteered to go check on the classroom, while Megan casually and unsuccessfully urged the boys to resume their work. "It's really probably nothing, or just a dumb argument."

"I don't know," the boy in the front row said. "Them girls don't fight much, but I hear that when they do, it gets *rough*."

Constance returned and reported that one of the girls next door had seen a mouse behind the teacher's desk, so they all rushed to the back of the room and were up on the counter. (A few weeks ago, the social studies teacher had left an open bag of chips in his bottom desk drawer overnight, which some members of the building's stubborn mouse population had located, and now the animals seemed to hang around that room.) The boy in the front row climbed onto a table himself—"I'm not taking no chances with those creatures around"—and the class resumed working.

The boy in the back had been writing on his own for a few minutes. He suddenly asked, "If I apply to the police academy, can they see my record?"

"The police can," Megan replied. "Any civil service can see your record, I'm afraid."

The boy scowled and began erasing most of a page, working his whole shoulder into the act.

"You think you might want to join the police?" she asked. The concept wasn't uncommon in exercises like this, but the details could be complicated to discuss. "Because you shouldn't erase your work just because of that."

"I don't think it's a real idea, though, if they're gonna see all the times I've been here."

"I think things are changing a lot, the way some people look at other people's experiences. There are people who might look at your record and see how your contact with the justice system could help make you a wonderful policeman."

He laughed benignly and shook his head, as if she were striking him as a little dim-witted. "Yeah, I'm not so sure about that, Ms. Mercurio."

"I think it's totally legitimate and also viable," she said with a shrug. "I would keep it if I were you."

He regarded his half-erased paper. "So I gotta write all that again?"

"Georgetown basketball and the police force. You're an ambitious person."

While these conversations happened, Constance patiently and methodically coaxed the new kid through his sheet. They weren't necessarily making progress on his chart, but he was beginning to speak in full sentences, and he seemed to feel seen and heard by her. He smiled faintly. The class was easy, fast, light, and productive—particularly as they entered the forty-year time frame and were unbound from realistic thinking, could blurt out any dreams that flitted across their minds: host a reunion of eighty-seven grandchildren; sign a law guaranteeing reparations for slavery; finally get Beyoncé to go out on a date. The boys wrote sentences and their banter in between was complimentary. The room held no tensions. The minutes passed quickly and pleasurably and also felt useful.

By the end of class, the new kid was speaking just loud enough for everyone to hear him. He said that he liked computers, and part of his five-year plan was to build one from scratch so that his mother and even his grandmother—who didn't know how to use a TV remote, let alone a computer—could both learn to use it, and then he could sign them up to have email accounts and be in touch with them from wherever life took him, including juvenile hall. He thought that he would be less homesick that way.

*   *   *

It was just one day in early December, and a rather unremarkable one: the girls of Unit 5 in the library, the boys of Unit 7 in the max-security classroom, Unit 6 in the education wing, plus some individual work in between. Two unrelated fights occurred: the attack on Darian Slay in Unit 7 and the blacktop skirmish among a few Unit 6 students. Megan hadn't witnessed either and never heard much in the way of specifics, except for the most important one, which was that neither students nor staff had been injured. At the end of the day, she straightened the chairs in her classroom, and she worked on a grant application to an organization called DonorsChoose through which she'd been successful in procuring hygiene items, and she chatted with Constance about the new kid in Unit 6 and his sweetness and astonishing turnaround, and she listened to the melancholy tune floating out of the office where the math teacher played his fiddle during rare quiet moments.

Megan reflected on this one day—one of two or three thousand days she'd taught English here—and she hoped above all that she'd simply done a decent job educating, maybe reached a child or two and made them feel all right about themselves, even if they hadn't necessarily learned much. She hoped she hadn't made any mistakes unawares or missed any warning signs that one of her students was in real trouble. In this emotional gray zone where she spent most of her time—the place of hoping without ever really knowing—she switched off her classroom light and left the education sector just before the shift change from daytime to nighttime staff at 4:30. She walked down that long, dim hallway, recognizing different voices of her students reverberating through the unit walls, and she passed through that series of double-doored security points and out into the city's cool, overcast, oxygenated atmosphere. The choked intersection offered a preview of her long commute home to her husband and daughter on the city's outskirts.

Days possessed a different character now that they were numbered. Though two years still remained before the official school closure, the atmosphere at school already felt elegiac, as if they were all mourning the sudden loss of a way of life while their daily rhythms remained exactly the same. These rhythms were decidedly erratic, revolving around an ever-changing collection of young people in moments of peak crisis being forced to learn rudimentary math and writing and history. But the staff at Woodside who lived those rhythms had come as a whole to depend on them, and on one another, to perform their jobs. And their jobs were not, in fact, to teach said rudimentary math and writing and history; their jobs were to make sure that the kids being locked up with so little certainty in any area of their futures could at least understand that there were adults in the world without any self-interest at stake who cared about those futures.

These same kids would say vile things (astonishingly creative and penetrating in their vileness) to their teachers and to one another. They would threaten violence and on rare occasions carry it out. They would form grand plans for themselves and then drop those plans as soon as they realized how many obstacles they contained. They would be active, full-throated students at Woodside, and then they would be released and a week later shoot a gun at someone.

Teaching at Woodside was an utterly irregular career marked far more often by failure than fulfillment. The eight people who'd landed in this career and persisted within it hated the physical structure they entered each morning, which they'd had no hand in constructing. They often hated the system that governed their work, which they'd had no hand in designing. They kind of hated a society that, after three hundred years of trying, had yet to learn that locking errant children in small rooms was neither a moral nor effective solution to discipline or safety. But their classrooms were in that building, and their jobs were a part of that system, and they themselves were products of that society. They came to work every day.

Although they were adults who understood that jobs ended sometimes, what felt painful and frustrating about Woodside's hard end date was that they had each spent years of trial and error figuring out how best to do this specific job, in accordance with their own contrasting personalities and sensibilities, within the small grim spaces of their assigned classrooms. They'd had a principal in Chris who'd encouraged this process, who chose not to have cameras in the rooms or to constantly critique their pedagogy. They'd honed different approaches to their students: strict, paternal, emotional, sardonic, intellectual. The building may have been terrible and the penal system archaic, but they'd figured out how to make the school within resemble an actual school. But because the school was part of that building, under the umbrella of that system, it was being disbanded.

None of the teachers knew what the reimagined version of court school would be in San Francisco—not even Constance, who was on the working group—but they knew that their work with young people would no longer be the product of so many enclosed individual days such as this one, the summation of all the invisible patterns of its small moments. The reimagined version would be closely observed, strictly dictated, and engineered by a committee disapproving of their work— those were three certainties right now. Those certainties were difficult to carry to and from school each day. They were not nearly as difficult as the certainties carried by the kids held at Woodside—every teacher acknowledged over and over, silently and aloud, that their struggles *in no way* paralleled or otherwise compared to those of the students—but they were difficult nonetheless. They rendered the days a little longer, the atmosphere a little tenser, and the moments with students a little more precious.

*   *   *

"I COULD NOT imagine a better start to the holiday than a room full of brilliant people strategizing to close down juvenile hall. This is about the best thing I can think of, pretty much." These words more or less christened the first meeting of the Close Juvenile Hall Working Group in January of 2020, spoken by the San Francisco supervisor who was the driving force behind the movement. The working group characterized itself multiple times during this meeting as having the eyes of the nation upon its work. The founding notion was that these select people—lawyers, educators, corrections and probation officers, social workers, advocates, and activists—could potentially provide a wholly new model for juvenile rehabilitation in America. These ambitions were probably a bit grandiose but certainly noble and motivating. They also belied that this was still a committee, governed by the dynamics between individuals in a political setting: some dominant and others passive; some well versed in the political language of a public forum, others total neophytes; some already comfortably set within alliances made over careers spent in and around the juvenile courts, others isolated and wary.

This meeting, the first two-hour session of a planned twenty-four over the next two years, was primarily spent setting a businesslike tone for the process. Under the guidance of hired consultants, the assembly members introduced themselves, reviewed the legislation that was the genesis of the working group, elected a chair, and began discussing the subcommittees that would be managing the minutiae of work in the months ahead. The structure dictated that these subcommittees, which had been streamlined from a planned eight to the current four, would meet and work independently and then convene on the third Wednesday of each month to update one another on respective progress and keep their trajectories aligned. The subcommittees—Programs,

Labor, Facilities, and Data Collection—each covered a deep, highly specific field that was intricately entwined with all the others. At these subcommittee meetings, the members were expected to sort through data and generate detailed plans of action. Then, in theory, they would marry these ideas with those of the other working groups in monthly, two-hour full-committee sessions. The process, as it was explained by the consultants during this first meeting, should happen seamlessly, transparently, with consensus and without overlap. The tone of this meeting was polite and hopeful, with only faint hints of interpersonal tensions around the edges, whenever a comment began with some variation of the words "I will of course go along with whatever the group ultimately decides, but I'd first just like to state . . ."

Constance Walker spoke three times during the opening meeting. The first was to declare herself present. The second was to introduce herself as a teacher in juvenile hall of twenty-two years. The third was to accept her assigned position on the Labor subcommittee. She stated her agreement that the current system was broken, citing the simple evidence that "we see the same faces over and over again." She added that she was excited for this opportunity, and that she hoped "there would be the resources and money to do the work that has to be done that this gets fixed, you know, because there are a lot of initiatives like this that sound good but don't really have an effect because it's not big enough, so I think this has got to be huge."

Hers was the only reference to either funding or execution, and the sometimes tenuous relationship between the two, that anyone on the working group would hear for months. Otherwise, the operating language of their meetings presumed that whatever they decided should happen, would happen, and that the outcomes of the city's youth would exponentially improve as a result. This mode of thinking vexed Constance from the beginning. The working group as a whole seemed to commence under the conjecture that simply because they were here trying to solve a knotty problem with deep experience and great intentions, the problem would be solved—that their being here was the solution.

Constance knew from her job at Woodside that just showing up with deep experience and great intentions, which she did with her colleagues there every day, was not nearly enough to treat a problem this intense, one ingrained from the very advent of the country for which they in San Francisco were presuming to light the way.

Chapter 5

◆

February 2020

THE MAN AT the front of the Unit 7 classroom sat in a regular desk chair with his feet flat on the floor and his back perfectly vertical. His body was all straight lines and ninety-degree angles—an otherworldly posture in an environment where everyone slouched all the time. He folded his hands placidly in his lap and seemed to take in the entirety of the room and the boys in it without swiveling his neck. His head was shaved and almost glossy. His skin was very pale. His eyes glinted with alertness, and his serene expression had the faintest touch of bemusement.

His name was Kodo. Megan introduced him as a meditation expert from the San Francisco Zen Center, where she sometimes practiced.

Kodo interrupted her gently, "It's not really possible to be a meditation 'expert.' There will always be far more that I don't know than I do know. I'm more like a guide. Our time together works best when I'm saying nothing at all." He smiled at what might be called his meditation humor, and suddenly the boys in Unit 7 could see him as a fellow human and not a living art piece. With that barrier broken, the boys began bombarding him with rapid questions.

"How much do you meditate?"

"What's the longest you've ever meditated?"

"Do you have, like, visions? Or do you enter, like, dimensions?"

"Have you ever seen the movie *Get Out*?"

Kodo's smile was steady as he answered in succinct, fluid sentences without pretension. He explained that many people saw meditation as an exit, a substanceless escape from the world they lived in, and that promise was almost always its initial draw. He saw it as the opposite, an effort to travel ever further inward. It was a confrontation with one's self and, with practice, a melding. It was a means to exist in the instant that was happening rather than to flee it. This was why, he said, many found consistent practice challenging to maintain: most people were not terribly comfortable just being with themselves, alone. During his first decade or so as a Zen student, he himself had been challenged. Now, he could meditate for as little as a few moments on a bus, or as long as ten or twenty hours at the Zen Center. Generally, he practiced for ninety minutes in the morning and ninety minutes in the evening. He added that he had seen and enjoyed *Get Out*—but, no, there were no visions or alternative dimensions in his experience, just his own rather plain consciousness.

"Does it hurt?" asked a young intake. He was fourteen years old and small for his age, with an overgrown rat tail hanging over his shoulder and down his chest. To be here, he had punched an elderly woman in the stomach at a gas station while stealing her phone and wallet.

For the first time, Kodo seemed slightly unsure of his words. "That's a difficult question. Physically, no, we're just sitting here. Your back might grow stiff, but it's okay to bend a little if that happens. You want to be comfortable. But maybe there are other kinds of pain, even some that might surprise you. Maybe things you've experienced in the past, or even things you fear experiencing in the future . . . it can happen fast." Kodo paused and seemed to gauge the measure of foreboding he'd brought into the room. "If it does, just say something. That's why I'm here. As I said, I'm like a guide. If you feel stuck, I can bring you out of it."

A few kids laughed, and another mimed paralysis with his eyes rolled back and tongue sticking out. Even with the joking, the Unit 7 boys, on paper among the roughest youth of San Francisco, were perhaps a little intimidated by this visitor.

Due to backlogs at the court building, the group of boys in this room had been together without turnover for just over two weeks. Consistency like this almost never happened at Woodside, but when it did, a classroom could assume its own personality. This group was relatively open-minded, curious, and lacking in the tensions that usually kept kids from voicing any thoughts that might invite derision. They also had a clear leader in Lawrence, the boy here for murder. Upon finishing the previous lesson block, David and Megan had asked the class to decide what they would study next. Lawrence had expressed an interest in the Dalai Lama, and the class deferred. They'd watched a documentary film called *The Dhamma Brothers* about a high-security prison group that engaged in meditation retreats. The boys began asking if they could venture their own retreat; they'd pleaded actually. Lawrence lobbied for ten days; Megan and David granted one class. Then Megan had reached out to the Zen Center, and Kodo had volunteered to visit—under the condition that he be permitted to come for two consecutive days, the first as an introduction and practice session, the second as a full-scale meditation. Otherwise, he felt, they wouldn't accomplish much.

Today was the practice session, and Megan had been gripped all morning by the certainty of disaster. She observed from the corner of the room, leaning casually against a bookshelf, trying (and mostly failing) to hide how nervous she was. She envisioned the boys refusing to take Kodo seriously due to his softhearted nature and overt Zen affect, or the actual meditation time turning into an obnoxious joke with kids making fart noises and such, or—most likely—one student who'd received bad news from court or from home taking it upon himself to ruin the hour for everyone else. A few dozen other forms of upset to the class dynamic could make this go poorly, and Megan couldn't help seeing them all unfold in her mind's eye. Only rarely during her twelve years at Woodside had any effort like this gone the way she'd hoped. She was accustomed to this reality and no longer overly bothered by it.

Yet she was particularly anxious about today, which probably signaled how much import she ascribed to the exercise, how much meaning she believed her students could draw from peering inward if they assumed enough vulnerability.

Vulnerability among their peers was one of the most difficult of all traits for these boys to embrace; within themselves, it was nearly unseen. A fundamental requirement of vulnerability—part of the word's definition—was to enter a physical or emotional area that wasn't safe. The majority of these children had been born into unsafe worlds, worlds in which asking an adult for help could be unsafe, walking out the front door could be unsafe, any unknown person or place could be unsafe, closing their eyes could be unsafe. These everyday realities were pertinent in this classroom today, where they were preparing to close their eyes and seek a space they'd never before been and encounter whatever spirits lurked. The source of Megan's fear lay there: neither she nor the boys had any idea what those spirits' temperaments might be.

She worried in particular for Lawrence. Through conversations happening around her and through the boy's own writing, she'd learned more about his background. The boy he'd killed—the boy Megan had taught and adored—had killed Lawrence's brother years earlier by stabbing him in the heart with a knife. This violence had happened right in front of Lawrence, in a convenience store. Twelve years old at the time, Lawrence had been with his brother, holding his hand, while he bled to death in his friend's car on the way to the hospital. He'd idolized his brother, who was a football player with a scholarship to a private high school. Six years later—this past summer—Lawrence had avenged him, been subsequently identified and caught, and now was here in juvenile hall about to meditate.

A little more than halfway into class, Kodo commenced the practice. The goal was ten full minutes. Megan didn't expect anyone to make it past five, but the time passed quickly and quietly, except that halfway through one large boy lumbered out of his chair and onto the floor to attempt a slumpy lotus position.

When the session ended, Kodo prompted the boys to open their eyes and allowed them some amused silence. Then he asked how it had been for everyone.

The big kid on the floor raised his hand and complained that the white noise from the air vent and the buzzing fluorescent lights bothered him.

Kodo nodded knowingly. "We become much more aware of sound, don't we? And that's important, it's part of the atmosphere and our lives, and sometimes it can really inhibit us. Because sound is an agitator. It physically vibrates us."

"Man, I could *really* feel that. Like my body was a bass speaker: *Boom-buh-boom-BOOM* . . ."

Students began raising hands and explaining just how loud their lives were, describing various homes in which shouting voices, slamming doors, street altercations, bawling children, were constant. They'd all come to juvenile hall from deafening environments.

"As much as you can tomorrow, try to absorb sound. Be aware of the sound and the space in front of and behind you and don't fight or resent the disturbances, because they're always part of where we are. That's a really hard thing about this practice, and it takes a lot of time."

The smaller boy with the rat tail raised his hand. "What do you do if your mind, like, wanders? Or it was, like, maybe I started to see things behind my eyes?"

"That's really profound, this experience of seeing images behind your eyes. It can feel almost like watching a movie, right?"

The student nodded ardently, and others concurred. "That's exactly what it was like. On my eyelids."

"Except that's not actually what's happening," Kodo said. "Those images are unfolding far deeper. And just let them unfold. Our instinct as humans is always to fight, always to recognize anything new as unnatural. But this is natural. Let the mind wander and that movie play for you."

The smaller boy shook his head and smirked a little sadly. "The movie sucked. I was getting smoked in it."

"Oh, okay." Kodo nodded thoughtfully. He took a moment to discern what the term *smoked* meant.

The boy noted the pause. "I was getting shot. Like, six or seven times."

Megan knew that this boy had in fact been shot six times during an altercation last year, between two stints at Woodside.

"I'm sorry," Kodo said, appearing deeply troubled now, as if he were partly responsible for the content of the boy's waking dream. "One of the biggest challenges—maybe *the* biggest challenge—is when the body doesn't feel safe because of . . . things that have happened, or things that could happen. Meditation really exposes the body."

"Can't keep your head on a swivel."

Kodo glanced at Megan, again unsure of the terminology. Megan just nodded.

"Right," Kodo said. "Exactly."

A few other students murmured that their experiences during the ten minutes of silence trended toward the painful traumas they carried: neglect, abandonment, loss, violence.

From her vantage point, with her arms crossed and warmly admiring the students and what they were capable of, Megan made quick eye contact with the counselor on duty by the door, Maceo Johnson, who'd seemed lulled himself by the meditation. She nodded to him to be semi-alert should any anger tapped into during the silence suddenly erupt. She'd seen it happen a few times while volunteering at San Francisco County Jail: thirty minutes of serene meditation suddenly unlocking decades of gathered rage.

Kodo considered the boys' responses for a long moment, understanding that the moment held great consequence. Then he said, "The key gift of mediation is the ability to recognize when the mind wanders or veers away, particularly toward emotions like anger."

Kodo used the analogy of training a dog or a cat, which could be taught the exact same behaviors using either abuse or reward. Animals taught with the former strategy could become highly obedient—could behave identically to their counterparts—but would always carry stress.

Through absolutely no fault of their own, they could never be peaceful beings.

The boys thought about this, and animals they'd loved, and themselves. Someone blurted, "You know how they say cats always find their way back home? Well, mine left and never came back—maybe because my uncle beat the shit out of it. Man, I hope that cat found its happiness."

"It's the same thing with training your mind," Kodo said. "There's never any need to punish it, you can be kind to it. You have time. With time, you'll learn to steer around its obstacles. Or, to use the movie comparison, you'll learn to be able to change the channel. Or, like with your cat, find a way to a peaceful place."

Though Megan felt that a meaningful discussion that could take dozens of different directions was just beginning, the class time ended, and no amount of meditative reflection could alter the schedules that governed them here. A door slammed outside, and loud voices began sounding in the kitchen about lunch prep. The atmosphere grew noisy again, as it usually was. But in this moment, the regular noise felt particularly loud and bothersome.

Kodo said, "Tomorrow, if you find anger entering your mind, focus on breathing through your mouth. If it keeps going, open your eyes and focus on your thumbs. If it keeps going, then stand up and let it flow out of you. Let peacefulness flow in."

They all stood, and as the students filed toward the door, a few bent their paths wide to give Kodo a high five or a fist pound or to thank him for his time.

Lawrence had been uncharacteristically quiet throughout this recap, as if sorting through even deeper ideas. Megan had to wonder if this was a good or bad thing for him to do.

The following morning Megan and David, for the first time in their joint memory of over ten years apiece working at Woodside, found Unit 7 students trying to begin class on time. The teachers had spread out the room's chairs to the extent that they could (they'd briefly discussed arranging them in a wide circle but realized that having kids in one another's direct sight lines would be distracting). Kodo sat in his unnervingly upright posture in front, as if he'd been there all night. The boy who had yesterday spoken of being shot asked to remove himself from class because he was still feeling agitated and didn't want to disrupt anyone else. Megan felt sad watching him leave, while the rest sat still and quiet, desiring to spend every moment available in meditation.

Megan said, in a tender plea that seemed generated deep in her heart, "It's really important to remember that you're all safe here. That during these next forty or fifty minutes, you don't have to worry about anything happening to you. We're all in this room to help each other and watch out for each other, and no one is coming in the room. I know it's really hard to feel safe sometimes, or a lot of the time, because things do happen and you have to be able to protect yourself. But nothing's going to happen here, I promise. You can really let go and try to do this. I know you all can do this. . . ." She trailed off when she realized how almost desperate she sounded, how she was striving to encapsulate challenges far beyond meditation class. Nothing she said now could dent even slightly the armor her students had to wear to keep living and enduring beyond this moment in time.

A quietude fell over them. The boys began gesturing for the session to begin. They all closed their eyes together.

Kodo said, "Focus on your body. Focus on your feet feeling your shoes." Then: "Stack your neck and head, and feel as though your mind is stacked on your body. Focus on where your breath is; focusing on breath gives your mind a point to look at."

Kodo opened his eyes and scanned the room. He ceased offering instruction. For almost fifty minutes, the class meditated in absolute silence: eleven young men, locked in jail, testing out the walls and barriers within their minds, maybe within their souls.

David participated while Megan again remained standing and cognizant throughout. She scanned the room and kept returning to Lawrence. He was still, almost statuesque. She waited for some kind of disruption, which seemed inevitable until about ten minutes remained, when she began to suspect that the class might get through the whole session smoothly. With five minutes left, she became sure that they would. With one minute left, she found herself wondering why she'd ever been worried in the first place, despite twelve years of precedent. Then she softly dinged the singing bowl and watched with a massive swell of something more powerful than just pride—wonder, maybe—as the boys began blinking their eyes and slowly drawing themselves from whatever unseen places they'd sojourned. They needed a full three minutes to resituate themselves within the classroom they spent most of each day in. Megan, beaming, said that they had only a minute or two for reflection.

"I felt my blood moving in weird parts of my body, like in my forearms, and my vision was, like, wavy the whole time," said a boy in the front row.

"I almost cried," said the kid with the rat tail.

"What made you?" the boy next to him asked.

The kid shrugged. "I don't know, I just did."

"I felt like it almost hurt sometimes—not, like, *ow!* But a different kind of hurt. A quiet kind." Others nodded toward the sentiment. "It was cool, though. I liked it."

Kodo said, "It sounds like you all noticed that it's not easy. It doesn't necessarily feel good or pleasant, this existing inside."

"Does it ever get that way?" the boy who'd talked about his own blood flow asked. "Like, when you did it for a year without talking—did it get easy ever?"

Kodo shook his head. "It never gets easy. But it becomes more comfortable. It's like moving to a new city. At first, you're maybe just lost. You spend time each day exploring, a little farther each day, and you learn your basic way around. You know where the groceries are, where the school is, you make friends. And after that, you can still explore and find new places and meet new people, unexpected and even scary places and people, but you have the known streets to always get you back home. With practice, that's what it becomes."

"Ms. Mercurio," Lawrence asked as they were summoned to the

lunch area outside, everyone somewhat loath to exit this space, "if I want to practice this for, like, thirty minutes a day, can I get room time for that?"

His eyes held a certain yearning. She smiled and told him that if he was committed to that, she could figure something out with the counselors. The kids goofed a bit on their way to lunch, ten feet from the room. She and David began pushing the desks to their original alignment, while Kodo gathered his jacket and bag, looking satisfied in his humble, Zen way. The three of them spoke casually about how well the session had gone and how impressed they all were by the boys.

Behind the banter, Megan hid that she was more than impressed. She was swollen with love and admiration and hope. But she wanted to contain these feelings, keep them as her own, keep them from pouring forth and bolstering her reputation among her colleagues as "the one who cried a lot." Maybe it was because she'd spent the class observing, rather than participating. Watching the boys sit still and silent for all those minutes, watching them and imagining what measureless universes their minds encompassed, had stupefied her. Those eleven young men were the products of massive tides of history, of the immovable forces of poverty and racism and apathy, of a society trying over and over and over to alter the outcomes of tragic scenarios and seeing the same outcomes persist. The young men were right now entangled with a justice system that assigned them to a locked facility before they'd even been judged by it, knowing that the judgment, whenever it did come and whatever it portended, would trail them all their lives. They were angry and scared and helpless. As their teacher, and as a human being, Megan's primary directive was simply to see them. Here, they'd asked her for the opportunity to see themselves, to create some time and support to check out what was going on beneath the masks of their faces.

Megan and all her coworkers could feel like ants sometimes: busy and tired and colossally productive in the microspaces of their classrooms, yet also purposeless in that their work could be and often was dismantled by far more powerful entities to whom they remained absolutely invisible and insignificant. The teachers worked every day in the knowledge that within a few years, most of these boys would not have graduated from high school, and a certain number would be in prison, and one or more might be dead. But Megan now held this new knowledge: her Unit 7 students had just meditated together for nearly an hour. In this moment, as she waved to them while passing the lunch area and waited for the great door to let her pass through, she felt as if each of them could accomplish anything if their worlds might provide them with anything to accomplish.

Chapter 6

◆

March–May 2020

"Y OU CAN'T HAVE school."

Chris Lanier processed the words and stayed calm. A fiery component to his personality gained satisfaction and energy from argument, but almost thirty years in the public school system had taught him how counterproductive this instinct almost always was, and how to curb it. He said evenly, "I was told the other day that we could. The shutdown isn't supposed to apply to us."

"Things are moving really fast, Chris. This is where we are now. We just have to listen and stand by."

"Well, what are the kids supposed to do today?" He couldn't help adding a trace of petulance to the question.

His supervisor passing the news along sighed. She'd probably been up most of the last few nights amid the disarray that was early March of 2020 in America. Chris didn't just trust his supervisor, who was in charge of all alternative education in San Francisco. He admired her as well. She was responsible for ten different schools for children requiring special education. Chris was responsible for twenty-nine of those kids at the moment. He shouldn't be needling her at all. But he felt helpless, as most people in the world did, and he was venting.

"Just get on the phone, talk to staff while we all figure out how long this is going to be. But you guys aren't allowed in the facility until further notice."

Chris had known this was going to happen—San Francisco had logged some of the first official COVID cases in the country six weeks earlier—but he still had trouble grasping that it was now happening.

Across the district, schools of all kinds were mobilizing tech support, hardware, and software to transition to remote learning. Administrators were sending mass emails and organizing the distribution of laptops and internet hot spots for low-income families. Technicians were building platforms on Google Classroom and some app called Zoom. Educators were writing up take-home lesson plans and even figuring out how to make PE virtual. Meanwhile, the kids at Woodside weren't permitted to use the internet unless closely supervised. They couldn't have pencils outside the classroom. They couldn't work independently. Except for the security system, the whole structure was intentionally low tech, largely disconnected from the outside world. The teachers were the conduits: to the internet, to world events, to high school credits. Now the teachers were to be locked outside while the students remained locked in. Even the library would remain closed, since it could only legally be opened by the certified librarian.

Chris was about to be the nexus of many dozens of frustrated, isolated, confused, scared people demanding answers that he simply wouldn't have because he himself was frustrated, isolated, confused, and scared.

Throughout his career, he'd learned intimately all the densely knotted contradictions of education, and special education in particular. During his first placement in a special ed classroom in Oakland, he'd been left on his own with almost no classroom experience with upward of forty second-graders who had various special needs. Before he'd taken the Woodside leadership position, he'd been in charge of support for special ed students throughout the SFUSD. Every day he visited different elementary, middle, and high schools, assessed the needs of individuals, and made recommendations for improved supports. And every day he'd creatively grappled with the challenge of balancing the individual attention that these kids deserved with the resources these schools were allotted.

Chris knew the particular expansion of his soul that occurred when a young person overcame unsparing struggles through sheer force of spirit. He'd once been charged with assessing an illiterate fifteen-year-old girl who was raising an infant and had been disowned by her entire nuclear family. Her child was asthmatic, and she was suicidal. He convinced her that she needed to learn how to read if only to be able to decipher the prescription labels on her baby's medications. Four years later, that girl enrolled in community college. She now worked for Amnesty International, and that baby was a repeat Student of the Month in middle school. Chris also had felt the pieces of his spirit that dissolved when he'd tried to help a young person—when he'd promised that he would help—but couldn't. Another high school student had extricated herself from a severely abusive boyfriend—Chris had snuck into the house to help her move her things when the boyfriend was out—but a full day and night of traversing the city's network of shelters and social services produced no space to take her. She went back to her boyfriend's. Three years later, she died of an overdose.

All his teachers were intimate with playing some small role in these rolling narratives of triumph and failure. Hundreds of them unfolded at Woodside annually (the school had repeatedly been dinged in the media for the resources used to teach less than thirty kids on any given day, but around four hundred different kids might pass through the school in a typical year). Overall, the teachers' experiences trended toward sadness and loss. The key to persevering in their work lay in being there and living through it all with the students; the key lay in the students' knowing that, whatever the outcome of a class or day or court appointment, the teachers would be there tomorrow. That simple dependability helped the students be less fearful.

What Chris was metabolizing now was the reality that, due to a few bits of RNA that had originated in a bat or some creature on the opposite side of the world, he and his teachers would not in fact be there tomorrow. And the kids—though they would never admit it, though they might not even be aware of it—would miss them. The kids would be afraid.

*   *   *

THE FIRST FEW weeks of quarantine were deeply strange because everything felt chaotic, but nothing much happened. The kids in juvenile hall had rec time all day, but the temporary lockdown measures decreed that they could use neither the gym nor the outdoor blacktop yard; absolutely no one understood why. The kids remained in their units. To prevent close gatherings, they were placed in small groups that rotated between their rooms and the common area and the eating area. Nobody was allowed in the classrooms.

The Juvenile Probation Department worked on amending its strict no-internet policy so that the teachers could begin implementing some form of individualized remote learning, but this process stretched on and on, frozen by the many technicalities surrounding juvie kids and the World Wide Web. The working assumption, based on sometimes specious amalgams of past experience, was that any Woodside student allowed on the internet would immediately begin organizing gang activity. Every second in which a student had access to a linked device was supposed to be monitored by a counselor. The department decided that, during the COVID-19 shutdown, this required a second counselor to monitor the first counselor who was monitoring the screen, to ensure that there were no attention lapses. The necessary manpower led to much debate over how many computers with internet connections could be permitted inside the residential units.

In the meantime, the counselors were deemed essential workers, but most were frightened and wary of spending too much time too close to the kids. Ominous numbers and theories had seized every tier of the news. The consensus seemed to be that young people were immune to most symptoms but transmitted the virus easily, while adults faced scary fatality rates. Such narratives could cause even the most devoted counselors to enter the units only for the amount of time required to switch out a DVD beneath the TV set. The kids at Woodside watched an awful lot of movies during those weeks.

School—or whatever vestige of school the teachers and counselors could improvise while tech guidelines were worked out—consisted mainly of short handouts with math problem sets and writing assignments. The counselors would print these, coerce the students one at a time to do some work in the eating area, then take pictures of the sheets with their cell phones and text them to the teachers. Megan received many dozens of JPEGs of blank sheets of paper. Some students were too depressed to even write their names.

The boys and girls at Woodside outwardly didn't seem to fret much. In late February, just under two weeks before the system locked down into near-total isolation, the students seemed only vaguely aware that some sort of virus in China had people in a stir. Immediately post-lockdown, even as the teachers ceased coming to work physically and the counselors were flummoxed by the logistics of spacing and risk, students displayed only a casual interest in what this virus was and how severe of a threat it posed to them. During those first two weeks, they were mainly pissed that the showers—normally such a frequent part of their daily rhythms—had been designated unsafe. They were permitted to bathe, but only during a short period once per day, with the requirement to clean their stall with disinfectant afterward. With another fragment of choice removed from their lives, kids began to forgo showers altogether, and they began to stink.

The common areas in the units had already become tense places due mainly to stasis and ennui. Minor disagreements, such as over the way someone might be lounging in a chair, erupted into unitwide tantrums. Kids were complaining about virtually everything: food, the tone of the overhead lighting, the paint color of the walls and the roughness of the carpeting, one another's speech patterns and acne, the court system, the toil of being alive. And quickly the rank odor of unwashed bodies settled throughout the entire space. Oddly, the smell was so prevalent that the kids ceased to be aware of it, and it was one of the few things they didn't complain about. The counselors, however, were struck by a noxious burst each time they entered Unit 6 or 7, where the boys lived. The mandatory face masks helped marginally. Weeks passed.

The court system devoted those weeks to releasing as many incarcerated kids as possible: basically everyone who hadn't committed a violent crime before or during their time at Woodside was hustled into the probation network. By early April, one girl and thirteen boys remained in the building. The two boys' units merged into one, mainly so that available staff could be more efficient. The prisoners were constantly moving among the facility's eight different living units so that different areas could be deep-cleaned regularly.

New intakes continued to arrive regularly; person-to-person crimes fell significantly at the outset of the city's stay-at-home measures, but crimes such as shootings, burglaries, and arson rose by over 30 percent from the same month a year prior. Arriving prisoners faced mandatory two-week quarantine periods. Lengths of stays became even more unpredictable because in-person court appearances were temporarily suspended, as were lawyer visits. Therefore, none of the kids at Woodside, old or new, had any idea when they would be leaving—yet another bruise to their sense of having any control over their existences. For the moment, while the teachers outside spent twelve-hour workdays striving to establish an allowable technology platform, all the boys had to depend on was three meals a day, a stack of random DVDs played over and over (they were on their twentieth or thirtieth viewing of the Michael Mann remake of *Miami Vice*, and it hadn't been any good the first time), and their own company.

They also had Maceo Johnson, who had been counseling at Woodside since he was twenty-six. He'd applied for the job as a lark because he'd become melancholy managing an Enterprise rental car branch and no bank would give him a loan to start his own venture, even with a business degree from San Francisco State University. Maceo also felt a personal draw emanating from the stint he'd done himself in juvenile hall as a kid. The facility where he'd spent months incarcerated had not (in his opinion) employed any adults who'd seemed genuinely interested in connecting with kids—or at least not with him, as he could be (also in his opinion) unruly and willful. Idealistically, Maceo had felt that maybe he could be that adult, the one who reached out to the unruly, willful kids and convinced them that they were not alone. He'd felt that maybe he could try to do a few good things for a few young people while he was still in his twenties, with some time and energy. Then he would go ahead and launch his business empire. That was his plan then. Maceo was thirty-nine now, having never left juvenile hall.

While he no longer felt young, he was still well south of fifty, the age scientists were using as a cutoff between low- and high-risk in the event of COVID-19 infection. He'd been working primarily in Unit 7 for most of his Woodside tenure. He'd developed the tricky skill of being both friendly and authoritative with his charges, of connecting with individuals without giving up the discipline he needed to maintain for his and their safety. Early on in the pandemic, Maceo felt the responsibility to take ownership of the lived-in units, both to protect his older colleagues' health and to help the kids not to lose their minds.

But watching kids watch TV for the bulk of each day for almost a month was not just sad but soul crushing. Juvenile hall was a place of locks; the psychology of everyone in the building was dominated by locks constantly opening and closing. With the coronavirus now in the air, it felt as if the locks had virtually ceased to open.

On the outside, Megan and David were working to adapt remote-learning platforms to the facility's infrastructure, and Chris focused on the bigger picture of mapping a course should the shutdown last into the summer (however unlikely that seemed at the time). On the inside, Maceo was lobbying the Juvenile Probation Department simply for the means to move the kids outside their units for a few minutes of outdoor time a few days a week—even just to water the garden. All of their efforts were inhibited by the leadership's faith that the lockdown would shortly end, that there was no way that the city, the country, and the world could fail to subdue this virus in a timely fashion, and the status quo would suffice until then.

For Maceo Johnson and others struggling to accomplish anything educationally within the building in the interim, the dilemma utterly crystallized what made working in the system so difficult: the constant nullification of trust. The kids Maceo took care of for a living—both pre- and post-COVID-19—did not have many adults they could trust. Maceo knew this about them before he met them upon intake because kids who did have those adults in their lives didn't often end up in jail, even when they made terrible choices. All the counselors and teachers had nuanced strategies for building trust—Maceo would share fragments of his personal story, but the boys could only unlock the next passage if they shared pieces of their own stories—so that they could then provide some form of an education, which was the only hope in all this. The regulations of the system made this dynamic—the maintenance of trust—exhausting on a normal day. The response to the virus rendered it nearly inoperable and turned Maceo into a liar who constantly assured students that they would have real school and was then left helpless when no school happened—when the kids not only had nothing to do, but no one whose promises they could believe.

Still, he toiled and hustled to establish some link to the teachers that might consistently work, so that school could come back. Almost the entire spring passed.

*   *   *

"THIS IS SUCH strong work, Isaiah. It's really powerful."

The boy's eyes darted around, returning now and again to a downward angle, which must have been where Megan's and David's faces appeared on his screen. The biggest frustration out of the many frustrations of remote teaching was the impossibility of making eye contact. If the student was seeing her eyes, it meant that he was looking at his screen while she peered into the curiously disorienting camera lens on the upper edge of her laptop. If she saw his eyes, which she almost never did, it meant the opposite.

"I'm really impressed," David added. "You clearly worked really hard."

"Thanks," the boy mumbled. He'd written a few sentences in response to a writing prompt they'd assigned: *What do I need to forgive myself for? All of us have something that haunts us . . . something we continue to beat ourselves up for. What is it for you? Use this time to put it on paper and start the process to MOVE ON!*

Isaiah had listed punching his father, failing to avenge a friend who'd been killed, and being overweight as experiences for which he needed to forgive himself, though he hadn't used any language of actual forgiveness in his sentences. Megan's instinct was to start their session by focusing on the line about being overweight, then segue into the story of losing his friend. But she hadn't been able to discuss this tack with David beforehand because they didn't have time to prepare much in between individual meetings. The setup was akin to speed dating.

With a touch of levity, and hoping that David wouldn't mind following her lead, she said, "I have to tell you that you're not overweight."

The boy laughed, then seemed to peer down at his torso and be revolted by what he saw. "I'm soft as hell. We don't get to work out here for one second. I feel gross."

"We really are trying to fix it," David said.

Maceo, who was sitting just behind Isaiah in the classroom, muttered, "I'm about to bust a hole in this wall myself, just so you all can play some basketball for five minutes."

"Five minutes would be good."

The four of them spent a moment commiserating virtually about the absurdity of the situation. Then Isaiah had to switch out of the classroom for the next student. Megan thought that Maceo appeared tired, and she implored the counselor to take some shifts off and get some rest.

"I'm good," he said. "We're all running on fumes a bit. You both must be, too."

"But we're not there," Megan said, though she was stating the obvious. To disentangle from their small apartment in a city that was one of the nation's viral epicenters—and also to secure free child care for her daughter while she taught—Megan had brought her family south to her parents' home outside San Diego. The weather here was conducive to a positive mood, the streets were wide, the people spread out. Her daughter was living as if in an especially pleasant dream: travel, grandparents, no real school, and no real end date. Megan was racked with guilt every time she saw the empty classroom in the background of her screen, and the other boys sitting around the rec area, hair unkempt and postures bent as they continued to do nothing when they weren't on the computer with teachers. Maceo was also slouched and a little puffy in the face. He'd been working every day for almost two months. He had a fifteen-year-old daughter, and Megan wondered if virus protocols permitted him to see her at all.

"I'm good," Maceo reaffirmed as the next student entered the classroom with a wrinkled sheet of lined paper and sat to go over writing prompts.

"I didn't get to write anything," he said immediately. "I've been too busy."

David couldn't help laughing good-naturedly even as the response's preposterousness saddened him. "What have you been so busy doing?"

"Stuff," the boy said with the faintest note of defiance. "Lots of stuff."

At the same time, the lone girl, Cynthia, remaining in Unit 5 met online with Constance Walker to attempt some independent English work. No one knew why every girl at Woodside save for one had been granted release due to COVID-19. But Cynthia was absolutely on her own in jail—on her own except for Mama Rose, the elder counselor in the girls' unit, who like Maceo hadn't missed a day of work since the coronavirus had first appeared in San Francisco. Eyes bright and encouraging behind her surgical mask, Mama Rose kept Cynthia constant company. They'd been having a continuous running conversation for days, mostly about loneliness and what it was, what it meant. Loneliness was the subject of the free writing that Cynthia read aloud for Constance today:

"'I get sad when I think of my mom. She is alone at home. The state put my father in prison and put me in jail and won't even let her leave her apartment now, so it's like she's in jail, too. I'm sad she can't be with family and she's probably going to get sick. She doesn't even have a Mama Rose or somebody to talk to and I'm scared she's going to go crazy in the apartment and worrying about me and go out with her friends, get drunk, probably get the virus. I wouldn't blame her because that's what loneliness does. We make bad choices and act out. Why I got sent to jail the first time is I was lonely and saw some friends and went with them just because. And that was it. I'm almost to being not scared of the mice in here at night anymore, because at least they company. I wonder if my mom even has that much to not feel alone.'"

Cynthia had been holding the paper in both hands, rigid in front of her face, such that Constance's screen was blanked by it. Cynthia lowered the paper now, bashfully, and through the computer Constance studied the girl's expression in the cold, empty jail unit and grieved for her, even as the girl forced a smile and awaited the teacher's comments on her written work. Constance had grieved for many, many children over twenty-two years teaching in juvenile hall: for children losing parents, losing friends, losing their futures, losing their minds, losing their lives. But the wave cresting over her now was almost frighteningly unfocused. Because she was looking at this wonderful young woman—but not really looking at her, looking at some pixels that depicted her on a flat surface—and she had no idea what would happen or what sort of control any of them might have over what would happen.

"I really like it," she told Cynthia. "I'm so impressed with how hard you worked on it."

"Mama Rose helped me with some of the spelling. And verbs and stuff."

"I didn't help barely at all," Mama Rose said in her hoarse, sage voice. "She didn't need it. This one's really bright. Some things she says to me in here are just . . ." Mama Rose looked upward and widened her eyes to suggest a spirit-altering epiphany. "She just understands so much. She's as smart as they come, this girl. She's got to get back in school."

"Me and all the other teachers are calling every day to try to get you home," Constance said. She wasn't supposed to say things like this; she wasn't supposed to give specificity to hope. "It's just so hard to get through to anyone, and then you don't know whom you're talking to, and they themselves don't even know the answers or who has answers. It's all a mess right now, but we're all trying to get it right for you, because it's not right where you are."

"Thank you, Ms. Walker," Cynthia said with the minimum of audibility.

After the class ended with the teacher's face frozen on the screen in an eyes-closed instant that made the girl laugh, Cynthia folded the laptop shut and moved from the eating area to the common area. Standing rigidly pencil-like with her arms at her sides, she let herself slowly topple backward into the cushions. Then she curled up and let both her legs slide over the arms of the chair. Mama Rose handed the laptop off to another counselor at the unit's front door, then returned. She walked slowly and breathed heavily. She sat near the girl in a plastic foldout chair because, at her age and weight, she had trouble rising from the softer, lower furniture. The two women, one old and one young, simply sat there for a time in the quiet of the huge space.

Gazing upward, Cynthia asked, "Why do they put the ceiling so tall?"

"It's to make it so you all can breathe a little. The building they had before this one . . ." Mama Rose grimaced and made a pained noise, thinking back to the nineties, when teenagers from certain neighborhoods were sent to juvenile hall for any transgression greater than loitering, when a bunch of kids fighting in Hunters Point would be arrested and dropped off at juvenile hall together, and as soon as their intakes were complete, all the same kids would resume fighting. "Those ceilings were *low*. Those kids were *unhappy*. That's when they *should* have closed juvenile hall."

Cynthia studied the room intently. "What I don't get is, if they wanted to make it nicer here, how come they didn't, you know, make it *nicer here?*"

Mama Rose tilted her head, not totally understanding the question.

"Like, okay, they made the ceiling tall to make the room feel bigger. That's nice. But all the walls and stuff are still plain old concrete. The paint is still ugly old gray mostly. Doors are all scratched and big and loud. Rooms we sleep in are just closets. The bathrooms are terrible, not even toilet seats. So how come when they made the place, if they wanted it to be nice enough to have high ceilings, they didn't just do a little extra all around?"

Mama Rose shrugged. "I honestly don't know how they think. I've worked for them for more than forty years and I don't know. . . ."

"Like, how come all the teachers are white and all the counselors are black?" the girl blurted. "They think high ceilings makes us not notice that?"

Mama Rose peered at the ceiling along with the girl. Last week, a pigeon up in the metal rafters had made for an entire day's worth of entertainment. Unlike the girl, the bird had since been freed. Today, nothing of interest was happening. The question Cynthia had asked was one of the most visible questions in the school, and one of the most ignored. "Not all the counselors are black," Mama Rose deflected. "There's Mr. Ian."

"C'mon. That's one."

"Mr. Padilla and Ms. Rayikanti teach. They aren't white."

"They're not black."

"All right, all right." Mama Rose's head tilted back and her hands were laced over her stomach. "I think with most of us on the counseling side, it starts as just a job. Like in my case, I was twenty-six years old, I had two kids, I just needed a real job, and the training for this one is not that hard—it should be hard but it's just not. And I got the job and I had a knack for it and I've been here with you all ever since. A lot of us are like that. We fell into it maybe out of being young and needing to work and not having a lot of options, and after the fact, we found meaning in it. All right? And people who are young, need work, and don't have options tend to be black. You follow?"

"Mm-hmm." Cynthia seemed only dazedly interested now.

"Teachers, they have to go to real school to do what they do. They have to have a plan and at least some money set aside, plus time, to get that degree and training. I think it takes two years. And so most people like that tend to be white. And that's the way it is in this country. . . . But don't get me wrong—the teachers here are good sorts, really good sorts. And almost all the counselors are, too, though some with the attitude could use some shaking. But they care. I know you feel that."

"I guess I do. What's the garden like these days? Is anyone watering it?"

Cynthia was all over the place this afternoon, but Mama Rose was content to follow her rapidly roving thoughts.

"I've checked a few times. For a bit, it looked like no one was watering. Now, lately, someone has been. I don't know who."

They were quiet together for a few minutes until Mama Rose's back grew stiff and she had to stand up. "Get your shoes on. Let's go check ourselves."

"Check what?"

"The garden, see if it needs watering."

Cynthia shot upward from the chair. "We're not allowed, I thought."

"The people who say what we're allowed and not allowed to do don't even come in here. They maybe don't even understand what this whole thing is." Mama Rose radioed ahead to clear the hallway. Her colleagues were confused but obedient because she was Mama Rose and people here, children and adults alike, generally did what she told them to. The elderly woman's energy and initiative seemed to fill the young girl and activate her. A few moments later, the two walked together in their masks about thirty feet down the hall. They turned left and Mama Rose pressed the call button to have the door unlocked, waiting to see if whoever was running the main console would hassle her about regulations. Then that awful buzzing noise sounded and the counselor took Cynthia outside. The sun was bright and absolutely clear in the early afternoon. In its light, Cynthia did a little twirl and emitted a not too loud *whoop* sound. But she only basked for a couple seconds before heading to the first of the planters to begin inspecting the lavender and sage, which were both lush looking. She appeared to be inspecting each leaf individually, frowning.

"Whoever's been watering them hasn't been giving them much attention," the girl called out, shaking her head.

"That'll be your job from now on."

Cynthia suddenly looked up with concern. "What about your job? I don't want you to lose it breaking the rules for me."

Mama Rose laughed, a hoarse, jolly grinding from deep in her throat. "If I lose my job letting a girl take care of this garden, well, I'd say I had a pretty good, long run here."

Chapter 7

◆

June 2020–April 2021

O N A BIG day, the swells at Ocean Beach broke a hundred yards off-shore. They were loud and unrelenting. To reach the surf lineup just beyond the break, one could only press headlong through the eight- or ten-foot walls that weighed thousands of tons each. Chris Lanier had been paddling out often since the school closed, either right before the workday began or right after it ended. Sometimes he joined friends or surfed with his eighteen-year-old son. More often, he surfed alone. The frigid water was invigorating, the ocean's forces powerful and compli-cated and uncaring. He depended on these forces to keep his soul intact, because he felt that juvenile hall was a mess of hurting children whom he couldn't help.

Chris didn't hold any pretensions that he could fix the juvenile justice system in America. At every single point of contact, kids in crisis needed individual attention, they needed intellectual stimulation, they needed unconditional love, they needed one another. These simple tenets were expensive, and they were administered—or not administered—in dif-ferent modes everywhere. But he had myriad ideas for improving schools like Woodside, which were embedded in the system and yet separate. His ideas—most of them scrawled somewhere in his trusty Moleskine—ranged from the books they read in class to the longshot

prospect of guaranteeing kids jobs with the city parks and rec department upon release. He believed that Megan Mercurio's minute of silent breathing should be used to begin every class in every juvenile hall
in the country; that students ought to be asked in advance whether or
not they were comfortable being called on during a discussion in order
to alleviate stress; that every curriculum needed to include some form
of empathy training and peer coaching; that project-based learning and
service learning were invaluable, as was the concept of "guest learning,"
or inviting visitors from the community and other sectors of the justice
system to come to classrooms not to talk but to listen while students led
their own lessons. He and his staff had incubated all of these strategies
and dozens more over the years at Woodside, and all were effective with
their rapidly rotating, conflict-prone students. Chris was confident that
they could be transferred into most any other facility in America to improve teaching and learning.

The Close Juvenile Hall Working Group had drawn enough public
attention to give him a coveted, valuable platform on which to model
some of these concepts and exhibit his staff's talents to critics who were
still reacting to anecdotes from the 1990s. But now the safety protocols
for the virus had them all refreshing frozen video feeds from their living
rooms instead.

He'd tried to obtain special permissions for himself and teachers who
were willing to enter the classrooms; that request had flatly been denied. He'd asked for multiple internet-connected computers from the
school district to be set up around the living units, at appropriate social
distances but visible to counselors, so that students could all log in to
Google Classroom and have virtual classes together during structured
time throughout the day. His superiors had made some effort on that,
but the anxiety surrounding juvie kids being on the web persisted. He'd
tried to procure headsets so that students could simply listen to pre-
recorded lectures from their teachers, on their own time, even in their
rooms at night. That plan was deemed too expensive. The students at
Woodside, even with their numbers down in the low teens, were still

mostly watching TV between their turns at the one computer in the unit with Wi-Fi software.

The Close Juvenile Hall Working Group was not delaying the mandated deadline, now a year and a half away, even though the group hadn't met virtually in three months. The lack of meetings meant that any progress or decisions or even data collection was happening out of the public view. Chris couldn't learn anything without directly leaning on his relationships, and he couldn't lean on his relationships without appearing meddlesome. He didn't even aspire to influence the working group via backdoor channels, the way politics in general and San Francisco politics in particular worked. He just wanted to keep reminding the people in power that two dozen working educators were in the current juvenile hall facility, teachers and counselors who were with these kids every day and were skilled at being with these kids. Those skills had to mean something as the system's redesign carried on.

As a classroom teacher, and later a special education coordinator, and now the principal of juvenile hall, Chris had seen the extremes of human nature at both ends—these extremes made for his most gripping and resonant stories—yet most of what he'd seen day to day in his career lay in between the poles. The triumphs lay in simple promises kept: staying out of jail and away from guns and earning high school diplomas. The disappointments lay in simple promises broken: adults vowing to support a child whom they then abandoned, a kid determined to go to school every day lasting only a week before resuming truancy. The vitality of Chris's job depended on being present through all of these moments, absorbing them, finding some meaning in the frenzy of them, and conveying it on through new ideas that might irritate his teachers but might also create some kind of novel energy.

But really, Chris's job—his core value to the students in his school and their families and maybe to society—was to deliver these kids school credits. No child arrived in juvenile hall who wasn't behind in his or her high school accreditation. Most were severely behind. Chris's program was designed to catch them up as thoroughly as possible for as long as the courts kept them in his school. Even though Chris was not the one locking them up and didn't believe they should be locked up, he took advantage of the fact that, as long as they were locked up, they had no other choice but to earn the credits he lined up for them.

High school credits sounded like a banal metric of success considering the depth of experience the Woodside staff collectively wielded, the profound leaps in self-belief they sought to stimulate. But in Chris's orbit, his purpose and the kids' futures depended on these credits. Because as long as they were behind in those numbers, as long as they remained on the path to *not* receiving a high school diploma, their court outcomes didn't matter: society would not permit them true entry. Credit totals, once committed to the system, became tangible and permanent and thus powerful motivators. Right now, he was unable to provide those credits in any consistent or meaningful way. The situation was racking him inside, causing him pain.

That pain was perhaps why, out in the ocean, he foolishly oared his splayed hands for the first massive ramp that arose in the dusky light, which became a drop as it heaved his small body on his small board. His timing and position were way off, and he never even attempted to gain his feet before flipping and plummeting over the falls, driven deep into the cold darkness. The wipeout—so bad that he had to humiliatingly sputter assurances to the concerned surfers around him that he was all right—felt symbolic of everything right now.

*   *   *

BABY RAMSIE—THE kid who'd orchestrated Darian Slay's attack right after Darian expressed his ambitions for credits and college the previous December—had never failed to explode the dynamic within Unit 7 whenever he arrived. Over his teenaged years he'd been sent there probably every three or four months, for a few weeks at a time. His older brothers and cousins had done more or less the same, as had his father and uncles; the family had a wide footprint at Woodside, hence the nickname Baby. The boy was haughty and bombastic, and he giddily made

life difficult for the teachers and counselors. Yet he had a gentle child-
ishness about him, as well as an innate intelligence, that made them all
believe that one day, once he outgrew his family's criminal sphere and
had the chance to make his own choices, he might thrive.

They would never know now, because Baby Ramsie was dead. He'd
been shot in a car while crossing the Bay Bridge. The shooter had been
in another car that had pulled alongside after following him out of the
city, then weaved on across the bridge without being stopped following
the shots. The killer was still at large.

Megan learned of the death while driving east across the country
with her daughter and another family, all crammed into a small sedan.
Every few hundred miles, they would pour out and walk around a national park or small town where the sky was huge and the land mostly
empty of people. The school shutdown promised to last indefinitely,
and Megan also had a mandatory three weeks off from teaching as the
result of a new schedule meant to keep Woodside in session year-round
(another of Chris's ideas, unpopular with staff, to replace summer
school, which was expensive and a little meaningless in juvenile hall).
So Megan was heading for a long visit to her sister's farm in Massachusetts. When David called her to say that Baby Ramsie was gone, she was
wedged in the back seat between her daughter and her friend's daughter
while they descended the eastern foothills of the Rockies onto the plains
of Colorado. She wept so hard that they had to pull over along a steep
shoulder, and Megan squatted behind the car's rear so as not to upset the
kids. She convulsed with grief while peering at the farmsteads stretching
out a thousand feet below.

Baby Ramsie's entire family was so embedded in criminal occupa-
tions that he had considered school utterly irrelevant, and the family
was so successful at crime that he had held sway over other boys in
the unit. In juvenile hall he might have had more control over his life
than he did outside. He'd been Megan's student for a few months, cumulatively, over the previous years. She'd spent dozens of hours with
him and knew him well. She'd liked him. He was funny and sharp and

skilled at reading people. He'd engaged deeply in poetry writing units, not just in writing rap lyrics as most kids did but in different forms of poetry: sonnets, haiku, villanelles even. He'd always been a sensitive listener when other students read aloud from their own work, which was one of the most vulnerable tasks they were called on to do in her classroom. He could be kind, albeit largely contained beneath the indifferent veneer that was required of someone whose family's livelihood was selling guns and drugs. While he had also no doubt indirectly injured and perhaps killed others through his family's trade (he'd told Megan that he'd never killed anyone himself, and she'd believed him), Baby Ramsie was still a child and had never made his own decisions regarding what kind of person he wanted to be. The bullet on the bridge meant that he would never reach an age at which he could consider any existential ideas for himself and atone. But maybe he never would have; maybe he would have continued to harden, inside and outside jail, and maybe his premature death had saved a number of lives. Megan didn't know.

Such was the great, irresolvable contradiction of caring about her students. On the lower slopes of the country's highest range, driving away from California and the jail and the virus, Megan grieved. The following weekend, while passing through the farmlands of Iowa, she watched a YouTube video on her phone in which hundreds of teenagers from Hunters Point—Baby Ramsie's neighborhood—walked across the section of the bridge where the boy had bled out. For the marginalized, poor youth of San Francisco, snarling traffic for an hour upon a busy roadway spanning a gorgeous body of water was their mode of paying tribute to a lost friend.

Four weeks later, teaching remotely from a barn on her sister's property, Megan learned that Mama Rose had passed away from a non-COVID-related respiratory infection. The nature of the loss was different from that of the student: Mama Rose had given the entirety of her life to a dignified calling, while Baby Ramsie hadn't had the time to live beyond the prescriptions of his birth; Mama Rose had died naturally, surrounded by loved ones, while Baby Ramsie had died violently on a curb while strangers gawked at him; Mama Rose would be missed dearly by thousands whose lives she'd touched, while Baby Ramsie would be forgotten by all but a small few. In the wide, lasting footprint Mama Rose had left, there was some solace and much to cherish. But still, a loved one was gone.

The counselors were able to organize a ceremony in Mama Rose's honor outside Woodside on the blacktop. The jail had no alumni network or social media presence, but the flow of teenagers and their families between the facility and neighborhoods such as Hunters Point meant that information found its way to people who were listening for it, and a few dozen young adults who'd once spent time at Woodside—whose lives had been touched and in some cases even altered by Mama Rose— showed up at the school. After much lobbying, the district granted waivers for these visitors to be in the yard.

Adjacent to the planters that Mama Rose herself had kept watered throughout the shutdown, now overflowing with splendid blossoms, a few dozen people from inside and outside the building gathered. They took turns extolling Mama Rose as not just wonderful, but a wonder: how she'd projected positive energy while working in a jail every day, how she'd navigated the drastically different personalities of both students and staff to foster a feeling of community, how just by sitting and listening she'd allowed young people to transfer their heavy burdens onto her, how she'd believed in those young people and hammered them with her belief. The more defiant and lost they were, the more she'd believed. The coldest young criminals in San Francisco—people who had murdered other people—would turn soft and deferential the moment she saw them being hustled down that hallway in their shackles, when she would shake her head and say, "You here again?" and begin muttering to her God. "I'm sorry, Mama Rose," they would say back to her, those four words a refrain echoing through the school for four decades. *I'm sorry, Mama Rose.*

The gathering was livestreamed so that teachers such as Megan, unable to return from Massachusetts, could watch. During that hour, de-spite its terrible occasion and being twenty-five hundred miles away, she saw that the place still had power over her. So much emotion was still locked up in it. On the computer, she listened to the words of people in their twenties whose lives had intersected with juvenile hall, for better and for worse. Megan knew again what was so easily forgotten when she wasn't physically in the space, physically near the children, which was that they couldn't submit to the virus, and they couldn't submit to the school closure, and they couldn't generally submit to the statistics of trauma and loss and recidivism. The whole job, in its heart, was about refusing to submit to reality. The job was to always give more time even to the most hopeless cases—to believe against all reason that they still had time, the way Mama Rose always had, until her time ended.

"I love you," she'd said in the library that morning late last year, words that would forever echo within that room and within Megan. *"That's the point of everything in this place."*

The death of Mama Rose left a vast physical and spiritual absence, but it nestled into Megan's chest in an almost gentle way, with the en-chantment that grief and grief alone could cast, and settled there among all the many other absences. Somehow, Megan still had space for them. There were so many losses in the world she and her colleagues had cho-sen to live in. Whether they manifested as an unjust court decision, the irrecoverable dissolution of youth, or any of the other different incarna-tions of human fatality, Megan carried them.

All of the teachers and counselors did. They didn't have to grade dozens of papers each night or deal with parents on the phone upset over their child's poor grade, the way "normal" teachers did. Their working hours ended definitively each day around 4:00 p.m. But they had to carry loss, and—more challenging still—they had to carry the weight of their utter ineffectuality in preventing it most of the time.

They no longer carried the weight together. As in any workplace, the Woodside teachers didn't always agree with one another, but they always seemed to admire and bolster one another, and their shared challenges made for powerful bonds: in the entire city, they were the only people who entered a jail each morning to teach lessons in core subjects to kids who didn't generally desire to receive them but could perhaps be saved by them. That was the work. It required a great deal of energy, reassurance, and inspiration—what might be encapsulated as *heart*—and the teachers relied on one another for that.

Communication via screen did not entirely eliminate these channels they shared, but it narrowed them severely. Each teacher was managing over a dozen one-on-one classes per day. The casual stop-bys to discuss the possible roots of a student's acting out in class, the delicate yet powerful art of team teaching, the essential hilarity undergirding all the sadness, the math teacher's melancholy fiddle solos wafting from his office in between classes—these rhythms were gone. While they worked closely to iron out the technology platforms and exchanged dozens of emails each day, emotionally they were each fading further and further away from their cluster of rooms at the far end of the great hallway. The various spaces of Woodside might have been depressing places to spend time—they were specifically designed to discourage anyone from ever wanting to be in them—but they somehow fostered a sense of investment in the present moment, of being in school and nowhere else for those hours each day. Even the staff bathroom, which had neither a lock nor a toilet seat, contributed to this shared feeling of doing something as hard as it was valuable, as valuable as it was invisible.

The new distance diffused that focus because not only were they quarantined to their homes but their homes required more attention. Chris, David, and the social studies teacher had teenaged children who couldn't be at school. Constance had three adult children navigating the effects on the job and housing markets. Megan had her young daughter and, recently, a failing marriage. The cinema studies teacher had four roommates. The pandemic intersected all the different sectors of daily life; it did so abruptly and relentlessly as the summer of 2020 progressed and viral surges returned and the temporary shutdown kept failing to end—all while the permanent shutdown of juvenile hall inexorably neared.

First the math teacher left, then the cinema studies teacher: the first nonmedical staff departures Chris had approved in his nine-year tenure as principal (though the cinema studies teacher, Mr. Diesel, continued to work with youth in San Francisco's largest group home, where he maintained some synchronicity with Woodside). Megan remained in Massachusetts throughout the summer and into the fall.

Maceo Johnson and the counselors continued to bear the load of both day-to-day living and education within the units, where COVID-19 regulations began to relax such that students were permitted more movement in the yard and in the gym—but incoming students still had to complete a restrictive two-week quarantine period in a separate unit. By the time they were transferred into the main units, these students tended to be depressed and highly reactive, so the units were in a constant state of upset even though the number of students remained low throughout 2020.

While the courts were succeeding in diverting young people from incarceration postarrest as both a response to the pandemic and as a precursor to the Close Juvenile Hall Working Group's creation of the nation's first juvenile hall–less major city, the courts were also severely backlogged. Kids who did end up in juvenile hall were being kept there for far longer than they would normally have been for low-tier crimes. Yet the teachers could only come to know them as well as their short visits on computer platforms allowed. Entreaties to finish worksheets and write essays and stay positive felt increasingly feeble. The various, contourless faces on the teachers' screens often froze due to the facility's low internet bandwidth. Logistically, technologically, and emotionally, everything at Woodside felt irrecoverably out of sync, as if this was how the school was fated to end.

* * *

CHRIS HAD SPENT the summer ruminating as much as his time allowed about the concept of *agency*. The word was one of several used ubiquitously in the education sector. *Equity, inclusion, success,* and *potential* were others. They all had their blanket meanings and stigmas, yet as a career educator he'd learned how vastly different their interpretations could be to each family and individual. As a principal in juvenile hall, he'd seen these words warped entirely from their societal definitions. For instance, *success* in the greater world meant decent grades, college admittance, a job and stable income; in juvenile hall, *success* meant not returning to juvenile hall. *Inclusion* in the world meant having a reliable group of friends and taking part in school clubs such as drama or sports; in juvenile hall, the word meant not being totally alienated, harassed, and physically attacked. *Potential* in the world meant finding a clear pathway to all of the above; in juvenile hall, the word was basically an abstract term that existed in the furtive space beyond immediate, life-threatening emotional and legal challenges. *Equity*—perhaps the most overused word in all of education—broadly meant access to basic opportunities and treatment regardless of class and race; in juvenile hall, a system founded on limitation where white children of any means rarely, rarely landed, the word was treated by the students as a macabre joke.

Agency, by definition, was the ability to take action to achieve a desired, realistic outcome. Both components of that definition—choice and efficacy—were elusive in jail. Chris had the budget, system support, and professional network to offer a few choices, such as a basketball team coached by a former counselor, or yoga in the early mornings. But for the most part, his students couldn't even pick what movies they watched. The notion of efficacy was even more amorphous, as the structure and statistics of jail gave Chris little credibility in convincing kids that anything they did here could alter anything that happened to them out there. No poems they wrote about their broken families could unbreak their families. No sage plants nurtured in the garden could undo a decade of not going to school. A feeling of absolute futility—agency's opposite—pervaded the spaces of Woodside. Hence Chris's heavy focus on credits, maybe the most basic form of agency in education. When a kid went to class, he or she earned a fraction of a credit in that class, and the accumulation of those credits led to better job prospects, maybe even a diploma and other life milestones. That feeling lit the kids' spirits in ways they didn't anticipate, which was why Chris poured his own spirit unglamorously into fueling it.

The kids were still earning their credits through one-on-one meetings with their teachers. Yet Chris wanted more for them, as he always did, even as the pandemic made less available for them. While inequality in education had not exactly been well camouflaged in cities such as San Francisco—cities all but lorded over by the very rich—the transition to remote learning had laid bare many of inequality's quieter, more insidious components. All one had to do to grasp it was contemplate the difference between forty teenagers competing for space on a teacher's fourteen-inch laptop screen versus twelve teenagers doing the same; all one had to do was compare a carefully curated "learning pod" complete with parental oversight and expensive tutors to a single mother in a small apartment with multiple children, a menial job that exposed her to the virus, and no internet.

Such contrasts were not hyperbole. They were defining education in America right now, and they were entrenching future disparity in ways that the most esteemed social scientists were only beginning to contemplate. In talking to other principals and simply reading the paper in the morning, Chris saw the children of San Francisco—including his own son, a college-bound, public high school senior—participating in communal virtual classroom scenarios while Chris's charges at Woodside learned in isolation, mumbling into a computer screen as the teachers working marathon sessions strived to create and maintain some emotional connection through pixels that were constantly glitching since concrete walls and metal doors did not lend Wi-Fi signals any clear pathways.

Chris became angry, almost as his resting state. Like countless people nationwide, he was homebound and upset about how absurd America could be, about his own powerlessness to change anything. All he wanted was extra computers and some policy tweaks that would enable the kids at Woodside to maintain a safe distance from one another and yet be in a class together online, the way other kids were going to school. He lobbied with great effort in multiple arenas. *Equity* was the key word he kept lobbing about. The word he kept hearing back was *no*. Not enough counselors were working at juvenile hall to monitor that much internet access, and no platform existed that could block web searches while still allowing students into a virtual classroom—and the kids in juvenile hall were given absolutely no concessions when it came to web searches. Too many shenanigans had occurred in the past.

Chris remained on this crusade until his teachers gently told him to stop. They didn't want to study how to use yet another learning system and then teach the kids how to use it. They didn't want to lose any more days—any more minutes—of class. While the teachers' hours had been long with one-on-one sessions, they all felt that the one-on-one format was working as well as any other format did. The kids who would typically be jockeying for attention in the classroom had to somewhat focus on instruction now. Even more powerfully, the kids who tended to cordon themselves off in classrooms—the ones who stayed silent to avoid ridicule—were beginning to open up in these closed sessions with teachers. These kids were reading their own prose and reflecting on identity. Given these increasingly apparent trends, the teachers didn't want to create virtual classrooms. They didn't want equity, didn't need the same formats or resources that other students had. Right now, each individual youth prisoner just needed to feel engaged. The arrangement built around Woodside's strict regulations regarding technology—and Woodside's lack of technology—was accomplishing that.

Chris listened to the teachers and dropped the fight immediately, which was strange for him. So much of his job involved battle: for budget and programs and different ways of thinking about the same problem that had vexed or corrupted centuries' worth of its overseers. As much as he battled for certain materials, he battled against societal stigmas about youth and mistakes and race and who does or doesn't deserve more chances. This rhythm was exhausting but also energizing, and he liked it. He was skilled at it. He saw Woodside and the kids locked inside as perennial members of that redemptive, underdog narrative that most Americans found captivating. That framing gave him the mandate to constantly tell other people—typically people more powerful than he—that they were wrong. They were wrong to assume these kids to be irredeemable or that redeeming them was too expensive, wrong to withhold learning tools from them, wrong to question the pace at which they could learn or seek the lowest common denominators of what they should be learning. Much of his professional self-worth came from making such righteous declarations. But in the middle of the pandemic and a little over a year out from the school's closure date, he ceased making noise and let the teachers craft their work from the means they had, which was one computer linked to the internet and the courage and care of Maceo Johnson and the other counselors inside.

But Chris wasn't capable of sitting idle, and he quickly generated a new idea, a bit of an absurd gambit that he shared with no one. He began to imagine a postpandemic world in which schools reopened but kids in special circumstances still had the option to attend by remote. Those in jail at Woodside could remain linked to their local schools, then return upon release, such that their schools wouldn't even have to know that they'd been arrested and detained. He was ignoring the reality that Woodside would cease to exist before a scheme like this could be tested, though he felt that with a little creativity this vision could be adapted to group homes and any probation arrangement. He was also ignoring the legacy of a system that didn't permit incarcerated young people to shed associations with the sphere of criminal justice and imprisonment. Boys or girls placed in secure confinement, even for a few days in their early teens, would always be a part of juvie—or, rather, juvie would always be a part of them.

*   *   *

MEGAN BEGAN THE email with *Wow*. She ended it with *Thank you from the bottom of my heart*. The message was just a short expression of gratitude, but she'd spent some time writing it. The correspondence would change a lot of things, she hoped. From a professor at the North Carolina State University College of Design, she'd just received confirmation of a collaboration in which he and his students would share virtual reality game programming geared toward her students. She'd initiated this by sending a completely out-of-the-blue message to his university email explaining how the kids entering the facility still had to endure a two-week quarantine entirely in one unit, and how she was flailing for ways to make this time not quite totally miserable. The professor had replied that this would be a wonderful opportunity all around. Megan then turned her attention to acquiring funds from the district for VR headsets. This part was surprisingly easy, too. Success without resistance almost never happened here. She was nearly confused.

After the pandemic began and the juvenile courts prioritized the diversion of younger offenders, Woodside was being sent older boys, nineteen- and even twenty-year-olds known as Transition Age Youth— or TAY students. The broader thinking was positive: to steer those in their early teens away from incarceration entirely while providing a lower-grade confinement than adult jail for those in their late teens. Within Woodside, the change was dramatic. A fourteen-year-old in jail was usually sad, capable of massive amounts of trouble, and often irritating in the way fourteen-year-olds were. But a child so young, even one in the midst of a dreadful youth, at least had some awareness of the value of youth itself. That energy caused problems in a confined space, but it also contained hope. In contrast, a nineteen-year-old in jail had almost always been in jail before, and his eyes could hold a nearly impenetrable fatalism. Even through the computer screen, Megan looked into the faces of these new students and saw hard souls that had peered into the human abyss often enough to grow accustomed to what they'd seen. And the physical differences could be scary for counselors in the units, as intervening in a fight between fully grown men was far more treacherous than separating boys. Locking these men into a single space for two full weeks all but assured regular fights, if only to relieve tedium.

Megan knew that a box of VR equipment wasn't going to resolve any of these challenges, but the novelty might help alleviate a few of them for some short time. She was still at her sister's rural property in Massachusetts. She was getting divorced and concerned with her daughter's well-being above all. But she studied the technology late at night while jumping through the many, many administrative hoops to secure permission to use it. She imagined these young men locked up, young men she interacted with every day, prone to loathing Megan and loathing one another and loathing themselves. She imagined them able to slip some odd-looking goggles over their eyes and suddenly be in the middle of a Martin Luther King Jr.–led civil rights march, or on the Wright brothers' first flight aboard their paper airplane at Kitty Hawk, or in a Japanese cherry-blossom grove during its full bloom. She imagined them not only seeing and hearing these settings, but walking through them, angling their heads around, peering upward and downward, exploring. The technology might offer only an illusion of what Chris called agency, but the illusion was advertised as being tremendously vivid. A well-crafted, high-tech, far-reaching chimera might be the best that they were all capable of right now.

*   *   *

A LITTLE LESS than one year later, Chris was in a quiet restaurant with a few friends, ostensibly enjoying the slow reopening of the city's communal spaces. They were talking anecdotally about the usual topics of the day—how their children had fared during remote learning, national politics, San Francisco's homeless crisis—when he felt that subtle pressure, familiar from childhood, behind his cheekbones. It was an involuntary quiver of his lower eyelids that meant he was about to start weeping. He excused himself from the table to do so on the sidewalk outside.

Throughout his decade-plus of working in special education and his near decade of running the school in juvenile hall, he'd been good at not doing this: showing emotion. He was skilled at identifying emotion, exploring it, controlling it, or at least wedging it into the corners of his consciousness while tending to the immediacies of on-the-ground education among at-risk children, and then, afterward on days that he could, surfing. He definitely didn't cry. And yet right now, crying brought him nearly to his knees as he faced the restaurant's recessed delivery door.

He didn't know why, specifically, this blanket sadness had seized him. Life and work were both going well. School at Woodside had reopened in April of 2021, and he'd been heartened to see the teachers and the students physically sharing space, amazed to see kids in the quarantine unit baby-stepping around the common area in their VR headsets, warily feeling their hands through the air in front of them, audibly gasping at times at whatever visions were being synthetically cast inside the plastic. In the broader landscape, the school's transition from serving younger inmates to older inmates, clumsily spurred by the pandemic, looked to continue beyond the juvenile hall's official closure date, which was still scheduled for the last day of this year.

The Close Juvenile Hall Working Group had been accomplishing a great deal of broad, innovative work on its envisioned programs for younger kids, but had lately become bogged down in details and regulations and various subcommittees' feeling "siloed," particularly over the establishment of a new physical facility that needed to be adequately supervised but wasn't intended to have any locked doors inside or feel at all jail-like. Accounting for possible contingencies and emergencies was thorny, and despite the progressiveness of the intention, the language surrounding the new facility began to sound similar to the language that had always surrounded the old facility, and the facility before that, in some ways dating back cyclically to the houses of refuge in the nineteenth century. The word itself—*facility*—caused resonant unrest in the community. During one Zoom-hosted public-comment segment in May 2021, a dismayed mother had lamented, "I don't want to be part of just planning the next thing people hate."

Chris was ultimately glad to have been passed over for the working group; while its members contended with the convoluted minutiae of government, the teachers and counselors remaining at Woodside would continue to teach and counsel, and they would be doing so for the TAY population that would otherwise be serving time in adult prison, which felt like a valuable application of their collective experience and of the space. The educational work was harder because problems grew larger as people did, but it was urgent and necessary and thus meaningful. Personally, Chris's son would begin college in the fall, on a campus near plenty of pristine surf breaks. Despite the last few years' worth of rapid-fire challenges and the weight of an entire city questioning the validity and dignity of his work, Chris genuinely felt as if all fronts of life were relatively healthy.

His girlfriend—who'd been his partner for twelve years—texted from inside the restaurant to see if he was all right. He wasn't finished weeping and didn't text her back. He walked around the corner so that they couldn't see him through the window.

Chris knew this: the pace of the work in the juvenile justice system, the secondary trauma, the exigence, and the stress were all-consuming. They were ceaseless, brazen, and had to be managed steadily, even defiantly. What he learned tonight was how stealthy and sly the sheer sadness could be—how it might hide dormant for days or months or years and then suddenly incapacitate a person. He'd seen this occur in others, people he cared about deeply, who'd had to take absences to settle their minds in order to be with kids again. He'd always assumed—foolishly, it turned out—that he was somehow hardened against it, inoculated, because he'd been in the trench of this work for so long. Like many of the kids locked in the units, he'd considered himself tough enough to absorb all the challenges these spaces contained—and like many of those same kids, he learned that he could not. Nor could he outmuscle the sadness or turn away from it or sidestep around it. He knew immediately that he had to just exist with it blooming in his heart.

The next day, he was at work. He had tasks and communications and paperwork, and he ground through it all at a measured pace. The building was quieter now than it had been before the shutdown, or perhaps ever. Fifteen prisoners were there, all of them men in their late teens, four recently arrived and thus in quarantine and working mostly with

Megan. Because only necessary staff were allowed in the quarantine zone, she continued to teach remotely. Chris called her spontaneously midway through the morning.

"I'm just checking in with you," he told her, even though he was really calling because he knew that she felt almost every day the way he had felt the night before. He did not want to tell her about the episode, but he thought maybe just her voice would help him settle the lingering hurt and shock.

"Things are going well," she said, before mentioning six or seven specific elements that weren't going well: forms she needed filed and students who required legal attention and some mess about another student's credits evaporating during a transfer between schools he'd attended years earlier.

"I'll handle all that," he assured her. "Yup, I'll handle it and let you know."

"Okay, I've got another student."

"I'm here."

The late morning found him sitting in his plain office in between phone calls. He had enough time to feel compelled to accomplish something, but not enough time to begin a new to-do list item. The residue of last night's attack still clung to him, so sitting still and unoccupied did not seem wise. Chris rose and took a round of the building.

As ever, he marveled at the height, length, and breadth of the central hallway as he passed down it. He listened as if for echoing voices of the 160 kids who used to be incarcerated here at any given time when he first became principal. He heard only the sound of his own footsteps until he reached Unit 3, where the eleven nonquarantine students were living. In the unit's classroom, David situated the chairs and folders in his focused way while Maceo Johnson called the young men into the room. The TAY prisoners looked drowsy and stoic and adultlike as they made their way in—not like kids. Chris was glad that no children were in this building anymore. But these were not men, either, even though some of them inhabited men's bodies. They were in that strange period of being no longer young but not quite old, and they needed counsel. He greeted each of them individually as they passed and grabbed pencil stubs from Maceo's jar. A few responded to him with head nods or grunts. He wasn't sure if any of them recognized him as their principal. He watched from outside as David began class with "We're doing your very favorite thing today: *personal essays!*" The students groaned, full force. The teacher grinned back at them.

With his remaining free minutes, Chris detoured outside and sat at one of the picnic tables in the yard. He was alone in the vast space. Constance had tried to organize a cooking class with the older group, but there'd been no traction. The garden was unused, but someone had been taking wonderful care of the plants since Mama Rose had passed. He didn't know who, but he was grateful, because as he reclined amid the floral scents and watched the bees and butterflies drawn from the hillside woods, this moment cast an utter calm over his soul and the building behind him and the city below.

Book III

◆

Exile

EXALT YOUTH
NEW YORK, NEW YORK

Chapter 1

◆

April–August 2019

A LITTLE FIGHT was all that the afternoon had presaged.
Ian Alvaro had been lying on the sofa in shorts and a T-shirt, playing a FIFA soccer game on his Xbox, occasionally palming a handful of Flamin' Hot Cheetos from the bag nestled against his leg. His phone vibrated with a text from a close friend saying that he'd been out walking and a dude from Paterson's south side had threatened him. Ian, who lived in a town house with his father on the north side of Paterson, New Jersey, replied that he would come out to see what was going on. As he lazily dressed, his friend continued texting in some kind of escalating fit: *Shit's about to get real* and other messages to that effect. Ian wasn't taking any of the content too seriously. In his strong opinion, the kids from the south were punks—mostly rich Arab kids—and they'd been talking a lot lately for some reason, but that was mostly all they ever did: talk. Ian figured that he was only headed to calm his friend down, restrain him from sending wide any texts that were so delusional or boneheaded that he would be mocked eternally for them, and that this was also an excuse to not be gaming alone all day on a Sunday.

As he walked from north to east Paterson, checking his phone constantly, his friend began creating new text chains with more and more people, all of them loosely part of a local group who called themselves the 493s, which was a derivative of an actual gang that had originated in Virginia. (The number was an area code in Guanajuato, Mexico.) In Paterson, the kids associated with these digits did not consider themselves a gang. Some dealt weed or the like at Paterson high schools on their own, but they were not organized. Mainly, the 493 teenagers in Paterson just liked being on text threads, email lists, and Instagram hashtags via which they received a stream of dumb YouTube videos and memes.

By the time Ian arrived at his friend's, about a dozen kids he knew had congregated around the stoop in front, all posturing over the prospect of a real fight. At first, Ian tried to settle everyone as they schemed to march together to the south side. "This is a really terrible idea," he announced outright, repeatedly. "We have basically no information besides someone talking shit on text." He knew that, should they all venture southward, the most likely scenario was that those kids down there wouldn't even show up to fight, and his friends would have gotten all fired up and walked a mile and a half for nothing—and that was assuming that the Paterson police would take no note of so many teenagers in a herd together. Ian said, "Why can't we just chill here?"

But teenaged life in north Jersey, like teenaged life most anywhere, was characterized by long stretches of utter sameness punctuated with the occasional opportunity to do something memorable, something that would be worth retelling throughout a school week. And Ian's friend was hell-bent on fighting, and this friend had unequivocally been present for Ian many times—when his mom left, when his eighth-grade girlfriend shattered his heart, when he'd been embarrassed in the quarterfinals of the city wrestling championships—so Ian went along with the group. Per his counsel, they splintered into smaller groups of four and five for the trek. Constant, rapid screen-thumbing recruited more kids, while Ian's friend established a meeting place with their supposed adversaries, the parking lot of a shuttered office space surrounded by six-foot walls that would mostly shield them all from street view. By the time the 493s arrived, their ranks had swelled to something like twenty kids.

Ian was surprised to find the south side group not just already waiting in the lot, and not just outnumbering the 493s, but also bearing arms. In a quick scan, Ian saw many knives of various lengths and serrations— some designed for combat, others for dicing vegetables—and pieces of timber, lug wrenches, tire irons. One kid had an actual mace—not the pepper spray but the medieval weapon, a studded metal sphere fixed to a handle. The south side group formed a sloppy triangle. The leader, with whom Ian's friends had been in constant logistical communication, stood at the apex with a smug expression and a bat through which a number of four-inch nails had been driven, such that their points stuck out at all angles. Ian didn't see any guns.

"The fuck," he hissed at his friend. "You didn't say anything about all this."

His friend made a flabbergasted, helpless gesture and held up his phone with the string of messages on the screen facing Ian. "He didn't say anything about it on text."

Ian's discombobulated group quickly began to disperse, backing away a few steps before casually turning. A few ran fast. Ian followed. Behind him, he heard laughter and an exchange in Arabic. To Ian the language's rapid cadence denoted haughtiness, and he was angry.

He and a group of about fifteen 493s, the ones who hadn't fled completely, reassembled in a weedy alley a block away. Ian, who'd been only mildly invested in the confrontation until he'd keyed in on those muttered foreign-language wisecracks a moment ago, said, "Let's go back."

"The fuck did you say?" his friend asked, wide-eyed.

"A bunch of them started leaving, too, when we did," Ian reasoned. "They don't want to fight. That's why they brought all that shit with them. Who the hell even owns a mace? We're playing it how they wanted, making it easy for them, and so all the talking shit is just going to continue." The others were listening now, all their eyes fixed on Ian. "What's the worst that can happen?" he asked rhetorically.

"Police," someone proffered.

"Or dead," someone else added.

Ian shook his head and grinned. "No, the worst that can happen is some of us get tapped"—meaning, knocked unconscious or otherwise disabled—"and the rest of us win."

His rationale didn't make for the most inspirational of speeches, but his friend whose texts had initiated the outing began nodding excitedly, and then the dynamics of being sixteen years old unified them as they all followed Ian back to the parking lot and incited a brawl.

When it was done, as Ian had loosely predicted, one of the 493s had been tapped and the rest had won. The south Paterson contingent backed toward the lot entrance and trotted off in different directions. Only a few lingered, all gesturing toward the boy unconscious at Ian's feet, the one with the nail bat.

The skirmish had unfolded fast; not two minutes had passed since their consult in the alley. The 493s had rushed back into the lot without ceremony, catching the others off guard, and begun punching and kicking and tackling. Even those brandishing deadly weapons—including the mace—had not brought them with the intent to actually use them; like the north Paterson kids, they'd come here mainly for something to do on a Sunday in New Jersey and for the prospect of having a grandiose story to tell afterward. Also like the north Paterson kids, none of them wanted to go to jail.

Ian's initial target, the leader with the souped-up bat, had taken a swing—a clumsy one, poorly aimed, probably made more out of confusion at the singularly focused kid in the Starter jacket rushing him. Ian had dodged it with a foot to spare. Even though the strike had been noncommittal at best, Ian was astonished by the resultant rage that coursed through him. This rage thoroughly seized and controlled him and made him dangerous. He landed a roundhouse kick to the boy's face (Ian had been practicing Brazilian jujitsu for five years, the training originally intended to help him, as an overly physical preteen, to control his body). The contact hadn't been powerful, but had stunned the boy and caused him to stagger backward, and Ian had tripped him, pinned him to the ground with a knee set upon each arm, punched him twice directly in the face, then used the boy's hair as a grip by which to pound the back of his head three times, hard, against the asphalt. Then Ian stood and took stock of everyone else.

Those who weren't watching him in modest horror were already gloating, making *woot-WOOT* calls with arms raised, shouting every derogatory name for the female genitalia they could think of. Following Ian, they all left at a steady jog, which, fueled by adrenaline, they maintained all the way back to east Paterson. Astonishingly, they never saw or heard a single police car throughout the entire excursion. They disbanded with the relief of having somehow eluded all the potential consequences of a situation that should never have ended well: no hospitalizations, no parents finding out, no arrests. This reckoning carried an immense power that wedged itself into the way they walked and talked and regarded the gray afternoon sky above. This feeling required being young to experience it in its truest form, as Ian did now. It was a feeling of absolute invincibility.

*   *   *

FOLLOWING THE PARKING lot melee, Ian Alvaro resumed his video games for the remainder of the weekend, though hyper from the residual adrenaline. The following Tuesday, his 493 group began circulating, via text, an article on NewJersey.com entitled "Police Probe Attacks on Arab and Muslim Students in South Paterson." The article stated that "over a dozen black and Hispanic" students wearing John F. Kennedy High School uniforms surprise-attacked four Arab students walking home from school. The police claimed to possess a cell phone video of the incident and to be working with the JFK High School administration to identify and punish the attackers. One of the victims' older brother was a local Paterson politician, who was quoted in the article as saying, "Kids around here are traumatized by what's happening." The south ward's councilman declared, "I have a zero tolerance approach to any attacks like this. We've got to make sure that the people who are responsible for this are held accountable." A photo of the mayor of Paterson headed the piece, even though he was not mentioned in it, presumably because the mayor was Arab.

According to the journalist, the fight had been a merciless and cowardly hate crime, a swarm of armed black and brown kids falling upon a few defenseless Arab kids for no reason. Ian found it absurdly reported on many levels: no black kids had been present, John F. Kennedy students didn't wear uniforms, his group had been baited and outnumbered and faced with lethal weapons. He had trouble comprehending that any kids who'd been beaten up like that would have admitted it to anyone, even the police, and lied about it so radically. Ian fumed over the framing of racism, which was an undercurrent but not the main driver of the conflict between east Paterson and south Paterson, and which definitely flowed in both directions.

By midweek, the police had found Ian's friend who'd initiated the whole ordeal due to his detailed text exchanges with the south side group and had already interviewed him.

What did you say? Ian thumbed into his phone.

Nothing. Then: *I said what happened.*

You told them what I did?

I didn't say your real name. I just said some kid called Feud.

Feud was Ian's 493 moniker and was used mainly for video game play. He cussed at the phone. That was worse than having his real name revealed—because if the police were serious, as they seemed to be, then they would have no problem figuring out who Ian was. In addition, a code name would make it seem as if he were part of a real gang as opposed to a bunch of dumb kids pretending to be, and the denotation of the word itself would give the police all sorts of fodder to imagine the kind of person Ian was.

I wish you hadn't even texted me that day! Ian wrote in pissed-off resignation.

His friend replied with the question that would both haunt and baffle Ian for the remainder of his childhood: *Why'd you have to bust his head like that when he was already on the ground?*

*　　*　　*

A MONTH PASSED before Ian was arrested. He was scared throughout this month, but he still went to school at JFK and was obedient and kept earning the decent grades that he always had, mostly B's with an A or C here and there. He learned that the kid he'd assaulted had needed stitches and concussion treatment but had recovered. Otherwise, Ian lay low at home, texting little, hoping that people would forget about that ridiculous article and the police would have more pressing concerns in New Jersey's third-largest city than some kids fighting. But on a Thursday near the end of his sophomore year, Ian was pulled from biology class by his somber-looking principal and immediately handcuffed by four police—not one or two or even three, but *four*. These officers prodded him along the school hallways just as the bell dinged and kids poured out of classrooms between periods. People he knew and people he didn't all fell into a giggly hush as Ian shuffled along, shackled. He tried to smirk and roll his eyes at first, but even in the moment he knew that his wantonness was unconvincing. He wanted to cry, and he let his head fall during the final stretch to the school's front doors. "It was just a little fight," he kept murmuring. "Just a little fight. . . ."

The weathered adults at the police station planted him in one of their tiny interrogation rooms. Before permitting him to call a lawyer (not that he had or knew a lawyer) or his father (the school had notified his father, they said), two detective-looking types dryly laid out the information they'd gathered proving Ian's involvement in a violent crime: witnesses, statements, texts, emails, and a cell phone video. They possessed exhaustive, incontrovertible evidence that Ian had split open the cranium of a city zoning board member's relative. (To Ian, the words *split open the cranium* called to mind a far more dramatic image than the cut scalp he remembered.) They said that if Ian simply confessed, then he would be put on some form of probation and largely spared a long, expensive, life-altering navigation of the judicial system. He'd be able to go back to school almost immediately. He would carry no lasting record of the incident or charge.

These bullet points all synced and felt conclusive. Ian did not have enough experience with police to know that they were legally allowed to lie to people—even young people who were especially gullible—to solicit confessions. So he told his version of that Sunday's unfolding, beginning with some convoluted backstory regarding the tension between east and south Patterson, then offering a color commentary of the hours between leaving his video game console around noon and returning to the same game later that afternoon. The detectives only interrupted in instances when he referenced the 493s. They wanted to know more about the 493s—though they never once mentioned the word *gang*, and that omission was important, because if Ian had heard or thought of the word, he would have shut up immediately. In his thinking, by elaborating on the nuances of his social circle, he was putting distance between himself and that word. So he described the 493s as a "kids' group that a lot of people were in, kids from all over, kids who didn't know how to not act like they were at school." He meant: nerds. The detectives asked if Ian was the leader of this large group. He'd never considered this question before as the group had no established hierarchy or directive; it was more of a dynamic in which one bored person texted another bored person and before long a bunch of people were hanging out somewhere or playing a game online. But, upon consideration, Ian nodded. "I guess I had some pull. Like, if I suggested something, a lot of people listened." They asked about this name they'd heard of, Feud, and Ian laughed: "That's just like my code name. Like, with games. Like *Call of Duty* and all that." The detectives laughed along with him. Aside from his being alone in an interrogation room in a police station with seasoned investigators asking him questions, he felt fairly comfortable.

They seemed sympathetic to the plight of having to defend your friend, as if they'd all been in that situation before. They seemed similarly angered by the online article's blatant mischaracterizations and errors. They seemed to understand that the sequence had not been organized or premeditated and was certainly not a hate crime—that it was just a bunch of kids being kid-like. Ian was careful to repeat many times that the kid he'd beaten up had been brandishing a *baseball bat* with *nails sticking out of it* that he'd *swung at Ian's head*. The only question they asked from what struck him as genuine curiosity came near the end: "Why did you decide to go back? I mean, you said all those kids had weapons, a bunch of your friends had taken off, you were outnumbered. Why did you go back and fight?"

Ian replied decisively, "I mean, you can't just not go back . . . right?"

The detective who'd asked the question nodded as if he understood precisely why you couldn't just not go back.

Later, they placed a few sheets of densely worded paper in front of him: a statement for him to sign. He was tired from the long morning at school and the longer afternoon here. He skimmed through the document, which, while not verbatim, seemed to basically sum up what he had told them. He missed or failed to register the significance of the repeated appearance of that word they hadn't used at all during the interview: *gang*. He also missed a word that appeared adjacently more than once: *leader*. Ian just wanted to go home. Instead, moments after signing his name at the bottom and moments before his father finally arrived at the station, Ian was handcuffed again and booked into county detention.

*   *   *

THE ESSEX COUNTY Juvenile Detention Center in Newark, New Jersey, was a low-slung redbrick municipal building on a residential stretch of Duryea Street, a block from the city's gorgeous Branch Brook Park. The facility was not physically imposing. Aside from the few strands of barbed wire atop the fence, it didn't appear punitive. Ian, upon arrival, thought it looked like a DMV.

In his general life, Ian experienced the same erratic emotional highs and lows that most teenagers did, often disconnected from the real-world consequences of a given situation. If a girl he liked failed to respond to an overture he'd made, it could close him off to his surroundings for weeks; when his family's landlord had raised the rent of their apartment almost 10 percent one year based on some loophole and they'd had to move quickly, Ian had barely registered the drama. But in juvenile hall, he consciously took a line directly through the center of his emotional spectrum and hewed closely to it, forcefully willing himself to neither detach from the proceedings nor be overwhelmed by them. He kept to himself for the first weekend, saying nothing when he wasn't prompted. When he was, he carefully limited his responses to the minimum number of syllables necessary to answer a question.

On his first Monday in jail, he emerged from his room when summoned by a shrill, screeching noise through the built-in wall speaker and walked obediently in line from class to class, in which the various core subjects were taught to teenagers at what he guessed was a fifth-grade level: basic complementary angles in geometry, the definition of conjunctions in English, "Who was Alexander the Great?" in history. He ate the tater tots and dry chicken sandwich in between. He performed the fifteen minutes of simple calisthenics that comprised the kids' exercise for the day. In the evening, he grabbed a random paperback from the rack to which they were given a few minutes of access—a short novel called *Love & Hennessy*—and read thirty pages before trying unsuccessfully to sleep for more than a few minutes at a time.

Since he'd learned all of the academic content when he was in middle school, he mostly focused on carefully observing the dynamics among the five other boys in his residential area. He assumed that he would need to identify who the leader was and quickly establish good terms with him, as was done by new prisoners in all the movies. But there was no leader, and the dynamics more closely resembled a summer-camp cabin or a college dorm. They were just a bunch of boys thrust together by some administrative algorithm, perhaps loosely based on the quick psych exam each had been given on entry, as well as the timing, location, and intensity of their alleged crimes. Two of the boys were absolutely morose; Ian could count on one hand the number of times combined that they raised their heads from their desks each day, and he deduced that they were heavily medicated. Another was constantly blurting out jokes and rejoinders in a Pee-wee Herman voice, but he wasn't funny at all; Ian thought that the kid could have used some of whatever sedative the first two were on. The two others were acquaintances from the same neighborhood east of Newark, and their continuous running dialogue mostly had to do with street corners and gang member names from neighborhoods Ian had never been to and people he didn't know.

All were nonthreatening and (Ian felt) tiresome. All were also black—Newark's juvenile system held the nation's largest disparity between black detainees and other races—which was uncomfortable at first because Ian hadn't carried any black friends past elementary school. But no one seemed to harp on Ian's ethnicity, so he didn't. He figured that they were all here for some form of violence, and that on paper their charges stacked together must have looked quite intimidating. However, in person they were just an odd grouping of misfits from north Jersey.

Overheard talk among counselors and guards held as truth that the saddest, most pathetic, and most frustrating kids in juvenile hall were those with positive male influences and stable homes—the ones who didn't have to steal or hustle or fight but did it anyway to show off or fit in. So Ian worked diligently in group therapy to keep these details about himself secret, particularly those concerning his father, who worked and was home every night for dinner. Ian didn't consciously consider the possibility that maybe having no mother at home was its own tremendous fissure in his development—one relevant to his casual capacity for violence. He spent this time in juvenile hall nurturing a deep well of shame directed at himself alone.

Partly to quell that shame, and partly just to fill time here, he began retelling his act of dodging that bat and then knocking that boy unconscious against the parking lot pavement. His roommates thought the story was hilarious—also admirable.

On Sunday, less than a week into his imprisonment, Ian's father came. They sat across from each other at a plastic table bolted to the floor in the jail's most brightly lit room. Ian's father was shorter and wider than Ian and was nearly bald, with a gray beard and a cluster of freckles on either side of his nose. The father had always thought of his son as a knucklehead, one who got into some trouble now and again, never big trouble, and was fundamentally a good kid. In turn, Ian considered his father to be decent and responsible, even if his inability or unwillingness to discuss feelings much made him impossible to confide in and a little moody. The relationship between the young man and the aging man was not deep but had for the most part been sturdy.

The relationship was wrecked now—which was made clear by Ian's father's chilly greeting, slumped posture, and refusal to make eye contact.

"You good?" his father asked.

"I'm all right."

"Is it rough in there?"

"What kind of rough do you mean?"

"Bullies, I guess."

Ian coolly shrugged. But his instinctual machismo did not at all suit the moment they were in. He murmured, "Everyone's cool so far." Then: "How's home?"

Now his father shrugged, and their conversation became entirely informational. His father had no experience with the system, and so the last few exploratory days had been clumsy, but he'd been in contact with a public advocate, who had been accessible, seemingly invested, and also fluent in Spanish.

When Ian and his father's time ended, they both stood up and simply regarded each other for a moment. Ian suddenly felt that he needed an embrace, the kind his father always provided during powerful moments, pressing their foreheads together with one hand on the back of Ian's head. But Ian wasn't sure if any physical contact was permitted, so he just nodded and turned back toward the jail's interior.

*　　*　　*

His FATHER, MANUEL Alvaro, having grown up in the US territory of Puerto Rico, was technically a migrant within the United States—not an immigrant. But he'd come to the tristate area young, poor, and with a few unreliable distant relatives here and an infant's understanding of the English language. His continental-American experience had been immigrant-like, and Ian's upbringing had very much resembled that of his first- and second-generation, predominantly Puerto Rican friends. All of them struggled financially but were not abjectly poor, all were enamored of American hip-hop culture nearly to parody, all were quite determined to go to college, and the majority lived in single-parent homes. What seemed to set Ian apart was that his mother, not his father, was the one who'd been overwhelmed at a young age with three kids and an unsteady income. She'd decided in some astonishing detonation of logic to leave them—not to live nearby and care for them on assigned days, but to completely exit their lives with neither warning nor debrief.

Ian had been five years old then, and his memories were spotty and clouded by the vast range of emotions experienced in the years since. He assumed that alcohol had engendered or at least influenced the abandonment since his father had been an alcoholic at the time. Ian's memories of that aspect of the passage, with its slurred language and all the disgusting aromas and the passing out at 6:00 p.m. while three boys under five had yet to be fed, were clear. Ian remembered walking six blocks to McDonald's once—Dad passed out, no food or money in the apartment—convincing the teenaged teller with deftly improvised untruths to give him three free Happy Meals and also not to call child services; Ian had felt absolutely heroic, especially when his father had snorted awake and demanded food, and Ian had replied that he'd only brought dinner for the "real men" in the family.

Manuel had sobered within a few years of his wife's leaving and procured a union job at Port Newark that he'd now had for over a decade. He'd become what Ian would characterize as stable, boring, and good, which was also how Ian characterized his childhood, aside from the unique devastation of his mother leaving them, which he carried alone and unsupported through adolescence. But otherwise: stable, boring, and good. For Ian as a young child, these traits were wonderful. However, they grew depressing and stagnant as he entered his teens. His father was kind but not tender, talkative but not emotive, strict but not severe, and overall very, very steady. The man believed devoutly in the merits of a high school diploma, but seemed perplexed by America's higher-education system and its strange balances of pedigree, cost, debt, and employment prospects.

Before his arrest, Ian's plan had been simple: he would graduate from high school with his 2.8 GPA, satisfy his old man that way, celebrate with friends, then leave Paterson entirely. In his imaginings, an abrupt departure would be the stuff of high romance, the kind of event that his friends would wistfully tell their kids about one day: "Once I knew this amazing guy named Ian. Then he just got too big for Jersey, and he left. I wonder what that guy's doing now . . ." He would probably head west or south. His diploma and his physical strength would ensure him some kind of job wherever he landed along the way. Maybe he would even encounter his mother, though he'd promised himself hundreds of times that he would never actively pursue her. From the irregular birthday cards she sent, he knew that she lived in Tucson, Arizona.

*   *   *

IAN KEPT ADHERING to the schedule of his days in juvenile hall, up and down the hallway connecting his residential pod to the classrooms. He finished his book and began another, and another after that. The loud, unfunny kid left for what they heard was some kind of restrictive mental health center. One of the Newark kids was sent to a group home; he was livid about this—all kids reviled group homes, even those who had never been—and he vowed to run at the first opportunity. His departure happened at a fortunate time, as he and the other kid from Newark had been sniping at each other constantly, tiresomely. Other kids came through for a few days or up to two weeks, one of whom seemed full of rage and capable of real physical harm; Ian absolutely avoided him.

Ian's father came every few days, and their conversations were reliably distant and bland, and Ian settled into a fixed melancholy. His wasn't the severe depression that had some kids wailing through the night's loneliest points and subsequently placed on medication, but rather an abstract, growing remoteness from the words and events around him as he followed orders and moved about the facility. The lack of exercise during the day made sleep difficult.

The lawyer was, as his father attested, accessible and invested. She seemed familiar with the system and experienced at her job, though Ian didn't understand much of the legal language she tended to use.

She felt that they possessed some ammunition, particularly in the way that Ian's questioning was handled, sans lawyer or guardian. She told him to clarify whether the police had ever asked him if he desired representation before they questioned him or at any point during their questioning. Ian replied that he couldn't remember—it was possible that they had. He'd been so tense that afternoon that he'd just wanted to complete their business with him as quickly as he could. She moved on.

Ian asked about the bat. The kid he'd beaten up hadn't even known how to use the weapon, but Ian was convinced that had embedded nails not been in play, he would have been far more restrained in the blows he inflicted.

"I mean, if someone steps to you with a big piece of wood with a bunch of big-ass nails sticking out of it—shouldn't you be able to defend yourself? Isn't that, like, a right?"

She replied that the weapon element was tricky, because the victim denied having a weapon, the cell phone video was unclear, and no such bat ever turned up. She generally did not want to bring up the specifics of the violence, because those details called to mind the endemic problem of gangs and hate crimes.

"That's another messed-up thing," Ian muttered. "They're making it all out like it was a big gang thing. Like I'm some big gang leader. Like we all hate Arabs and go around just beating them up. But I'm not in any gang. We're, like, a fake version of the 493s, a pretend version. And

I don't hate Arabs—they hate us and they talk a lot of shit." A pleading quality flavored Ian's voice, and it tasted bad. He noticed his father shaking his downturned head ever so slightly, either in disappointment or embarrassment, but certainly not with any shred of confidence in his son's rendering.

She reiterated that they would be wiser to avoid invoking any of this.

She pivoted the conversation immediately back toward Ian's having been questioned without an adult present, and that he went to school and brought home decent grades and played sports. As an aside, she informed him that police had questioned his wrestling coach at JFK regarding Ian's general aggression.

"It's wrestling! The whole sport is being aggressive!"

Three or four meetings followed this meandering path, interrupted by frequent logjams of facts and reason. Ian's father grew increasingly antsy and distant during these times. Ian didn't know what the minutes were costing Manuel, either in missed work or legal fees. Days and weeks inside detention accumulated until Ian's routines assumed an upsetting quality in that they began to feel normal. He knew the counselors by name; he knew which showerheads had the strongest pressure; he knew which teachers would let him zone out without a fuss; he told new arrivals where things were; he was sleeping better and better. All of this familiarity was scary.

Then something happened outside, beyond his knowledge or ability to influence. He never learned what it was—a conversation, a threat, another witness statement, involvement of the south Paterson political establishment—but the lawyer suddenly became convinced that Ian needed to entirely avoid standing in front of a judge. In no uncertain terms, she said that if his case saw a courtroom, then he would spend the following nine months to a year in a New Jersey state care facility. At best, he'd be looking at six more months in detention followed by confinement to a group home.

"What do we do, then?" Manuel asked.

She promised to try to work something out. A week later, she brought them terms that she felt were quite favorable: Ian would receive indefinite probation. He'd be allowed to leave juvenile hall and go to school. He probably wouldn't be permitted to play sports or have his own cell phone. Obviously, he could not associate with any of his current friends in any manner. A probation officer would closely oversee him. Ian thought that all sounded pretty brutal, but he could do it. His father's sour countenance implied something more.

The lawyer then said matter-of-factly, as if it were some kind of afterthought, that Ian would not be allowed in Paterson for a year. Actually, he wouldn't be allowed in New Jersey, at all, for a year.

Manuel and the lawyer began to discuss some of the particulars. Ian didn't hear many of them. He processed this decree that his home was no longer his home.

He did register one word, if only because it felt so out of place in this depressing dialogue. It had something to do with the person who would be his out-of-state probation officer, with whom she'd been in contact and had informed that Ian was a smart kid. The PO had mentioned to her offhandedly a diversion program he'd sent a few of his charges through, a nonprofit with a focus on transition and reentry for kids embroiled in the justice system, called Exalt Youth.

Chapter 2

——————◆——————

October 2019

T HE CLASSROOM WAS nondescript: just two blank whiteboards and two windows that looked out on the bricks of the adjacent office building a few yards away. Its walls bore no inspirational posters, no rows of past student work, no American flag, no quotations from civil rights leaders. Ian gauged the room and the people in it; a person learned in juvenile hall how to measure the energy in a collection of humans, how to accurately discern who was a threat, who was an annoyance, who was weak, who was cool. But this room and the eighteen others there with him defied simple reduction, partly because they were not in a detention facility in north Jersey with wire mesh baked into the windows, but rather on the third floor of a luxury condo-and-office complex on the southernmost point of the island of Manhattan, one of the most expensive neighborhoods in one of the most expensive cities in the world.

The kids here with him were mostly his age, quiet and in various slouching or crouching poses around the peninsula of three abutting tables. Right now, during their initial moments together, each projected a guarded resignation, a sense of definitely preferring to be somewhere else—anywhere else—if not for having been screwed by the system.

The whole scene at Exalt Youth was quite bizarre and hard to read, especially with all the blithely cheerful grown-ups being nice to them while gliding around the posh and polished space in business casual dress.

One of these adults was Alex Griffith, who wore a dark suit and smiled continuously as he placed thick binders filled with blank paper in front of each student. He had very white teeth and very black skin.

"How are you all doing today?" Alex asked in his alto voice. He was tall and thin—six feet four inches and maybe 160 pounds. He was also young, twenty-nine. He spoke while continuing to place the binders and seemed to find the monosyllabic murmurs he received in response— "Good," "Cool," "A'ight"—to be unsatisfactory. He chuckled. "Listen, you all are going to be spending a lot of time together in this room—*a lot* of time. First thing we need to learn to do together is talk. I mean, a little more substantially than 'good' and 'cool.' I know you're able. In fact, I bet talking probably has a lot to do with why you're here."

As in any typical first-day classroom setting, Alex went around the room prompting introductions. There was Nahla, a petite girl with cornrows and a sardonic smile. There was Kyla beside her, with hot-pink press-on talons on the ends of her fingers and hot-pink hair to match. They were both from the East New York neighborhood in Brooklyn and were already friends from the same high school, able to communicate, it seemed, through a running exchange of short giggly bursts.

"I'm from East New York, too," Alex said.

"You still live there?" Nahla asked, a little bit of a test embedded in the innocent question: if he'd grown up in East New York but left when given the opportunity, then he wasn't really *from* East New York.

"I still do, with my wife and daughter."

"Cool."

There was Malachi from Cypress Hills in the corner still wearing his puffy gray winter jacket inside on a mild fall day, the garment like a cumulus storm cloud enveloping him. He seemed on the verge of sleep and incapable of more than a couple mumbled words. There was Jordan from the South Bronx, with thick glasses and short, spiky hair, soft-spoken. There was Kensi, also from the Bronx, whose faint, singsongy voice and gesticulating arms called to mind some sort of spiritual guru. There was Javi from Sunset Park, who, despite his toddlerish bowl cut and crooked teeth, projected high confidence and a light comic touch. There were others, male and female, gregarious and contained, grateful and embittered. When Ian's turn arrived, he leaned forward on the table and said, "Yo, I'm Ian, from Paterson."

Javi cupped his hand over his mouth and spurted laughter as if these were the most hilarious words he'd ever heard. "Paterson! Damn, that's gotta be, like, three hours from here! Dude's got dedication!"

Ian shook his head. The distance was more like ninety minutes on public transportation in the afternoon.

Alex regarded Ian seriously, though still with a hint of that easy smile. "Come on, Ian. You can give us a little more than that."

"JFK. That's my high school." It wasn't his high school—not anymore. In the two months since his release from juvenile hall and excommunication from New Jersey, he'd moved to the Brooklyn neighborhood of Brownsville, where he was staying with his father's cousin and her family. He'd begun the new school year at the local public school there. But he didn't desire to detail any of that information, nor the sadness, fear, and alienation that currently distinguished his life. He wished he could just pass.

"Okay," Alex—who knew about Ian's circumstances—replied, holding Ian's eyes in his until Ian quickly grew uncomfortable and glanced sideways. For months now since that afternoon in the police interrogation room, Ian had been avoiding eye contact with everyone—his lawyer, the judge, the guards and detainees in juvenile hall, his PO, his new teachers and classmates, his father's family in Brownsville, even his father. Eyes lately seemed to hold only threats or disappointment or hopelessness or—worst of all—pity. Most of those people seemed glad not to make eye contact with him, helping remove some portion of the emotional toll of difficult exchanges. Alex waited, however, calmly letting an awkward moment be prolonged in front of everyone else, until Ian's eyes reluctantly returned to Alex's. The teacher's look simply said, *Give me two hours, okay?*

They finished introductions and Alex launched into a quick and polished overview of the Exalt program. This group now commencing was the 108th classroom cycle in the nonprofit's fifteen years of operation. Over eight hours a week for four months they would be learning computer skills, interview skills, code-switching skills, résumé and letter-writing skills, self-advocacy skills, logic and problem-solving skills, financial-management skills, business skills—not to mention the basic skills of reliability, of being at a certain place at a certain time every day. In their binders were blank time sheets, with check-in boxes for every afternoon they were to meet here over the next four months. Each box signified time on a train, time in this room, time doing hard things instead of easy things. The pages contained a lot of empty boxes.

Ian reexamined the room, now padded with the scant knowledge he'd gained from introductions, particularly the various neighborhoods his classmates had cited. Alex had not specifically asked everyone to name where he or she lived, but it was the first piece of personal information each student had been compelled to share. In New York City, or any city, a person's neighborhood was closely entwined with a person's identity. Streets, storefronts, elderly people manning their stoops—all were sewn into the fabric of one's being. Ian had decided to invoke Paterson over Brownsville because Paterson had everything to do with who he was, Brownsville very little. Yet he'd been kicked out of Paterson, its parks and delis and spaces of comfort, his lifelong friendships there, the autumnal leaves along the bending roads. He'd had to leave most of his clothes and all of his video games behind. Even his father only seemed to communicate with him in the cursory, unloving language of "checking in." And Brownsville was an insular place, all concrete and asphalt and impenetrability. Ian didn't feel comfortable there, hadn't been accepted there, and didn't foresee either happening anytime soon. His identity was utterly scrambled. He clung to the word *Paterson* even as its homelike feelings had begun to elude him.

Alex was giving a serious coda to his program syllabus: failure to show up reliably or to participate earnestly would mean expulsion from the class. Exalt kept strict guidelines in this regard.

"So when do we get paid?" Javi blurted out, beginning to establish himself as the humorist of this assembly. The room chirped with teenagers excited about money: once a certain threshold was met in the program, the students would be paid $13 per hour to show up for two-hour classes four times a week. Being paid to go to school was captivating to all of them.

"We're not there yet," Alex replied. "We're a long way from talking about that. What I do want to talk about, now that we're a little bit introduced, is that you all belong here. I see many of you trying to act like maybe you don't"—Alex eyed Javi—"but you *do*. It doesn't matter if you were referred by your PO, advocate, judge, or even the police, and it doesn't matter what you did or allegedly did to get involved with the system, and it doesn't matter if you're only here for the money or to shorten your parole time. We here take the entry process very seriously, we've done it for thousands of young people, and we do not accept students who we don't think will make it through the end. You are all capable of quality work and you are all capable of life change, for real."

Amid the teacher's vaguely stirring assertions, Ian couldn't yet tell how he felt about Alex and Exalt in general. He knew that both were better than jail, and that together they could help him get back to Paterson, to reclaim the person he'd been before that march to the parking lot. Mainly, he continued dwelling on the neighborhoods he'd heard mentioned earlier: East New York, Sunset Park, South Bronx . . .

Even though he was from Jersey, he knew enough of these various places to understand that kids hailing from all of them couldn't gather in a contained space like this without a fight soon breaking out.

*   *   *

UNTIL AS LATE as the fall of 2018, New York City had been sending teenagers convicted of felonies to Rikers Island at a rate of four thousand youths per year. Over time, the city's media unearthed enough harrowing stories of depression, solitary confinement, sexual assault, and suicide among children locked up like adults that public pressure coerced the city to open smaller juvenile facilities throughout the boroughs. These offered high school classes, real exercise yards, recreational options, and some semblance of recognition of the realities of youth. The change happened quickly and clumsily, with juvenile justice jurisdiction transferring from the state to the city and corrections officers trained in the strict discipline required in a prison such as Rikers suddenly tasked with providing emotional counseling to fragile sixteen- and seventeen-year-olds. But the concepts were simple and progressive: small groups with project-based education and emotional support. The effort—adapted from the Missouri model over forty years after that model's inception—was a lofty political and financial risk in a highly segregated city of almost 9 million people and immensely concentrated wealth where systemic changes, when they occurred, were expected to bear fruit quickly.

Two years after the last group of juvenile offenders moved from Rikers, meaningful data regarding key outcomes like recidivism and graduation rates was still difficult to collate; such figures took five to ten years to measure meaningfully. The most highly touted, solid figure was 24 percent—that was the citywide decrease in arrests of sixteen- and seventeen-year-olds in 2019, and it seemed to refute the archaic, enduring argument that harsh punishment was a deterrent against crime. But arrest numbers had been trending downward for a decade, and local police grumbled that youth crime wasn't necessarily falling at all. Rather, the new system of paperwork was so onerous that law enforcement was more inclined to let young people go uncharged for all but serious crimes. Arrests were imprecise indicators in general. Theorizing on why some young people *weren't* arrested could sound heady in short news-paper pieces, but the exercise had no real correlation with the outcomes of those who *were.*

The wide-scale improvement of those outcomes required time and money to nurture, measure, and interpret. But in an absurdity perhaps typical in government, the powers that be needed to justify that time and money with promising numbers right now: numbers that were undeni-able, that spoke not only to hope but to progress, that made influential people in the donor class feel good when skimmed in an email blast, and that were nearly impossible to find in the city's juvenile justice system. They needed numbers such as 98 percent, which was the high school graduation rate of students who completed Exalt Youth cycles.

Exalt Youth had been operating quietly and efficiently and mostly invisibly throughout its decade and a half in existence. With devoted educators and a grassroots fundraising base, working out of a cramped, low-ceilinged office suite off Borough Hall Plaza in downtown Brook-lyn, the organization had already made a lasting footprint in this field. The data it boasted were superb.

Suddenly, with the highly publicized sea change in the city's ap-proach to rehabilitation paired with Exalt's stellar record in the sphere, the organization piqued a widespread interest. Its management had had particular success recently in public and private funding, business part-nerships, and attracting influential board members whose experiences ranged from advocacy to the arts. Less than a year before Ian Alvaro's referral and the start of Cycle 108, the group had moved from Brook-lyn to its fashionable and elegant new space across the river in Lower Manhattan.

The fancy building and the office's pristine Statue of Liberty view did not change Exalt's mission, program, or results. The new address did make that mission and those results easier for the ruling class to see. The expense of it felt superficial—to the teachers more than anyone else, considering the students they served and the distance they themselves had to commute—but being seen was vital in the competitive milieu of

New York City nonprofits. Thousands and thousands of .orgs across the spectrum of causes competed for the tax-deductible earmarks of the prominent rich people living on and around the island. The kids in Exalt's program, conversely, were among the city's most disregarded: nearly all of them black or brown, all of them poor, all from far-flung neighborhoods, all tagged as criminals. Bringing these two demographics together was challenging, strange, and absolutely vital. The office space felt ancillary to the work done inside it, but its charming effect on the donors, potential donors, foundation board members, government grant writers, and people of political influence was undeniable.

Far more important was the space's role in showing the children that they were worth the cost, that they weren't destined always to learn in dingy rooms without natural light, that they belonged in prime real estate, too.

Overhead costs were tight and arduous to procure, as benefactors of youth services always wanted their dollar spent on a student's work rather than the file cabinet in which it was stored, on the laptop that a student used rather than the electricity that charged the laptop. Harder was finding business owners in various fields—consulting, architecture, fashion, parks and rec—willing to employ juvenile offenders as interns during the second half of the cycle. Harder still was keeping track of a few dozen teenaged individuals and their daily journeys across the five boroughs to ensure that they could make it to Exalt when they were supposed to and were held accountable when they didn't. Four full-time staff members spent most of the day on the phone with students, families, parole officers, work supervisors, and school administrators maintaining this living map of schedules and whereabouts.

The hardest task would always be changing people's minds—those outside the program regarding what a teenager with a court record was capable of, those inside the program regarding what they could be as human beings living in a world preset to treat them with contempt or—sometimes worse—indifference. That task was accomplished wholly in the classroom, in the invisible currents running between teachers such as Alex Griffith and students such as Ian Alvaro as they discussed ideas.

In careers, changes such as these could take years of retraining. For alcoholics and addicts, they required lifetimes of maintenance. Marriage, parenting, financial management, fitness regimens—moving from one mode of being to another was grueling and easy to forfeit. Ian and the other kids at the outset of Exalt Cycle 108, who possessed deep knowledge of how messy and hideous the world could be, had four months to revamp their worldviews, self-images, and damaged interior spirits.

*   *   *

NOBODY FOUGHT IN the Exalt Youth Cycle 108 on that first day in October, or during that first week. In class, Alex, their teacher, often referenced *code-switching*, the abrasively clinical term for the behavioral alterations required for impoverished people from insular communities to navigate a greater world seemingly intent on marginalizing them.

"You all already have this skill," Alex said during the cycle's third meeting, pointing to the word he'd jotted on the board. It was one item in a list the kids were blurting out in free association of useful attributes in professional environments. They'd also listed *computers*, *eye contact*, *follow-through*, *language (no cursing/no slang)*, *fashion/dress*, *ask questions*, and *don't fight*.

"But it takes a lot of constant effort, right?" Alex asked. He tapped the word with the dry-erase marker in his hand. "The term itself, *code-switching*, is kind of deceptive, because it's not like there's an actual switch you can turn on and off. There's not an actual code or switch anywhere. Walk in a room, flick the switch, all good. We all know it's not like that, right?" Nods rippled around the room. "It's something we have to think about and make an effort toward every second we're in that room, because the rules are different in each room and they're always changing, too. It's a huge, *constant* effort that people who maybe own apartments in this building never have to contemplate, they can spend that same energy on the task at hand. So you all have to already have more energy than the people you're competing against for school, jobs. I have about ten thousand stories from law school. You all must have your stories." Alex raised his chin to indicate that anyone desiring to share one should.

Kyla, whose small head poked up from the neck of her gigantic sweatshirt, shook her head. "I never really leave East New York except to come here. So mostly I can just be myself." She twirled a pencil around her long, fake, neon fingernails; Ian thought it was astonishing that she could even hold the implement. Her hair, hot pink a few days earlier, was now dark purple. "Except maybe with my grandma or something. Then I act very polite."

"What about when you were in court?" Alex asked.

She shook her head, made a sad *psht* sound, and looked down. "I just acted like myself in court. That's probably why they sent me to jail instead of probation."

Alex nodded grimly. "Listen, we'll get to how the justice system is and ways we have to help make it work better for you. I know we all have *a lot* to say on that. But that's another lesson."

Ian ventured to raise his index finger from the desk. "I've got one just from today." Then he described emerging from the subway on Wall Street and entering this building: "Just walking, like, four blocks, you feel like, if you act how you act at home or even at school, you'll get in big, big trouble from just walking. Or even if you don't get in trouble—people call you out, mad-dog you, walk wide around you, you're different. Basic things like buying food in a store are harder." Ian gestured sympathetically toward Kyla. "And then it's like everyone's always telling us we got to get out of our neighborhoods, like that's the key to everything, the key to the world. You know, *get out. Escape.* But why would we want to get out when it means we have to deal with all that, all the time? To be stressed and not be ourselves—all the time?"

These sentences were probably the most Ian had spoken in a single burst in many months. So he'd spoken tentatively, questioning each word as it had exited his mouth, doubtful of each word's value. Voicing serious thoughts hadn't felt so fraught before jail. At his former high school in Paterson, he'd frequently offered prolonged monologues in class while assuming that if a thought was important enough to spark in his brain, then it was worth the attention of others. He no longer made that assumption. People who talked too much in jail had a terrible time.

After a moment of quiet, Alex said, "It's a really hard question and we'll be asking ourselves that a lot, looking at the different sides of it. The important thing is you all can already do this very well. You all got here today. You got *here*." Alex pointed emphatically downward, as if through the building's lower floors and into the bedrock that kept the waters at bay from this thin rectangle of dry, valuable earth. "Just to do that, just to get here, takes a certain amount of courage, and it also takes *skills*—skills that you have that you don't even know you have because a lot of people don't even recognize them. Skills that most people around this neighborhood can't even imagine." When phrased like this, with such sincerity, it was energizing for the students to consider competencies they possessed that many others did not—energizing because they spent so much of their psyches, both conscious and unconscious, dwelling on all they did not have. And they were here because they'd broken laws to obtain these things: money, accoutrements, respect, maybe some agency in their lives.

This first sequence of classes in the Exalt program was called the "pre-contemplation phase," because no one was yet asking the students to adopt a specific model for how to be or how to think. The purpose of these discussions was to introduce the concept that different methods of being and thinking did exist, to let these conversations carve their own routes, to soften these kids' exteriors through safe, free-ranging discourse. Alex had taught fifteen Exalt cycles before. He'd seen all manner of energies rule this introductory phase. So far, he was pleased with 108.

* * *

IAN SLIPPED INTO the apartment a little after seven thirty. The two-bedroom was a typical New York City walk-up, with a narrow living room overlooking the street and a long hallway that passed a kitchenette and two bedrooms, ending in a bathroom in the floor's rear. His clothes were semi-neatly piled on top of his suitcase in the corner of the living room. A bedsheet and two pillows were draped over the sofa's armrest, where he slept. His aunt (technically his second cousin, but he called her "Aunt"), uncle, and two younger cousins had already eaten dinner. Music played, soft-pop hits. The adults were on the sofa thumbing their phone screens while his cousins fought over a soccer game on the video console. Ian's father, who was keeping his erratic schedule at the port in New Jersey and still living in Paterson, would be here tomorrow for some of the weekend—though Ian didn't totally keep track of their text message threads, which focused exclusively on where Ian was and where he was going. Ian's cursory replies in these exchanges, indignant in their brevity and their slang, made for a written record of his regimented, monotonous days. School, this apartment, PO office, Exalt, or in between any two of the four—that's where he always was.

He didn't quite know why he was distancing himself from his dad, who was not responsible for the situation, and who'd spent a lot of time and money and had upended his life to salvage Ian's. The nature of fathers and sons was that neither could be the first to attempt to bridge or even acknowledge the expanse. The modern passive-aggressiveness of text-speak certainly didn't help with understanding. The only substantive content of their communication lay in his father's incessant pleading with Ian to be gracious to his host family, to help them keep the apartment clean, to sleep at normal times and not play his music loud (or at all), to never for a second forget the kindness they were extending.

Ian interpreted these missives as his father's lack of faith that Ian would do any of these things, that Manuel thought Ian was doomed to screw things up.

Ian spent most of his free time texting with his friends in Paterson. This was technically illegal. But he doubted that the overtaxed legal system of New Jersey would be obtaining warrants to search the phones of Paterson teenagers for correspondence with Ian Alvaro regarding who had broken up with whom at school, Spotify playlists, fast-food joints visited. He maintained running text exchanges with two dozen people at a time this way—though he'd begun noticing that these people whom he'd grown up with were slowing down in their responses as weeks passed, providing less detail, letting the ellipses indicating a message in progress blink on and off (as if they'd started writing to him but then became engrossed in more pertinent matters midsentence). After less than two months, they were all, maybe, beginning to forget him. Or at least his life held less relevance to theirs, was just a voice echoing faintly from Brownsville. They couldn't even sync video games to play together, since his friends used Xboxes and his cousins had an old PlayStation.

While clinging to the frayed strands of significance he still had left in Paterson, almost frantically producing fresh message content, he usually sat in the windowsill above Amboy Street and peered out at Brownsville. This cityscape was astonishing with its dozens of project towers, most of them midrise. Brownsville remained one of the most consistently impoverished, high-crime neighborhoods in all the five boroughs of New York City, thus far resistant to gentrification because of those towers. Ian stayed inside at night, so he didn't know how closely the actual street life hewed to the mythology. But he'd been observing from a distance, five floors high, entranced during nocturnal hours by the yellow lights glowing within kitchens and bedrooms up and down the tenement-style buildings on Amboy, and across the massive facades of the projects, each space containing its own small dramas like his. The landscape of the city was so vast. Its population was so colossal. Its windowsills were so terribly lonely.

In the city's thrall, he was no longer a leader or athlete or person of influence. He was no longer Feud of the 493s. He was just a kid looking out through the glass, waiting a little desperately for people to respond to his texts, clinging to a sense of his own consequence, watching it slip away into the great atmosphere above Brownsville at night. He was a speck.

Chapter 3

———————◆———————

November 2019

E ACH AFTERNOON AFTER school, Ian climbed up into the subway
station over Saratoga Avenue and waited for the 3 train. Street noise
drifted upward to the elevated platform: from car horns and diesel engines, mostly, and there was always someone yelling at someone else,
either in agitation or in greeting. After a time, the train would clatter in.
Though Saratoga was near the beginning of the Manhattan-bound train
line, there usually wasn't any room for him to sit during the forty-five-
minute trip across Brooklyn. The majority of these minutes were under-
ground, so there wasn't much to see, either: just people, most of them
on their phones. The crowd inside the train thickened further as Manhattan neared, collecting whiter and wealthier-looking people through
Crown Heights and Brooklyn Heights. Then the train covered the long,
uncomfortable stretch beneath the East River—invariably halting once
or twice due to dispatch signals, during which it was impossible not to
contemplate the millions of tons of water directly overhead—before
belching many of its riders, including Ian, out at the Wall Street stop.

The dichotomy between where he boarded the train (a neighborhood
with the highest concentration of public housing projects in America)
and where he disembarked (the nexus of the country's financial system)
was too intense and absurd to merit much in the way of intellectual con-

sideration. The weather was still warm and Battery Park was busy with people hustling for the Staten Island Ferry or perusing Lady Liberty tchotchkes. Ian worked his way to the Oceana, the building in which Exalt was located. Entry into this building proved amusing every day, as the outflow of suited downtown office workers in the gilded lobby and elevator bank reacted to the Exalt kids in their baggy clothes and braided hair and sneakers that squeaked loudly on the polished floors. The other tenants didn't perform blatant double takes or ask if the students were lost, the way they might in film portrayals of racism in America. But they definitely registered the seeming abnormality. Some smiled and tried to be progressively friendly in the elevator. Others whooshed past toward some urgent business, perhaps annoyed at having to weave around these children in no rush to be anywhere or to accomplish much of anything. Most tenants were conscientiously nonchalant, putting noticeable effort into not noticing the Exalt kids at all.

If Ian was early, which he was for the most part in the beginning, he would wait with the other Cycle 108 kids in the front room. Desks ringed the open-office-style area, occupied by an even mix of teachers prepping for the afternoon's lessons, staffers making their rounds of calls to check in with families, various actors in the legal system whose work intersected with the org's, as well as former Exalt students who were now interns. The 108s would sit or stand around a tall oval counter with built-in bookshelves stocked with literature: *The New Jim Crow* by Michelle Alexander, *Between the World and Me* by Ta-Nehisi Coates, *The Fire Next Time* by James Baldwin. They commiserated over stalled trains and stupid school days while snarfing processed food they'd picked up at overpriced delis along their various transit routes. At exactly four thirty, they were all summoned to their classroom.

At the outset of Cycle 108's second week—in transitioning from "pre-contemplation" to the "contemplation" phase—Alex told them about his own first contact with the legal system. He'd been fifteen years old, a gangly kid still learning to situate his long limbs, the son of Ghanaian immigrants who didn't speak English, a meek-voiced nerd in East

New York. He'd procured a date for the first time. After weeks spent summoning the courage to ask and days spent stunned by her affirmative reply, he'd then faced the horror of planning an evening in the city. He was going to take her out of East New York, maybe even to Manhattan, to show how worldly and sophisticated he was. He had less than $10 with which to do that, but he would figure it out. He picked her up in the late afternoon and walked her to the subway. She had a card, but he wasn't going to let her pay for anything. He swiped his monthly pass and gestured for her to go through. Then he tried swiping it again at a different turnstile, to save $2.25. He didn't know if a cop had been looking straight at them at that moment or if some alarm had dinged in the booth, but a moment later both he and his date were in handcuffs against a wall. They both spent most of the night in jail, in separate male and female cells, the fifteen-year-olds nestled on reeking benches among the drunk and transient and violent of far-east Brooklyn.

"Let me guess," Kyla asked after the story. "You two're married now."

Alex rolled his eyes upward. "Are you crazy? She never talked to me again. If she saw me in school after that, she'd turn and run in exactly the opposite direction. No, no, trust me, we didn't get married."

"They booked you for a double swipe?" Javi asked, aghast. "No sympathy for a brother taking a girl out, just charges?"

"No sympathy, definitely no. And they booked me, but they didn't charge me. They could have. I was lucky in a way."

"For a *double swipe*?" Javi repeated.

"Yeah."

"That the only time you've been arrested?"

"Yeah. I was careful after that."

"So why are you telling us this story?" Ian asked. "It wasn't that bad."

"Well, it was embarrassing and scary as hell."

"Yeah, but . . ."

"The point of the story—" Alex paused, backtracked. "Okay, there are two points to the story. The first is, don't double swipe, don't jump the trains. I know it seems easy and two seventy-five is two seventy-five.

But I tell you, it is not worth it. Don't jump the trains. That is why Exalt gives you loaded Metro cards to get here. Okay?"

He waited somewhat seriously for everyone in class to respond with at least a nod.

"The second point is, that night wasn't bad, like you said, except for the date. But it could have been. Maybe if I wasn't so skinny, maybe if I had a deeper voice, maybe if I swore at them or resisted in any way. If I wasn't such a lanky, dorky, terrified kid, it could have been really bad. And that realization changed me. It's part of what motivated me to go to college instead of getting some job like my parents had. Motivated me to go to law school instead of just getting some slightly better job than my parents had. Motivates me to practice law during the day and work here in the evenings. It's all because of how bad things *could have* been, but weren't, because I was lucky. I don't want you all to have to rely on being lucky. Because you all already know what it's like to be unlucky. Okay?" Most traces of levity vanished from Alex's voice. "And that is what this second week of class is about: beginning to think about how you can take luck out of the equation and put everything on yourself."

Ian nodded, because that's what he was supposed to do in that moment. But he refused to believe for one second that luck could be rendered obsolete. A few days earlier, a shooting incident between two groups of young men occurred two blocks east of Amboy Street where he was staying; Ian had walked past the same corner less than an hour earlier. In the meantime, Nahla and Kyla's East New York neighborhood was on the same subway line as Brownsville, so, if he timed his exit from Exalt properly, he'd have forty-five minutes each evening to hang out with two bright and pretty girls. Ian was fairly certain that luck, both good and bad, was very much an operative factor in life.

The class discussion moved on past Alex's narrative and into a tech lesson about how the program Google Docs worked. Document slides flashed on the Smart Board (an astonishing detail Ian had noticed about Exalt was that its Smart Boards always seemed to work). Alex clicked on different menu items to show how to save and share future work. Ian panned around the plain classroom at the sundry faces of his wayward cohorts. He'd only gathered small snippets of each classmate's experience with the system, but enough to know that they mostly hinged on some outlandish turn, similar to the way Ian's brawl had been framed as a gang-related hate crime. Nahla had used her shoe in a fight with another girl at school, which had been classified in court as an assault weapon. Jordan had been snitched on by good friends after robbing a store. Kensi had taken some money from his mom's boyfriend's wallet, and Kensi's mother had turned him in. There was luck, and there were their own active roles in what had befallen them, and there was the amorality of providence. Ian's mind digressed into an angry jag over the random intersections of the three, in particular that crazy chain of events with the nail bat.

Alex had moved from Google Docs to Google Sheets. He was nodding toward Ian in his reverie.

"Sorry, what?"

"I asked if you've ever used Google Sheets before."

"No—I don't think so."

"Anybody?"

A few hands raised.

"Cool. We're going to be using this a lot, to keep track of schedules, finances, your internships when those start. So listen up. It's pretty important, and it's pretty cool." Alex was still looking at Ian, as if fully attuned to his roving mind, the feeling of victimhood that had physically gripped him. "Cool?" Alex repeated lightly but with his eyes drilling in a bit in that way perceptive teachers had.

Ian nodded. "Cool. I'm cool."

He sat forward and focused on the screen and gripped his pencil, using that simplest of instruments as his anchor in the present.

* * *

THAT SATURDAY, IAN took the 2 train to Times Square, then switched to the A to 181st, then boarded a bus over the George Washington

Bridge. From the peak of its gentle arch, he peered up and down the Hudson River. The morning sun was painful to his eyes on the wavelets below. Boats cruised north and south. The Palisades looked at once mighty and delicate. He stepped off, illegally, in Paterson, and walked from the Main Street thoroughfare into the neighborhood of blockish apartment buildings in which he'd grown up. He felt more uneasy than he'd anticipated, especially when a police car passed now and then and he concentrated on appearing unstressed by their presence. Each turn onto a new block threatened recognition. Most of his life, he'd strived for just that: to be recognized in this small swath of America. During this passage, he sought only anonymity until he arrived at the stoop of an old friend, someone with whom he'd gone to elementary and middle school. This friend hadn't been part of the confrontation that had altered Ian's life; he'd been at a family gathering in Montclair. He was still a junior at JFK High School. He still played on the soccer team. He seemed generally unburdened, and Ian envied him this.

Together, they walked another mile or so toward the eastern tip of the town, Ian's friend updating him on the banal goings-on around here, Ian talking nonspecifically about what Brownsville was like. They came to a telephone pole in the middle of a block. A heap of withering flower bouquets had been laid against the cracked wood. A stuffed giraffe was soggy from the previous evening's shower. A placard read RIP MY BROTHA in brightly colored Magic Marker over a yearbook photo of a young man with glistening hopeful eyes before a generic blue background. The face had belonged to another friend of theirs. He'd been shot and killed last week in this nondescript place. Few details were known, but a group was even at this moment coalescing in the city to canvass for information and initiate revenge.

Ian would not be a part of this group, even though he somewhat longed to be. Geography and the terms of his probation made it impossible. All he could do was break the law and risk further incarceration to pay his respects here, then say goodbye to his friends—the one who had been murdered and the one who had risked seeing Ian today.

They performed the elaborate parting handshake they'd devised in fifth grade, and Ian trudged back to the bus depot for the journey to his interim home. With his hands clenched tightly in his pockets, he fixated throughout on all he'd lost.

*   *   *

"RAISE YOUR HAND if you're bilingual," Alex told the class.

"What's that mean?" Javi replied.

Alex cringed at him. "C'mon, you know what that means. If there's one thing to take from this class, it's to please stop acting like you know less than you do, like you're dumber than you are. A lot of you all do that, and it holds you back. I'm not saying to act like you know *more* than you do—a lot of you do that, too—but don't act like you know *less*. So, bilingual, raise your hand."

Six students raised their hands. Five spoke Spanish at home, and one spoke Haitian Creole.

"Well, good news: you all are about to be trilingual, because we're about to learn computer language."

The class was unenthused. Computer language meant typing, and typing was both boring and frustrating.

Alex pointed at Kyla, whose hair in the fourth week was now green. She was frowning. "How can you act in a bad mood about this when you said last week you wanted to start a gaming company when you grow up?"

"I like working with computers." She held up her inch-long fingernails. "It's just a pain with these."

"I don't know what you do about that."

"I have strategies."

"Anyway, most of you basically know what you're doing with computers, but we're going to do some work with certain programs they use in a lot of offices that maybe you wouldn't use at home or at school. We're going to get you proficient. Anyone remind me the definition of *proficient*? It's part of the new language we're doing."

Nahla—who had been imprisoned for striking someone with a shoe sole, who was always seated beside Kyla and always with extralarge sweatshirts wrapped around her small frame—said, "It means good."

"Yes. Anything more specific?"

"Fast," Javi offered, and then through his huge toothy smile: "I'm proficient at a lot of things."

"None of us need or want to know what they are," Nahla said.

"Knowledgeable," Jordan, in the back, murmured. He murmured pretty much everything he said.

"Yeah—*proficient* basically means all that: knowledgeable about something, fast, and good at it. We're going to get there. Oh, and I have more good news." Alex surveyed the room and the many sleepy pairs of eyes staring back at him without anticipation. "It's week four in the cycle, which means you all are about to start getting paid next week." Students who lasted a month in the Exalt program began earning $13 per hour for their time. This reminder was met with whoops and fist pumps. So far, the class had lost six students, who, overwhelmed by the commitment, had voluntarily left Exalt. Twelve remained to celebrate this imminent milestone—though only eleven were present right now. Ian had not shown up yet.

Alex began the lesson by reviewing the previous week's unit, which had encompassed all the subtle factors in earning and retaining a job. That week was always a crucial passage in the program since the internship phase of their cycle began in a month, when they would stop reporting to the Exalt office every day with their friends and instead be working in a professional office with strangers. The small nuances of that transition—the imperatives of language and dress, the invisible boundaries of appropriate humor, the sly and devastating racism embedded in office culture—would be difficult, and they would each be largely alone in it. To prepare them, Alex had to be redundant and repetitive in this class, reviewing the same concepts exhaustively.

The students tended to groan throughout these interludes, and those reactions were fine; Alex didn't expect to be appreciated by his students.

His job was only to make sure they knew these cues well enough, both intellectually and emotionally, to have them on hand when the stakes mattered and they didn't have people like him nearby.

So he spent twenty minutes rehashing the concept of professional dialect and how crucial it was to adopt the vocabulary and speech patterns of the people they would be working for, no matter how irritating or wrong it felt to do so. He reminded them that this obligation in no way detracted from or was meant to replace the way they talked at home and with their friends. He spoke of nonverbal communication and various silent methods by which to project enthusiasm for a job even when they weren't feeling it. "If you're working at Starbucks, both the managers and the customers want to believe that you like coffee." Alex used this metaphor often. "You might hate coffee. I hate coffee. Starbucks in particular smells, like, burnt. But you still act like it smells and tastes great or you won't be working at Starbucks very long." He mentioned open-mindedness and their own latent forms of stereotyping against, say, Muslims, transgendered people, and white people. He told them to pay attention to what they wore and how they smelled: "Don't go to work smelling funky, period." He reemphasized the truth that it was illegal for any employer to ask them if they'd ever been arrested. "You do not ever have to answer that question—because it's rude as hell to begin with, and also because arrest and guilt are two entirely different things."

Ian Alvaro trudged into the room then, about twenty-five minutes late for class, looking weighed down by his oversize Starter jacket and weary as if the world had just gotten one over on him in a significant way.

"Hey." Alex nodded to him with an intentional touch of frustration. Ian had been arriving on the latter end of the first half hour of class for a few days in a row. The boy found his binder in front of an empty seat and sat down. "Everything all right?"

"The trains were messed up," Ian mumbled. "No one was getting into the city from Brooklyn."

"Okay, that happens."

Nahla and Kyla shared a giggly expression between them. They rode the same train line and had arrived ten minutes early together.

"Mark your time sheet as arriving at four forty-five, okay?"

"Thanks." Ian shaved ten minutes off his lateness in the appropriate box.

"But starting next week, when you all start getting checks for being here, you don't get to cheat like that. All right?"

"Cool."

Alex's professional demeanor hid well his deep concern. The six students who had already exited Cycle 108 would have the opportunity to repeat the program with a later cycle, once they'd gained better control over their schedules and priorities. But students who dropped out or were kicked out after the internship phase of the program began were not permitted to return—mainly for practical reasons of finite space and resources, but also because those situations affected Exalt's reputation for dependable interns in the business community. Ian had only missed two classes so far in the cycle, with somewhat valid excuses, but he was consistently late with the troubling trend of becoming later and later. He'd begun rolling in five minutes late a week or two into the cycle, breathless and apologetic after sprinting from the Wall Street subway, and now here he was today almost thirty minutes late and thoroughly indifferent. The lateness bothered Alex only a little; time was a tool that children and adults alike used to assert some illusion of power. But Ian's uncaring attitude weighed on Alex. Apathy could become a lifelong affliction; Alex had seen this trait assimilate entire personalities, negate entire potential futures.

"So what were we talking about?" Alex asked.

"Computers," said Kyla.

"Right," he said. "The digital divide."

"The what-what?"

"The *digital divide*." Alex wrote the two words on the board. "This is what I'd say is one of the three main instruments that keep people who look like you and look like me and don't have much money from getting a foothold in the workplace. We're going to talk all about it, and we're going to do the best we can to eliminate it."

*   *   *

OUTSIDE THE CLASS and down the hall, past a nook with a coffee machine and the executive director's office, was a horseshoe of cubicles adjacent to the waiting area. Within these cubicles, the majority of the Exalt staff spoke into their phones and typed on their computers all day, often simultaneously. Some were not many years older than the students. Most were seasoned in the labyrinth of the justice system— through personal experience, their work at Exalt, or both.

These members of Exalt's staff had different job titles that all served the knotty task of tracking hundreds of young, kinetic bodies through the densest and most populous city in America. These hundreds filled four distinct categories: prospective students, current students in the classroom phase, current students in the internship phase, and graduates. Prospective students—young people in contact with the justice system, in the grip of the murky terrors of crime and punishment—had to be vetted, profiled, and interviewed, all in pursuit of answering the question *Does he or she want to do this?* Current students—not all or even most, but a lot—required relentless needling to make it to classes, parole meetings, and anywhere else they needed to be relatively on time. And even the most decorated graduates struggled in their post-Exalt lives and benefited from being checked in on regularly.

Patterns emerged in the kids who came through Exalt's program. Bright but impulsive and unfocused was a common archetype. Loads of potential but troubled at home was another. But much of the work was in gathering everything unique about each individual during a cycle and making the information purposeful.

The rigors of Exalt typically meant the lessening of probation, so the majority of students began the program with some eagerness based on that transaction. They didn't fully register the expectation to do more than memorize some things and nod their heads, as they could do in school. Exalt's mandate was to alter almost all of their habits and priorities. The first few weeks of the cycle could feel harrowing to students as this commitment set in. Depending on the deeply complicated circumstances surrounding this moment of their lives, not all were capable of processing these challenges.

That was why Cycle 108 had already lost six members. That was why Alex worried about Ian's growing fickleness.

The problem was that within the current structure of his relocated life, no one ever really knew where Ian was or what he was doing except Ian. His father continued to work his shifts at the port and visit Brownsville on off days. His aunt and uncle were kind to house Ian, but they had jobs and younger children and little bandwidth to help with Exalt. He was a new kid at a large public school. His parole officer, working in the Brooklyn office, was overloaded and only caught up with Ian during their mandatory appointments. Ian didn't have a job or any extracurriculars. In Brownsville, he was a seventeen-year-old free atom with a serious juvenile record.

Kymare Hutchinson was Ian's point person in the office and had been assisting in Alex's class. She was a licensed master social worker with a BA in deviant behavior and social control from John Jay College. She'd worked for the Center for Alternative Sentencing and Employment Services as an intern and later as a court liaison specialist, and she also volunteered for a coalition to improve the treatment of the families of incarcerated youth. She'd only been with Exalt for a few months, since the previous summer, and her smiley demeanor and soft voice emphasized that she was young and new while belying that she was experienced and determined. The question she wrestled with now was whether the time had come to confront Ian directly, and—if so—how hard to press him regarding his dedication to the program and his ability to follow through on its demands.

"I'm just afraid if I use a word he doesn't like, or something I say reminds him of something that happened that we don't know about—we'll get blamed in his head, you know?" Kymare reflected to Alex. The two were gathering folders and organizing time sheets after the most recent class.

"Yeah." Alex nodded, slowly collating papers in his hands, deep in thought. "If we challenge any small habit then we'll get blamed, you know, for *everything* that's going on with him."

"He's doing well, though. There's stuff we need to deal with, or at least know about, but I guess the danger would be him rebelling even more and taking steps back."

"He's doing well on paper—but is he believing it?" Alex spoke in an analytical, almost cheerful-sounding tone, the way students spoke of newly discovered ideas surrounded by unanswered questions. "Is he buying into anything we're doing, or is he just filling out the time sheet so his PO can check off on it? I really don't know with him."

"He's such a leader. Such a good example sometimes."

"Sometimes, not all the time. I would actually say less and less. Maybe for the moment I'll just say something offhand, you know, like, 'How about you try to make it on time tomorrow?' Call him out, but in a real soft way."

Kymare was doubtful. "I have a sense that he's going to hear it a certain way no matter what, and there's a fifty percent chance he doesn't make it at all the next day just to test you out."

Alex sighed. Then Kymare sighed. These were both audible, exaggerated, frustrated expressions in the quiet room. They had all the papers organized. Daylight saving time had passed and it was dark outside. They both had long train rides ahead to the outer boroughs where they lived. Alex's wife and one-year-old daughter were at home, and he was eager to see them. He had clients to meet with during the day tomorrow for his part-time law practice. Kymare had two cats and three volunteer positions for various juvenile advocacy organizations that had her writing into the a.m. hours most nights. Both of their slates were full. Both of their minds were bursting.

"Let's just finish out this week with him, see how it goes without saying anything directly," Alex said. "We still have another month before internships start. That's a lot of time to get things right."

"Yeah. I think with a lot of people I'd be more proactive. With Ian, I think it's probably best to stand back a little bit, but watch close."

"Hopefully he can kind of get things right on his own."

* * *

IAN WAS FIFTEEN minutes late the following evening, and his face projected brighter spirits.

Alex decided not to call attention to him, since Ian had arrived much earlier than he had for the previous class, but then Ian asked, "What should I put on my time sheet?"

He was clearly challenging Alex.

The teacher replied, "Put what time it is. It's four forty-five."

He watched Ian's reaction closely. The boy just nodded nonchalantly and wrote down the numbers.

Alex began class with a series of slides showing the technological disparity between the rich and the poor. The numbers were depressing: 94 percent of high school students in the top income bracket nationwide owned unshared computers, and 100 percent had access to them at school; in the bottom income bracket, the respective numbers were 17 percent and 58 percent. Ninety-six percent of top earners had internet subscriptions at home; 51 percent of low earners were connected. In households in which the primary provider possessed a BA degree or higher, 97 percent owned laptops or desktops; in households in which the provider had not graduated from high school, 46 percent owned computers. He clicked quickly through many more disturbing sets.

"I don't see the big deal," Nahla said. She had small eyes, an unassuming nose, and she always appeared to be amused as if by a joke that the others had missed.

"The difference between those numbers doesn't seem like a big deal to you?" Alex asked. "In a country where pretty much every job above minimum wage, and even a lot of minimum-wage jobs, require some type of computer skills?"

"I just mean, I think it would be kind of nice not to have a computer, not to be checking email and SNAP all the time, just enjoying life instead. I feel like owning one makes people dumber, in a way. That's my opinion."

"I see what you mean now," Alex replied. "Yeah, I'm sure we'd all like that to some degree. But for better or worse it's not the world we live in. It is really, really hard to get a good job without knowing computers. It's getting harder every day, basically. I mean, a well-paying job. We've talked about all the other hoops you have to jump through already: how you dress, how you talk, how far you have to ride the train, all that stuff. How to act different from who you really are, because that's what society demands of you right now. So adding a few computer skills on top of that, like typing and Google Docs, shouldn't be a big deal."

Alex casually began to leaf through his teaching binder. The digital divide was one of the more egregious forms of systemic inequality of the twenty-first century, encompassing all the poverty, racism, and inequity upon which America and its schools and its justice systems were founded. Alex's manner this afternoon suggested that a couple hours of class time focused on the matter would resolve it for the most part, and that he was antsy to push on to more interesting material. He acted this way intentionally, so that they would focus on overcoming the divide themselves rather than dwelling on the original sin of why it existed.

Nahla stuck out her lower lip and puffed a hard breath upward across her face. "I like the old-school way better."

"What, Microsoft Word?"

"No, writing with a pencil."

"Well, typing is faster. Most papers you write for school are typed."

"Not at my school. They don't have enough extra computers. So they don't make us use them."

"Doesn't your hand end up hurting?" Ian had been trying to interject in Nahla's various dialogues for weeks, usually with decidedly bland comments such as this one, just to be noticed by her.

Nahla more or less ignored him.

Alex said, "The city is really focused on laptops for everybody now. It'll be good for you to get ahead of it. You gotta change with the times."

"But a pencil you can hold in your hand," she murmured. She slid downward in her chair, almost forlorn.

Alex suddenly seemed to grasp some elusive aspect of this conversation's purpose. Slowly and seriously he said, "I'm sorry, I misspoke saying that, about the times. We are absolutely not here to change who you are or where you come from. I try to make that clear every step of the way, because we talk a *lot* about doing things different from how you grew up with and how you're used to and I know that's hard. But maybe I'm not clear enough."

"Nah, you're cool," Nahla assured him.

"It's like the suit I'm wearing."

"What?"

He gestured down across his outfit. "That's why I wear these clothes all day. It's not because it's comfortable. I mean, it's *all right*, but I'd be more comfortable in sweatpants and I'd still be the same person, with the same intelligence, able to teach the same things. But if I was wearing sweatpants, no one's going to hear a damn word I say. True?"

"I would listen to you," Javi said. "You're my man."

"Javi might because Javi doesn't have anything better to do. Most people wouldn't. I wouldn't be able to practice law or teach in sweats. We've already talked about this stuff. Computer skills are basically the same thing. If you're up for an internship, and the applicant next to you can type like this"—Alex mimed fluid, ten-fingered typing—"while you're typing like this"—now he pretended to clumsily hunt and peck—"even if you know more and write better, who's usually going to get the internship?"

Nahla nodded at the self-evident answer.

Alex added, "And remember what came up earlier this week: *proficient* doesn't just mean knowledgeable. It also means fast."

Following the extended metaphor, Alex began speaking about professional email addresses, and how IDs such as madbitches@gmail.com were also not helpful for employment. He went around the room, asking the students to say out loud their email addresses. Most were tame if obscure, with references to music they liked and neighborhood streets they lived on. One student's contained the word *thug*, which Alex advised him against using generally because of its ubiquitous connotations as well as because white culture had appropriated the word from rap as a permissible substitute for the N-word. Ian's contained the term *officialfendi*.

"What's Fendi?" Alex asked.

"It's, like, a brand, you know, fashion," Ian replied.

"Okay, that's cool, I know you're into that stuff. But for a professional email, we want to keep it to some version of your name. That way an employer doesn't even have to think about it, they just start typing your name, and your email pops up on their screen."

Ian nodded, but seemed inordinately doleful.

"You all right?"

"Say my professional email is, like, IanAlvaro86@gmail.com or whatever. The first thing an employer sees in that is *Alvaro*."

"You think that's true?"

"I know it's true. My dad told me. They see *Alvaro* and know it's Puerto Rican or Mexican and figure I must be lazy and shit, so they click on to the next without reading."

Alex replied quickly. "If you're worried about ignorance, then it can just say something like Ian-a-whatever."

Javi, trying to be helpful, said, "*Officialfendi* is not, like, a hood term. Why does it gotta be changed?"

"It doesn't," Alex said. "Ian should totally keep that for social correspondence. I have a Gmail address for friends and an Exalt address for professional. It's mainly to make it easy for professional contacts to remember, even if they lose your card."

"Wait-wait-wait," Kyla interrupted, waving her arms while Nahla chuckled beside her. "You're saying we got to *change with the times*, but now you're talking about *business cards*?"

"People still carry those," Alex said.

Kyla snorted. "People just text."

Alex moved ahead. This unit on computer skills was exhausting in its breadth and its intricacy and also the hundreds of fragile emotional points it seemed to press. Whether kids grew sensitive over their specific email addresses or over their educations' having been undergirded by systemic inequality and lack, he needed to treat their sensitivities with some care while also progressing through the lesson at pace. So Alex concluded this segment with instructions to manage three separate email accounts: one personal to use with friends and family, one professional to use with employers and school, and one a throwaway to sign up for potential spam sites, the kind that offered free iPhones in exchange for magazine subscriptions. "Chances are you never get that phone, but you never know."

Later in the week the students worked in small groups to research and create substantive PowerPoint presentations about such figures as Sonia Sotomayor and Maya Angelou (some students in the class had never heard of either, and others had heard both names but couldn't remember exactly what they did or why they were important). The students took typing tests (Javi outperformed Ian, which pissed Ian off). They spent a class on financial literacy and monthly budgeting spreadsheets in preparation for the Exalt paychecks they were about to start receiving—at $13 per hour and eight hours per week, each would earn $416 a month assuming they were consistently on time—and they wondered how anyone was supposed to save 10 percent of their earnings when, according to the charts they'd made, each and every one of them was already deep in the red, some by hundreds of dollars, before depositing a single check.

Throughout the various, sometimes heated discussions, Alex was insistent on reminding them all of their power, especially as he released them for the weekend. "Don't sleep on yourselves, even if you got a bad score on your typing test. Think about where you all were in week one versus where you all are now in week five. Think about how much the dynamic in this room has changed. Week one, I was standing up here ready to break up a fight if I had to. Now I'm talking about paychecks and résumés and saving ten percent. Think about that."

Alex gave them a moment to do so, hoping that each would spend that time in earnest consideration. Admittedly, earnestness was challenging on a Thursday evening, their last class of the week. And these kids knew the value of appearing absolutely stoic no matter what aches might be fevering within. They'd learned this skill to survive through their various turns in the juvenile court system and its different facilities of imprisonment. So Alex couldn't accurately measure what they heard and how they felt.

Ian was gazing vacantly at the top of the table in front of him. His hands were folded in his lap. He looked far away.

Chapter 4

◆

December 2019

W HAT IF WE take all these professional skills and all apply to the
same job that says *Resource Management?*" Nahla giggled, a full-
body laugh: both of her feet lifted off the floor of the subway car while
she wrapped her forearms across her stomach and her face tipped upward.

Ian enjoyed watching his friend become completely overtaken by
the mirth of her own joke. The two of them had been laughing almost
continuously since miraculously finding open seats together at Wall
Street station at 7:00 p.m. They'd made jokes about Alex and Javi and
the financial-literacy lessons they'd been having this week as well as
about more generalized truths of being a teenager in America. From
Ian's perspective, they were having one of those quintessential New
York experiences, constructing a small, warm, privately shared universe
in the middle of all the cold anonymity of the city. Every detail around
them romanticized the moment they were in, from the rocking of the
train to the tunnel streaking past the window to the gorgeous pinkish-
purple harbor dusk they'd just admired outside the Exalt offices. He
consciously willed all of life to pause for a time so that he wouldn't have
to exit at Saratoga Avenue.

"We'd have to know the *shit* out of Google Sheets to work in resource
management," he replied.

"Yeah, we'd have to get *proficient* as *fuck*."

Moments with Nahla around were a little better than moments that didn't include her. In this current window of exile that he lived in, Ian considered Nahla to be his closest friend.

Nahla had only spent two nights incarcerated before her diversion toward Exalt. She'd had a few run-ins with school resource officers and had finally been arrested in school following a fight with a rival girl during which Nahla's improvised use of a shoe had souped up the charges against her. In her opinion, the school administration used aggravated assault and weapons charges to prune kids they didn't want there; any regular school fight could become "aggravated" with the creative use of a few details. Even though Nahla's turn through the court system had been relatively brief and streamlined—the juvenile court prosecutor denied the law enforcement agency's petition and personally referred Nahla to Exalt—the route from arrest back into school was complicated and time-consuming. Without Exalt's motivation and care, she would probably just have dropped out of school. Her mom would have complained for a minute, but Nahla would have left their apartment and stayed with friends until the drama passed over, then begun piecing together days selling drugs on a small scale with her friends. Those days would have commenced the rest of her life. Nahla had an ability that Ian had not yet cultivated in himself, which was to take the long view of two divergent life paths and feel a deep gratitude to Exalt for holding her hand along the first stretch of the harder, better one.

When Ian confided his whole situation, he edited language and narrative to make the fight seem more a consequence of honor among young men, less an example of idiotic bravado among teenaged boys. He framed himself cinematically as a hero-victim of society. Subconsciously, he'd perhaps reached the thorny point of oral history in which he'd lost track of the actual sequence of events and subscribed instead only to the story he told. As a result of nearing this threshold, his propensity for self-righteous indignation—to see the entire world as a force working in direct, intentional, corrupt opposition to him—was burning brightly as well.

In that context, being late to his Exalt classes didn't bother him much, nor did acting out in school, ignoring his father's calls, or passing through the motions of each day resentful and alone. He did not share Nahla's gratitude, but he felt closer to it when he was around her— closer to a fairly recent version of his self that was lighthearted, creative, and forward thinking. He knew that feeling gratitude and grasping that self would help him exit this passage in life without deep wounds and maybe with some wisdom. But even when he brought himself there, he couldn't quite stay there.

"This is you," Nahla reminded him as the train slowed into the Saratoga Avenue station with its pleasant Brownsville views.

"I'll hang out a little longer."

He remained on the train with Nahla an extra three stops to Pennsylvania Avenue—which was the boundary of his known neighborhood. He was now contemplating a mile walk back to his aunt and uncle's in the dark. His other options were to pay the extra subway fare to cross back in the other direction at Pennsylvania or else to ride farther east to New Lots, where Nahla got off at a bigger station that would allow him to turn back without paying. But he felt like walking.

"You cool?" Nahla asked when he was about to disembark.

"Yeah," he said.

"Because you don't even have a real coat on. That stupid Starter jacket's, like, ten years out-of-date."

"It's vintage."

"I'm not sure if that's true, but *okay*."

He gave her a half hug, half hand-clench before leaving the train. Then he stood on the frigid, mostly empty platform and watched her waving to him through the window, the car all lit within. He wasn't sure if he would go to Exalt tomorrow, which was their last real class before the internships split them up. He wasn't sure when he would see Nahla again. So he knew enough to savor this vision of her, buried in her own winter coat, this small, cool person in the middle of this gigantic, difficult city, smiling. Then he tightened his Starter jacket around his shoulders—it really was old and pretty useless against the weather—and descended the stairs with other weary, freezing commuters. He took a moment to fix his bearings on the unfamiliar intersection and guess where home was, then he headed that way along Livonia Avenue.

*   *   *

CHURCH WAS A mandatory part of Ian's room and board in Brownsville. While his aunt and uncle's Catholicism did not govern every aspect of their lives—aside from a prominent crucifix in the living room and prayers before meals, he wouldn't have been able to peg them as God-fearing—they were in the pews every Sunday at 8:00 a.m., and they expected him to be as well. Ian's dislike of worship was tempered by the fact that it looked good to his parole officer.

Ian's father was coming to Brooklyn early from Paterson that Sunday, the second in December, to join them at church and spend the day with Ian. When Ian woke on the couch, the crisp winter sun streaming through the window felt like a weight on his chest, and he struggled to rise beneath it. The street was fairly quiet, belying the exhausting day ahead. His aunt and uncle were loudly exhorting his cousins to dress themselves, arguing over where the Sunday clothes were, stomping between the bedrooms. Ian lay with his head propped on one armrest and his legs hanging over the other until his aunt trained her stress on him. He acted more tired than he was—"All right, all right, I'm *up*"—then pulled his own set of church clothes from the duffel bag behind the couch that he'd been living out of for four months. He could not possibly imagine how he could live here for another eight months.

His father arrived in a sour mood because Sunday morning was the hardest time of the week to park. Manuel and Ian's aunt sparred over nonsensical gripes for a few minutes. It was lost on no one, not even the young kids, that Ian's living arrangement was causing possibly irreparable tension. Good, loyal Christian intentions often did. Ian was behaving well—keeping healthy hours, buying his own food with the

$13/hour stipend that Exalt had been paying him, performing any errand that came up. But the apartment was small and simply by existing in their space, living and breathing, Ian was testing all the various binds of family. In this morning's version Manuel was giving Ian grief about his increasingly unruly hair, while Ian mocked his father's baldness. These exchanges carried on until they were seated in the pews of Our Lady of Mercy Chapel on Mother Gaston Boulevard and the first notes sounded from the piano.

Ian performed all the rituals over the next hour and a half, standing or sitting or on his knees. Throughout, he remained keenly aware of and attuned to his father beside him: his restrained voice during the hymns, the way he knelt and rose again a few seconds behind everyone, softly groaning sometimes, as if he were carrying some weight so tremendous that God wouldn't understand it.

As much as Ian was bored by church, the atmosphere lent itself to a deepening of whatever mood and line of thinking he was in. This wasn't always a positive sensation. Today, he was anxious about his Exalt internship starting the following day, and he was upset at his father for no clearly defined reason. But ninety minutes spent dwelling on his annoyance took it to bitter places unmoored by rational thought. Ian suspected that Manuel was glad to have Ian out of his house and out of his town; he wondered if Manuel had let him spend those months in Newark's juvenile hall intentionally before enlisting an advocate; he conjectured as to how much better his life would have been if his mother had taken him with her when she fled; he blamed his current circumstances on his father's reticence and past behavior, and the drinking in particular; without any evidence, Ian wondered if his father was drinking again.

These were the ruminations that church wrought during this challenging moment in his life, and the two men spent the rest of the day avoiding eye contact and conversation with each other.

* * *

"YOUR JOB IS to get people inside, so that I can do my job."

Ian's Exalt internship commenced the next afternoon at a clothing store in midtown Manhattan. A sign outside on Thirty-Seventh Street listed all the many mid to low-tier brand names inside: Lee, Hilfiger, Skechers. The store was not quite as low-rent as it could have been but not nearly as upscale as it pretended to be. Normally, the wide doors would have been fixed open onto the street, but the cold kept them closed, and immediately upon entering Ian felt oppressed by the hot, unventilated atmosphere amid the densely packed racks of clothes. The mirrors that ringed the upper portion of the space's walls, which were intended to make the store appear much wider and deeper than it was, only made Ian feel more confined. He struggled not to betray his extreme discomfort while receiving a short tutorial from the guy in charge of the sales floor who had apparently been assigned as Ian's mentor.

"Are there any tricks to it?" Ian was sincerely striving to use the interpersonal strategies Alex had taught the students at Exalt: Ian made eye contact, spoke slower than usual and concentrated on his enunciation, asked questions that reflected both deference and a willingness to learn, made an effort not to say what he really thought. All of these skills required exhaustive concentration and were difficult to apply.

The sales manager squinted at Ian. "Just hand them out and don't do anything, like, crazy—right? Because people sometimes talk shit."

Ian's first station was outside on the sidewalk, where he handed out flyers to passersby. For two hours in the freezing, dark evening, he hawked sheets of paper advertising sale prices inside. He didn't have gloves or a hat because he hadn't been warned that he would be working outdoors. Worse than the physical cold was the mental toll that being ignored by hundreds of people wrought on him.

Ian took short breaks inside to warm his fingers and ears. He expected to be offered at least a cheap beanie from the discount bin, but he wasn't. He kept waiting to be rotated inside, but this didn't happen, either. The time passed slowly. He didn't meet the business owner or see how the cash register worked or how books were kept. He learned nothing and felt frustrated—more so when, at the end of his shift, he went to sign out and learned that the sales guy had forgotten where he was. Ian was incapable of looking past this thoughtless slight, of *not* seeing this single, crummy evening of work as a portent for an entire lifetime resembling these hours. That was Ian's struggle: grounding stray moments so that they didn't bloom into grander existential symbols and metaphors; simply letting an hour be an hour, a thought be a thought, a feeling be a feeling, a lousy two-month internship be a lousy two-month internship; permitting experiences to come and go without assuming a moral charge.

The entire train ride home, he projected this past evening onto his whole future and willed the train he was on to just keep going to the end of its line and past it, out of New York City, out of America, away from planet Earth.

* * *

NAHLA'S INTERNSHIP WAS with a property-management firm. This office had been taking Exalt interns for over five years and had a clearly defined space for her that was equal parts learning and doing. The learning mostly involved peering over the shoulders of professionals while they coaxed intricate charts and images from specialized computer programs. The doing mostly involved printing, copying, and disseminating those charts and images. Though she felt silly wearing business-casual slacks and blouses instead of her typical oversize jeans and sweatshirts, and the commute was long because every commute from East New York was, she loved it.

By the end of the first four-day week, she'd absorbed enough information to be given time to mess around with a personal idea of furnishing a communal game room within one of the properties. She spent hours alternately toying with a computer program that let her simulate a game room in different virtual spaces (foosball here, pinball there, a puzzle table in the center . . .), and penning a proposal as to what value a game room would bring to a tenant community in counterbalance to its expense. The computer-proficiency aspect of the Exalt curriculum, as much as she'd lightly derided it at the time as remedial, helped her immensely. She was not confident in her writing skills, yet building an argument was analogous to all the dozens of times in her life that she'd had to talk herself out of trouble, and she was highly self-assured in her ability to do that.

The firm's employees only treated her gingerly for two days while gauging her attitude and then, upon finding her inquisitive and bemused and quite amenable to listening, began assimilating her as just another part-time, low-rung hire. No one took it upon himself or herself to be her overseer. No one seemed interested in the role of counselor or surrogate parent or tough love–provider or—worst of all—savior. The space was open-air, mostly people working on laptops at long, narrow tables surrounded by tall windows overlooking Broadway in lower Manhattan. She loathed school and classrooms, but she looked forward to returning to Exalt on Friday so that she could share her experiences and hear from the rest of the class.

She'd been texting individually with others throughout the week, mostly exchanging different iterations of the sentiment *Fuck this working shit is CRAZY!* with emojis bracketing the words. When they all converged again with Alex in their classroom after the majority of a week spent at their various internships, the evening promised the comfort of being able to shed the restrained, decorous, at-work versions of themselves and commiserate over how peculiar the professional world truly was.

"How are you all?" Alex asked with a tight smile and eyes lowered as if in preparation for the inevitable stream of left-field complaints.

But the complaints never hit him. With their witty back-and-forth rhythms, the initial recap of week one of internships took the tone of a college sociology class: observations made in the field and brought home to be mined for patterns and, maybe, truths.

Kyla worked at a law firm that catered to low-income New Yorkers contending with typical legal matters—rent disputes, employer discrimination, unpaid tickets—that were often debilitating for people without disposable wealth. "People work there—like, they *work* work." A quick shake of her colorful hair signaled the degree to which she marveled at this aspect of white collar life. For emphasis, she added, "Like, *work, work, work.*"

Alex asked, "And what was it like for you adjusting to that kind of environment?"

Kyla breathed out and said pensively, "It's hard, you know. It's hard getting there every day—it's two trains plus a bus—and it's hard knowing that once I *do* get there, there's going to be no rest and no fun. But—I'm kind of into it, you know?"

She panned around the room, and mostly blank faces stared back. Alex said, "Clearly, we don't know. Can you talk a little about that?"

Kyla giggled nervously and stop-started a few times. Then: "People give me work to do, but it's not just, like, 'Have this on my desk by four thirty or else.'" She did her best impression of a crotchety male corporate drone's nasal voice, and it was pretty spot-on. "It's more like, they just *know* I can do the work, so they tell me what they need just straight up, and I'm like, 'Cool,' and I do it and do a good job on it and they're like, 'Cool.' And that's it. If I do have a question about something, I just ask, and somebody answers it. It's . . . nice."

"That sounds just crazy," Javi blurted.

"It sounds remarkably sensible." Alex added, "I actually know a few of the lawyers there, and that's how they came to be working with Exalt. They're focused but they're good people. They were the same when we were all in law school. I thought Kyla would do really well there—I knew it would also be kind of a trip for her—so I'm glad to hear it's going well." Alex asked Javi next.

"I get to order around kids *my own age*, and they have to listen to me, and that's basically the whole job." Javi was interning at an after-school program tailored toward students who needed as much structured time at school as possible to lessen their challenges at home, akin to preventive care. "I say, 'We're playing checkers,' and they go get out the checkerboard. I say, 'We're playing ball,' and they do that. I am *boss* there." Javi beamed with unadulterated pride, then his expression quickly soured. "But, damn, those kids do bother the hell out of me—for real."

"I love placing my students in schools," Alex said, "and watching as you all start to realize what your teachers have had to put up with. There's this empathy that happens. It's hilarious."

"I wouldn't go that far yet," Javi replied. "I'm not saying I'm the easiest, but these kids be *particularly* terrible."

Nahla appeared morose as she stated that her internship was awful: the people were mean, the work was boring, she was learning nothing, and she couldn't wait for it to end.

Alex appeared dad-like as he apologized. "You can talk to me about this stuff, and I can help change the situation—"

Then Nahla grinned, and he realized she was joking. "It's really good," she said, and then briefly described the game room she was lobbying for and designing. "It really is cool to be doing something."

Ian was a full forty-five minutes late, arriving after everyone had described the first week of their various internships. No one would have registered the time because he was often late and never seemed bothered by the docking of his stipend. But a faintly angry aura pervaded the way he walked in, with his head down, his fists stuffed in his pockets. He landed in his seat as if an invisible person had forcibly pushed him into it.

Alex, knowing better than to call any attention to a student who was clearly yearning for argument, just offered a head nod. "Ian, hey, do you want to say anything about your internship before we get into today's lesson?"

Ian shrugged and looked sideways at an indeterminate spot on the wall. "It's cool," he mumbled.

"Okay, good. Anything more specific?"

"Not really. Just, like, sales."

"Okay. I don't really know the company you've been placed with—they haven't worked with Exalt before—so I'm really curious to hear how it goes as you move forward. Now, we're a little behind so let's really get into the lesson. . . ."

Alex had one of those strange teaching sessions in which he was able to instruct a class on specific material—today focused mainly on the employer's perspective and what sorts of details the bosses might have on their minds, such as net-income receipts and employee health benefits—while another part of his consciousness was focused on concern for Ian Alvaro. So Alex animatedly moved around the room, asked questions and answered them, maintained an easy levity, and successfully brought his class to where they could attempt to look at their internships through the eyes of the people who held power over them. But every few seconds Alex would discreetly glance at Ian. The boy mostly sat staring at his notebook with his pencil in his fingers and the lead point actually touching the paper, but without taking a single note.

Alex had seen students look and act exactly as Ian did. Every Exalt cycle Alex had taught contained kids who exhibited his terminal uniqueness—the belief that their feelings and experiences were so deep and rare as to be inaccessible to anyone else. Alex could almost always connect with them through a few side conversations. Then he could begin to discern whether a kid might benefit from tough love or extra attention in class or any number of other well-honed, if slightly manipulative, approaches.

Alex's growing dread about Ian had to do with how late in the cycle Ian's discontent was manifesting and how erratically he had see-sawed throughout. Early on, he had been nicely focused and one of the sharpest kids in the class. He'd faded a bit, and then he'd made an effort to reapply himself and seemed fully capable of bearing the discouragement that internships could sometimes bring.

While Alex seamlessly taught that Friday class, he grappled internally with the possibility that Ian wasn't capable of bearing that discouragement, and that Ian was past the point in the cycle of being offered second chances. The teacher conceived of the conversation he absolutely needed to have with Ian afterward. Friday evenings were the most annoying time to pull kids aside for any serious topic. He suspected that Ian would sigh and eye-roll and ask why they couldn't just have this dialogue over text. Alex's task was to look this boy in the face with some gravity and tell him that the next years of his life would be determined by his actions over the next days of it.

Alex wasn't sure if he was prepared to communicate such an ultimatum in the precise tone that Ian's current state of mind—which Alex could only guess at—would receive. He wasn't sure if Ian would hear him regardless of tone. He wasn't sure of much at all because Alex had tripped into the irresolvable plight of all educators in and around the juvenile justice system: he had to stand in front of a young man who had yet to begin processing all sorts of deep emotional trauma—in Ian's case a mother's abandonment, a father's addiction, a violent peer group, railroading, imprisonment, exile, more—and take an uncompromising stance in holding that young man accountable, in drawing a sharp line between childhood and adulthood. Throughout the entire class of role play and other exercises, Alex dwelled mainly on the rhythm of the dialogue—the intervention—he would have at its end. Ian remained sullen and untalkative throughout the hour and fifteen minutes of class that he was present for. His only emotions involved scoffing at Javi's jokes.

When the time came, and the other kids jauntily filed out to catch trains home for their weekends and Alex lightly asked Ian to stay behind, the intervention only lasted about eight minutes.

"Back in October, when this cycle started, you seemed like you wanted to be here. You were talking in class and asking questions and getting here mostly on time. It's not like you were grateful, and we don't ask you all for gratefulness here. We just ask for a certain kind of attitude that's helpful. Kids who won't or can't show that attitude, they go home and try again later. Those who do, graduate. You had the attitude. And then you didn't. If you want to talk about the why in between, I want to listen to that and work with that."

Alex waited a moment. Ian shrugged and looked at the floor.

"If you don't, that's okay, too. But we have to figure out how to get you here when you need to be here, and get you to work when you need to be there."

"I get to work," Ian blurted with some defiance. "I got there all week."

"Tell me how it was. I don't know those people well, so it's helpful to hear from your perspective. We matched you there because you've expressed interest in fashion. If it's not working out—"

"I got myself there all week," Ian said again more softly.

"If it's not working out, just tell me so I can get on the phone and try to help."

"I'm good. The train wasn't working today, that's all."

"I—" Alex faltered and let up. "Okay. I know you're still kind of fresh to New York. The trains tend to work pretty well here, especially the two-three line you're on. But you need to learn to account for delays. Up to fifteen minutes late, people generally understand about trains. Over thirty minutes, people won't understand."

"Uh-huh." The syllables were Ian's reliable fallback.

"You know about the rule with dropping out of the cycle once the internships start."

"I don't get to come back."

"Are you thinking about dropping out of the cycle, Ian?"

"Nah, man. Nah."

"Because the way you're being when you are in class . . . it's hard for me to think that you still want to be here. That doesn't mean you won't get through the next two months, but it makes it a lot harder on everyone."

"I want to be here," Ian said softly.

Alex considered asking about Ian's home situation, and his father, and school in Brownsville. But Alex knew that Ian would just say that they were all fine, and Alex didn't want to cheapen his message. So he decided to let the moment end with those unconvincing words, *I want to be here*, and the image of the boy tiredly slinging his backpack over his shoulders and leaving the Exalt space. After a brief, head-shaking consult with a few of his colleagues, during which they scheduled customary calls to Ian's father and his internship supervisor, they concluded that all they could do right now was hope that Ian persevered. Sometimes, a child's success in the diversion program ultimately rode on only that: hope in perseverance, faith in the force of will required to show up again next week and the week after, the aspect of the human spirit that drove people—even young people who had been brought to their knees by a system that didn't much care whether they rose again—to complete what they'd begun. Then Alex left Exalt as well. His commute was long and crowded, but he reached his apartment in time to spend an hour cooing and reading to his baby daughter before her bedtime.

*   *   *

HEY, NAHLA TEXTED Ian two nights later, Sunday. She'd been unsure about reaching out to him. They texted with each other sometimes but never with any defined intent. Her intent now was to express concern, but she didn't want him to know that. Ian was smart, though, and able to see through most of the screens that people hung over various everyday interactions. He was also the type to be angered by any energy he took to be condescending, any inquisition along the lines of *Are you okay?*—no matter how friendly and mundane. He didn't reply for over an hour, which worried her. It was after 11:00 p.m. on a Sunday night, and a quick reply would mean that he was probably just home and bored. His not replying meant that he was out or upset with her or both.

Hey back, he wrote a little before midnight.

What you been up to?

Ian replied with a bunch of *Zzz* emoticons.

Cool.

You want to hang out? he wrote.

Now? Alone in her room a few neighborhoods east of Brownsville, Nahla wrote definitively, *No.*

So it's like that?

Like what?

U dont want to hang out with me?? He tacked on some scowling faces with turned-down eyebrows.

I dont want to hang out with anybody in the middle of the night.

It's early tho.

In what world?

Whatever. Go back to bed then.

I got work tomorrow. You too, she wrote.

So?

You going right?

I guess.

That means yes I hope.

You got a good job. Mine kinda sucks.

You still gotta go. She added five faces with gritted teeth and wide eyes that signified stress.

You sound like a teacher. He followed with a line of faces crying laughter.

Its like 6 more weeks. Just sayin.

7 weeks actually.

Makes no difference. You need 2 graduate that's all.

Why tho?

Nahla wrestled with this question for maybe twenty or thirty seconds, which was an eternity within a text exchange during which Ian was no doubt ascribing emotional significance to the bubbles on his screen. She knew the macro answer, but she couldn't articulate it within this medium's required brevity. They needed to complete their Exalt cycle to fulfill the bargain by which their probations were reduced, for the recommendations they would receive from Alex and their internship supervisors and, more important, members of Exalt's powerful board, who touched many of the city's exclusive, influential spheres. They needed to graduate so that their schools would treat them less scornfully and their guardians would worry less and they could activate the small yet definitive escape hatch from the system that the Exalt program, against all odds and reason in the beginning, provided. They needed to finish so that they knew, within themselves, that they had—so they could carry that knowing with them through all the future's undetermined challenges.

She eventually wrote, *U know all the reasons.* She added images of a black female cartoon figure with her palms raised and facing up on each side of a genial expression.

He didn't reply. She chose not to prompt him. She eventually turned to YouTube dance videos to pass the time until she was tired enough to sleep. Ian didn't text the next morning, either. Then she was busy making her way through yet another school day, the entirety of her focus on avoiding conflict with teachers and peers, and then she was rushing to Manhattan for another afternoon at the real estate company and further work on actualizing her game room project, which, as silly as the idea was, represented an actual physical mark she might make on the planet—and in that way was utterly stirring in her heart.

Chapter 5

———————◆———————

January 2020

THE HOLIDAYS WERE a reprieve from school and work. They were also frustrating for Ian because he made the mistake of asking his father over the phone if he could sneak back into Paterson for a few nights. He promised not to see anyone or even leave the home. His father told Ian that he couldn't. Ian interpreted the hard response to mean that his father didn't trust him, and Ian told his father this.

"You're right," Manuel said. "One of your boys calls, I'm asleep, you decide to go out—and that's it, it's over. They can send you back in a heartbeat."

"I been in Brownsville for months and I haven't gotten into any trouble, not one detention, nothing."

"That's because it's rough there, you're scared there. That's why it's a good place for you. Here, you're not going to be scared enough. That's bad."

"I'm going crazy here, Dad." Ian felt his voice quavering. He was about to cry. The urge made him angrier.

"I'd rather you crazy than going to jail."

"You'd rather just not have to deal with me," Ian said. "You'd rather I just stay anywhere you're not."

His father muttered something away from the phone's mouthpiece, and then: "That's not what this is."

"Yeah, you just want to sit with your TV and your drink and not have kids to deal with."

"I'm not drinking."

"How do I know that?"

"Because I said it, and I don't lie to you."

"You lie to me all the fucking time!"

"I can't help what you think. You're headstrong."

"You lied when you told me you were in this with me. You said we would get through this together. Remember that?"

"I don't remember what words I used. I am here with you."

"That's bullshit," Ian said, and hung up.

His ire was all-consuming mainly because he shouldn't have asked permission to go home in the first place; he should have just gone to Paterson on his own and stayed with a friend. A few easy lies to his aunt and uncle and dad would have enabled a quick sojourn home. Now, as Ian had realized would happen the moment their conversation ended, his father called Ian's aunt to make sure Ian remained in Brownsville over the winter break. He spent those days and nights doing what had become routine, which was mostly nothing: passing time indoors with his video games and text threads, accomplishing little emotionally or physically while remaining attuned to a vast, active ecosystem outside this apartment that he seemed to have no role in.

That was all Ian yearned for in the end: a part to play in life's unfolding. This yearning was why his thoughts bent so often toward Paterson. The city was small and grim in places and generally not an inspiring place to be. Most of the kids he knew there—including himself—aspired only to leave it for places such as New York City. He'd received hundreds of texts over the past months from friends who envied him for having "gotten out," even if his escape had been levied on him by the juvenile court and Brownsville was not exactly a destination of note. But Ian had a station in Paterson established over the first seventeen years of his life. His days had a scaffolding there. The character Ian Alvaro had already been written into the drama across the two rivers, and his great fear was in being written out.

Exalt asked quite explicitly for a reinvention of self. Ian desired a reversion to the self that had occupied the couch an hour before that fight last April.

Despite having placed his intentions on the adults' radar with the phone call, he still considered about a dozen different ways by which to go home over Christmas. These ranged from faking a friend's death to simply running away. His ability to pit potential consequences against concrete actions—historically not a strength of his but a skill the students practiced incessantly, hypothetically, in Exalt classes—overrode these schemes in the end, and he did basically stay in Brownsville. When his eyes grew bleary from screens and his thumbs stiff from texting, he gazed out the window at strangers on the slushy street below. His trancelike stillness began to bother his aunt and uncle. They complained, called him lazy, told him he needed to do something with his life. Ian was mostly amused by the distilled measure of contradiction. Whether loose in the city or supervised in the apartment, those who ostensibly cared about him the most figured out ways to be disappointed in him.

Juvenile hall did this, too, corrupting not only one's relationship with the justice system but with the nuclear family, fixing a residue of guilt over the most mundane and harmless behavior. As vicious as that parking lot melee had been, as uninhibited and objectively horrible as Ian's decisions within those minutes were, they might have unfolded without his having been entered into the system; they might simply have existed as shockingly dangerous, teachable moments that occurred between boys sometimes, when a person such as Ian saw the worst of who he could be. Maybe he would have run the other way. Or maybe his hubris would have been amplified and his behavior would have grown more reckless and harmful. He'd never know; he was in the system now. Consequently, every room he was in, every spot within a room—home, school, work, the street—was under watch. Not even completing Cycle 108 would ease that reality.

Such was his pessimism as the holiday passed and a new year began and the months of school and work and passivity ahead took an interminable shape. Within the confines of his seventeen-year-old brain, the few weeks remaining to complete his internship and receive his Exalt certificate seemed like an impossible stretch of time.

*   *   *

WHILE THE EXALT staff worked hard to create illuminating internship opportunities with nonprofits, city government departments, and the private sector, the goal was not necessarily to match every student with his or her dream job. Internships, almost by definition, were tedious and underappreciated positions. The working world in general was repetitious and not always managed by pleasant or even competent people. While being introduced to environments they'd never conceived of before, the Exalt students were dosed with those aspects of American life as well; the underlying purpose of the internship phase was to place young people in situations where they would struggle and then deploy all of the different strategies they'd been learning in the classroom over the first two months of the program. They were supposed to show up on time and with a positive attitude, even after humiliating days. They were supposed to separate facts from feelings. They were supposed to ask for help—and this was generally the most difficult action for Exalt kids: to admit they didn't know something or couldn't handle something.

American kids born into worlds in which they could comfortably believe, from the first moments of their lives, that the adults around them existed to help them tended to have little trouble with this concept. In contrast, kids who from a young age were forced by circumstances and ethos to see themselves as functioning adults tended to have an awful time with the humility and vulnerability required to seek counsel, which could be seen as an expression of weakness or even a source of shame.

Ian didn't consider himself the most mature kid, but he had grown up with no mother and an alcoholic father. As his saga with the justice system unfolded, most of what he carried, he continued to carry alone.

Exalt was filled with people motivated and equipped to aid him. Multiple liaisons were responsible for coordinating the internships. Family outreach coordinators had therapeutic training to talk about living-situation dynamics with parents and guardians. More-recent Exalt alumni had jobs in the office specifically geared to help current students withstand the trials of these weeks, through simply talking and listening. Support absolutely surrounded the kids who were receptive to it. But Ian continued to barricade his interior with absence and silence. The second Friday of January, he did not attend the scheduled Exalt class, nor did he send a message explaining why.

Once Alex realized that Ian wasn't going to show up at all, he left the classroom to task the entire Exalt team with finding Ian: "Call his dad, his aunt, his employer, his school, his PO. I don't care if we embarrass the hell out of him or get him in trouble or piss him off. Let's just get him on the phone however we can and get him here." Alex knew that something urgent and vital was unfolding, and that reaching the boy was colossally important.

They couldn't. Ian's father hadn't heard from him in a few days and couldn't elicit a text reply. Ian's school was unhelpful on a Friday evening. His internship employer hadn't seen him in the store for most of the week. His PO wasn't in the loop. His aunt said that he'd been in and out of the apartment but she didn't know where he was coming from and going to; she assumed work and school. Ian wouldn't reply to any correspondence—calls, texts, emails, Instagram DMs.

Alex continued to lead the classroom discussion energetically. These were the most thoughtful, elevated Exalt classes of the whole cycle, a fleeting segment during which students brought anecdotes from the professional world back to the security of their classroom and shared whatever they'd learned or were struggling to learn or were appalled by or found hilarious. Some stories were serious. Most were silly. A few were deeply poignant. Cumulatively, the sharing formed a catalog of how each of their domains—the portion of society with which they were comfortable engaging—was growing wider and deeper.

This broadening formed the heart of Exalt's rather unpretentious mission: to orient some kids so that they could complete childhood and with some measure of self-confidence initiate the adult lives that system contact had threatened to invalidate.

Alex paced around the interior of the rectangle of tables, and he could see adulthood gestating around him. Even as the kids gave wrong answers and made foolish observations and completely missed lessons that should have been easy to learn, they did so with a freedom to err that they didn't experience at home or in school or anywhere else in America. That freedom was part of the mission, too.

"Have you heard from Ian?" Alex asked Nahla after class. She and Kyla were walking out together. With a look from Nahla, Kyla moved on to wait outside. Kymare, the program coordinator for the cycle, remained in the room.

"Not really," Nahla said.

"I don't want to put you on the spot at all," Alex said. "I know you two text sometimes."

"Not in, like, over a week. Why?"

Alex quickly considered how much to involve her. He didn't want her to feel in any way responsible for Ian's absence or for convincing him to come back; she did not deserve that burden. But he believed that Nahla was intelligent and mature enough to maintain boundaries between Ian's problems and her own, and so he trusted her to help. "We're all just having a lot of trouble getting in touch with him, so I was wondering if you had an easy way of just seeing what's up."

"I can text him, no problem." She drew out her phone. "Should I tell him to call you or something?"

"At this point, it would be good just to know that he's all right."

She quickly thumbed some phone keys and sent a message. "He probably just went back to Paterson and has his phone off so no one can trace it, because he's paranoid."

Alex felt foolish for not having considered this possibility earlier, and glad for having sought Nahla's insight. "Right. That makes sense. I mean, not really—it's actually some really poor judgment—but I can see how that's making it hard for us to find him."

All three of them laughed somewhat mournfully. Nahla said that she would let them know if she heard back from Ian. She didn't sound hopeful. Then she rejoined Kyla in the front room and the girls exited for the weekend.

Friday nights could cast a slightly eerie, lonely atmosphere in the Exalt office. Some combination of the Statue of Liberty's distant glimmer and Brooklyn's southwestern front glowing across the harbor, and the financial district's being one of the few neighborhoods in New York City that quieted on weekends, and the kids' all being gone made the place strange. Also, the hour or two between the end of classes and the closing of the office were the only moments of the week in which no one at Exalt was on the phone. Courts were closed, internship offices were closed, schools were shut, families were having dinner, email accounts weren't dinging with incoming onslaughts. The silence was thorough when contrasted with the ceaseless, urgent matters unfolding at all other times. It could also be worrisome, because the challenges the students carried away from this place did not pause in tandem. They'd just been shepherded through another week of life on planet Earth, which segued immediately into another.

Alex sat in that uncentered feeling for a bit. The single most difficult aspect of his occupation was knowing that, at the end of all his annoying persistence and unreserved caring and subtle teaching tricks in imprinting the gospel of the program here, the most crucial choices that needed to be made belonged to Ian alone. The quietude amplified the likelihood that he'd already made them.

* * *

DURING THE THIRD week of January, after the school day ended in Brownsville, Ian bought pizza slices and sat for a while. He'd recently used savings from the $13/hour that Exalt had paid him through December, until he'd stopped showing up, to purchase a pair of sneakers that he'd desired for months. The sneakers were bright red, limited-edition shoes from a company called Cariuma Catiba. Just looking at them on his feet released dopamine bursts in his brain. These countered the negative feelings that had set in once he'd stopped receiving communication from Exalt, which had seemed to signify his official exit from Cycle 108.

When his phone had been lighting up with texts and calls—even though he'd left many of the texts unread and messages unreturned—he'd been aware that he was upsetting people who cared about him and were scared for him, and he was wasting an investment that had been placed in him. He was also loosely violating his parole, and being kind of a jerk. But the sheer volume of outreach gave him a strong if synthetic confidence, as if he had to be a pretty important person to stir this much commotion.

Now that the ado seemed to have subsided, and he was just sitting somewhere in Brownsville eating pizza and sporting nice shoes, he felt sad.

How complicated the chemistry was that governed his consciousness, and how easy and innocuous the choice had been to stop trying. Since the Exalt Cycle 108 had begun, he'd been surrounded by people striving to instill in him the belief that he was not only responsible for but capable of living a productive life with an upward curve. At some point recently—he didn't know quite when exactly, or how—he became fixated on simply living in the day he was in, not accomplishing anything of import, not contemplating anything intricate, not raising his expectations beyond modest. He'd concluded that days would be less stressful that way. In the end, that was the path he pursued. The alternative cost too much, and hurt in too many places, to sustain. He couldn't go back now anyway.

*   *   *

THE REMAINING MEMBERS of Cycle 108 convened for four final classes after completing their internships. These days were akin to the plays at the conclusion of a football game when, with victory secured, the quarterback kneels with the ball to run out the clock, or to the stretch of time in a normal high school between final exams and graduation parties, or to the last, safe miles of descent from a successful mountain-summit expedition: disasters could still occur, but not really. While graduation was not a total formality—the students were expected to perform somewhat for staff, donors, and board members—the atmosphere in the Exalt lobby before and after their class each evening was one of warm, grounded triumph. They savored the particular human feeling, both euphoric and mournful, that comes once all the work is finished but before the actual ending occurs. Passing through these days, Nahla was wise enough not to hurry—to understand that, as redundant as the program could be sometimes with its piling of school upon school and reviews upon reviews, she would rarely in her lifetime feel as safe and as valued as she did here.

On the last Monday in January, they further debriefed their various work experiences. Javi, who'd mentored for an after-school program, had decided that helping kids was rewarding but that he didn't like kids. Kyla, who'd interned in a legal advocate office, had been stimulated by being on the edge of fights picked against the larger justice system on behalf of people who couldn't afford the fight themselves, but she'd been intimidated by the hours worked and a little disheartened by the ultimate success rate, which was low. Nahla, at the real estate management firm, had been more inspired by the creative computer technology than the business of helping properties to function. She now desired to become an architect.

"What ever happened with that game room you were working on?" Alex asked in an early-week class. "Did they follow through with that?"

"I don't know if they did or not."

"Do you care? Like, would it mean something to you if they built that room?"

"I think it would be good for people who lived there. The building is not that nice, so I wanted people to have a place where fun could be had.

But it's kind of costly and I don't know if people would use it or how to keep stuff from getting stolen or broke after a while."

"Ah," Alex said. "So maybe you learned something about how people live in the city? What is required to upkeep housing, the costs and challenges?"

"Aw, shit." Nahla pertly placed her fingers over her mouth as if to snatch back the profanity. "It costs so damn much. There are so many challenges. This wasn't a really nice place, but it was better than most of the places I've lived. The elevator worked and everything. But, I mean, it's just a pretty regular building. And it is crazy how much work happens every day."

Alex pressed her: "Well, so, we often see landlords and building managers as the enemy. I mean, there is some *messed-up stuff* that happens in this city, with insurance and evictions and all around. Regular people do not usually like their landlords."

The groans that sounded around the room were unanimous in disdain. Living in combative rental situations was another commonality they shared.

Alex turned back to Nahla. "Do you feel like you got some new perspectives working on their side of the equation?"

Nahla shrugged. "The people at my office were mostly pretty cool. I didn't see anyone intentionally trying to hurt or screw over anyone else. When someone called about a broken pipe or busted light or whatever, the people I worked with got someone there to fix it. I think there were some eviction kind of stuff. I wasn't too close to that. I don't think they were trying to put anyone on the street—but I can't really speak to that. So overall, yeah, I guess I got some perspective."

Alex told her that her observations were interesting, and Nahla believed him. She couldn't recall ever having experienced that feeling in school, thus far.

On Tuesday, they watched clips from the TV series *The Wire* and segued into an exercise in which they were given ten fictional employee thumbnail profiles and told, as hypothetical managers, to choose two of them to promote. They'd performed similar role-playing earlier in the cycle, and they were clearly supposed to pay attention to how their work experiences had evolved their thinking. Apparently, the impact was huge. The class as a whole seemed to consider race and personal circumstances with far less weight than they had in the last incarnation of this exercise, which had been one of their first group activities during the cycle's early weeks. Back then, they'd chosen to promote characters they liked best or who inspired the most sympathy. Now, they homed in on how a business operated and what traits best served its purpose. One of the characters they declined was a black mother of young children who'd become unreliable due to her childcare situation; one of those they promoted was described as an arrogant, white, highly skilled and productive coder whom no one else in the (fictional) office could stand. After a few months' worth of half days in professional environments, their analytical thinking seemed to have shed much emotional weight.

Nahla asked aloud if they should consider this a signal of progress or even positive. No one offered a satisfactory answer.

During Wednesday's class, they wrote. All of the students were going to give a two- or three-minute speech to the ceremony guests describing how they came to be connected to Exalt, what they had learned here, how they had grown during their internship experiences, and what their plans were moving forward. Alex told them that they absolutely did not have to talk specifically about their arrests or the court proceedings leading up to their diversions to Exalt. The organization stakeholders would be much more interested in the details of their internships because they were professionals and most were active in this aspect of the program.

"Be specific," Alex implored before letting them free-write. "Don't just say, 'Exalt has made me a better person,' or, 'The most important part of Exalt has been the friends I've made.'"

"That's just what I was going to write, both those things!" Kyla groaned.

"I mean, those things are important. I'm just saying to *be specific*. What is it *about* Exalt that has made you better? How has friendship *specifically* improved your life and your decision-making? Does that make sense?"

Javi said, "It's kind of hard to talk about when we only have, like, three minutes."

"Don't worry about length right now. This should really be from your heart. Not, like, mushy—actually, you can be mushy if you want—but this is your chance after all these weeks of me telling you how to think where you can just be real."

Javi's face lit up as he seemed to be imagining a scene in which he said exactly what he thought to this collection of New York City's power players.

Alex caught this glimmer. "Not *all* real. Keep it clean and keep it respectful. But make it your own."

They each took a laptop and began to write, most kids settling into the comfortable chairs out in the office lobby. The sky was dimming outside, but the space was lively with all the phone calls that occurred every late afternoon with employers and families and people in every level of the court system. The entire office staff was exhilarated for the kids in this cycle—their coming graduation, the potential in their lives beyond that event—so the many side conversations rendered any sustained focus difficult. Nahla sat with Kyla and they were giggling constantly, writing little. Javi sat at an empty office cubicle. He put the landline phone to his ear and pretended to have an urgent conversation while also miming his fingers to be typing rapidly, as if he were multitasking at work. The chatty atmosphere was wonderful. Even the administrators who had nothing to do with instruction milled around as informal writing tutors, leaping at this fleeting opportunity to work directly with the young people they typically served from a distance.

Then Alex gently reminded everyone in the room—the students as well as the adults happily distracting them—that this assignment was not simply a throwaway essay. "You all will have to *speak your words* in front of an audience. And the Exalt board, these are not ordinary people. These are some pretty important people. They can give you jobs. They can take away jobs. If you all tank your speeches, I might not be teaching this next cycle. So, try to put some thought into this. Think of who you were walking in here for the first time four months ago. Think of who you are now. How are those two people different? Just as important, how are they the same?"

Then each member of the class began to write intently, which lasted about fifteen minutes before their attentions drifted from computer screens back to one another and muted conversations grew loud, prompting more of Alex's pleas.

The evening passed in this rhythm, and the following class—Thursday—began the same way. The students and staff communed while the sun set stunningly over the harbor. Somehow, their various individual essays did take shape. Instead of exhorting them simply to finish, Alex and Kymare and others began editing the students' work, helping to specify language and clarify points. The results, Alex felt, were strong. Exalt students did not typically have sound backgrounds in writing. The Exalt curriculum did not have the space for Alex to teach it, though writing was embedded in the units regarding communication: how to approach a job interview, how to compose a professional email, how to speak in public. Upon reading a few of the essays and suggesting possible improvements, Alex felt that the work the students had finished tonight reflected well the work the class had conducted since the previous October. With the wistfulness that always accompanied the end of a cycle, he stumbled into the knowledge that was ever in doubt until these last days, which was simply that they'd done all right in the time they'd had.

Four months was not enough time to supplement the unique assortment of developmental work each student had missed over his or her lifetime. It was merely enough time to support broad growth and introduce some fundamental skill sets. The essays generated were a modest testament to the power of such support. Even Javi, who had spent most of the writing time physically spinning around in his borrowed office chair, had crafted a solid sequence of introductory sentences that he would have to finish at home that night. The grammar and diction the students used were elementary; the stories they told were profound—at least to the adults in this space, people who knew them well enough to know what such phrases as *I used to get in trouble a lot at school* really signified.

Ian was not overtly missed. Since he hadn't grown close to anyone in the class besides Nahla and the students hadn't spent much time in the classroom since before the holidays, any mention of his name tended to be pitying and not much more. Ian had become that guy no one wanted to be, that symbolic person at whom most kids in school were apt to shake their heads sorrowfully and then brush past. A handful of students in Cycle 108 couldn't even remember his name unless prodded.

Chapter 6

———————◆———————

February 2020

W HILE HIS FORMER classmates worked lackadaisically on their speeches in the office, Ian worked hard in his soul to sever attachments to the past year.

In February of 2020, he couldn't think of many minutes since April of 2019 that hadn't been horrendous and damaging. Well, he could— subway rides with Nahla, moments at Exalt in which he'd voiced some novel concept or laugh-inducing aside, times when he'd been acknowledged by anyone around him as a person of worth—but he strived to avoid such reveries, as they only caused him loneliness and guilt. Without formal support, Ian was attempting a difficult, often quixotic psychological maneuver that members of the upper class might pay tens of thousands of dollars to supplement with therapy: he aspired to cease dwelling on the past, particularly the blame embedded there, and turn forward wiser but unencumbered. In a subtle contradiction that wasn't totally lost on him, Ian held this aim in tandem with his overarching goal of returning to Paterson. Since exiting his Exalt cycle, he'd divided his hoped-for trajectory into three doable subcategories: he would finish the school year in Brownsville with solid attendance and passing grades; he would meet all of his probationary requirements, Exalt notwithstanding, and expunge his record;

he would do his very, very best to mend any wounds that had been festering with his father.

With his life thusly organized, his days became both more immediate and more purposeful. In reflective moments, he considered that the purpose was a bit amorphous, that returning to Paterson would only open up further quagmires he would need to resolve. But he was confident that, once there and legally permitted to wander the streets he knew, he would be filled with such self-assurance and security that further aspirations—college, maybe, or a job that could be leveraged into a career, or a girl he might want to date for a while—would just unfold before him with a clarity that wouldn't occur anywhere else in the known world, and certainly not in Brownsville.

Throughout February, he focused on creating and sustaining a rigid routine: school, check-ins with his parole officer, a conversation or at least a text sent to his father, some homework, and taking care not to impose on his aunt and uncle too much. During those weeks after his unceremonious exit from Exalt, Ian did what the ruling sector of his consciousness had always commanded him not to do: he deferred entirely to each of the various structures—school, justice, family—that purported to administrate his life. He made himself small, and he tamped any rebellion of his inner spirit by framing these months as a transitory expense toward a coveted end. Outwardly, he was generally capable of eliding the knowledge that, had he made this decision a month earlier, he would be graduating from Exalt. Inwardly, he struggled.

Hey, girl, he wrote randomly to Nahla. He didn't expect her to respond. The frame of life in which they had reason to be friends had passed.

You coming to graduation tomorrow? she replied quickly.

For real? I forgot it was tomorrow.

You should come by.

That would feel weird.

We would all be happy to see you.

Maybe I'll roll through. Don't you have to give a speech???

I'm nervous!!!

You'll do great. He then repeated, *Maybe I'll roll through.*

He missed Nahla. He missed Exalt. He missed Alex and his dry humor dusted with dad-jokes. Ian mostly missed hanging around the office, not because the conversations were extraordinary but because of that sense of having access to a safe, social, openly accepting space. The world contained few such spaces. Ian was a self-admittedly self-righteous person, capable of defending even his most objectively irrational decisions with biblical determination, but he already knew that he'd made a weighty mistake in exiting Cycle 108.

What made his self-diagnosis more enduring was the knowledge that his ability to recognize it could be fully credited to the work he'd done and lessons he'd learned in Exalt.

To Nahla, he just wrote, *Proud of you girl.*

She wrote back, *Thx.*

He scrolled through his emoji list and sent her a bunch of graduation-themed images: bound diplomas, a black female face staring from beneath her tasseled cap, multiple hearts of various colors, fireworks, a cake, the columned facade of a classical court structure. She replied with her own images—nervous face, disco ball, a bomb about to explode, some double-underlined *100s*—and a command to him: *COME THROUGH TOMORROW!!* Then the correspondence ended.

Ian, who knew that he was not going to attend the graduation, considered that this might be the last time he would ever hear from his friend and classmate. He had always had the ability to move on from faded relationships—childhood friends who'd changed cliques, girlfriends who hadn't worked out, people who'd moved or been arrested—without lasting entanglement, almost as if certain people ceased to exist once they ceased to directly affect his life. But he knew that he would continue to think about Nahla throughout this last, dwindling phase of his youth—and probably well into adulthood, whatever that looked like.

* * *

"MY NAME IS Nahla. I am seventeen years old. I am from the East Flat-bush section of Brooklyn, New York. I currently live in East New York and I'm a senior in high school. I am interested in gaming, a bit of sports, and exploring. When I get older, I will own my own game lounge and I will be an architect. I have critical thinking skills, I learned how to use my resource management skills, and I've used my creative problem-solving skills the majority of my life. I was oblivious to the name of these skills, but Exalt helped me put a name to my skills and Exalt staff assisted me in enchanting them. My weakness is my attitude, but I've also been working on my temper. . . ."

During her graduation presentation, Nahla spoke only vaguely of her "trouble with the criminal justice system." She spent much of her allot-ted time describing an app that architects used to test out their ideas in virtual spaces, called Rhino 6. While mentioning the early weeks of the cycle, she said, "When I began seeing people getting dropped out of the program, I just continued to work hard and stay determined. It's safe to say I earned this." Crowded into the lobby, the audience of board members, donors, legal advocates, POs, police officers, and prosecutors all nodded along.

Nahla concluded, "Exalt encouraged me to recognize the skills that I had and bring them to the surface and that is what I did. I feel as if there should be more programs like Exalt around neighborhoods of poverty, because not only will it help mature the minds of young men and women but it can help slow down the school-to-prison pipeline. If I had an option, I would stay in this program forever. I thank each and every staff that works at Exalt because not only do they show that they care about youth but they are making a difference getting youth off of the streets and from behind bars."

Though the last bit sounded a bit cursory in the room, Nahla had moved people. Her words were effective, but more poignant was her proud, nervous, giggly, absolutely sincere manner as she read too far from her prepared sheets. The ceremony's format carried a performar aspect—that of gratifying deep-pocketed and/or politically persu

supporters—which belied the deep authenticity of the students' dozens of hours together, but the class members carried the evening wonderfully while remaining themselves. After four months of relentless, varied challenges—four months of analyzing their failures and shortcomings and the obstacles America pitted against them daily—these last moments as Exalt students were designed for them to succeed.

Twenty minutes of mingling followed the speeches. Students and their families fielded compliments and softball questions: *What are your future plans? Are you thinking about college? How can I help?* Alex had prepared the students for this dynamic, too; networking was a necessary if unpleasantly self-conscious aspect of professional aspiration, and tonight was an ideal opportunity to practice with an audience primed to adore them.

The presence of individuals from various layers of the justice system who had helped place the kids here lent the atmosphere a feeling of reunion and accomplishment. The donor class comprised a diverse lot, both in race and experience, and they seemed uniformly interested in the kids and their plans for conquering high school and the world beyond. The people who gravitated toward Exalt for charitable giving were not generally compelled to talk about themselves exhaustively, or to dominate rooms, or to demand recognition for the social good they were realizing with their largesse. They were there to help. Nahla left the graduation ceremony feeling as if there were a group of people in the world sincerely interested in her, and in kids like her. She had fourteen business cards in her jacket pocket as a testament.

She said as much as they sat down for the traditional postgraduation class dinner. "Not one person asked me what I did, or anything about jail or my court case. I thought that was pretty cool."

"Do people you meet generally ask you if you've been to jail and what for?" Alex asked.

"No. But you can tell when they're kind of wondering. I didn't feel that from anyone tonight. They were just chill."

"They were chill, but my face still hurts from making eye contact and smiling that entire time." Javi made a zombielike expression of keen happiness to illustrate, a squirmy child posing for a school photo he didn't want taken.

They had walked from the Exalt office to an upscale pizza restaurant in the lobby of a nearby hotel. Only Alex, Kymare, Exalt's CEO, and the class members were there. Stakeholders weren't invited so that students could cease performing, and family members weren't so as to preserve a reflective atmosphere. This hour was for the students alone to properly feel the exultation of these four months.

"Back in October, where were you?" the CEO, Gisele Castro, asked. The kids mostly knew her as the regal woman always talking animatedly on the phone or hosting important-looking people behind the glass of her office. "What were you going through?"

The kids took turns mumbling and shaking their heads: "Just out of jail . . ."; "Still in group home . . ."; "About to drop out of school . . ."; "My ma had actually kicked me out the apartment . . ."; "I was just high as shit all day—sorry!"

Gisele—who seemed to be as relieved as the students for this reprieve from work—laughed. "That first night in class at Exalt, that very first Monday, what were you thinking?"

Nahla blurted, "That we were going to seriously fight."

The nods up and down the table signaled unanimous agreement.

"I even thought that might happen, to be honest," Alex added.

Gisele said, "And what are you thinking now?"

"I don't even know," Javi replied. Of them all, he'd probably undergone the most noticeable changes. He still had the compulsion to punctuate every exchange with a joke, but he was less desperate in his attention seeking, and he'd come to exude a serious thoughtfulness. "Like, overwhelmed, I guess. Like, I can't even believe this happened."

Kyla, sitting beside Nahla and picking at a bread roll with her long nails (a low-key purple for the occasion), said, "I feel like, back then, I was happy to be here and all because it meant less punishment and also being paid, but I didn't actually believe anything teacher Alex was saying about life or what we could be. To be real, that first week of classes just sounded ridiculous. Like, 'All right, sure, Alex, we'll turn our lives around, whatever you say.'"

"I felt that," Alex said seriously. "I feel that every cycle."

"And then tonight," Kyla continued, "I'm like having conversations with all those rich people, and even with policemen and like prosecutors, just like regular conversations, and it didn't even seem strange, that group all in a room just talking."

They paused to order their dinners. In class, they'd discussed these sorts of service-sector interactions, and how to be respectful in addressing waiters directly and not hemming and hawing over their orders. *Act like you've been in a restaurant before* had been Alex's headline. Tonight, officiously, they ordered mostly plates of spaghetti and cheese pizza.

When they resumed the table conversation, Nahla said, "I'm starting to get real nervous, though."

"I think that's normal," Alex said.

"I'm interested to hear you explain why, though," Gisele said.

Nahla was wearing an ankle-length dress that her mother owned and had hemmed for Nahla's first internship interview two months earlier. She squirmed a bit, perhaps not wanting her words to be misinterpreted as ungrateful. "It was hard to be here every day, just, like, drop whatever I had going on at three in the afternoon and get all the way here. But then it became kind of, like, the opposite of hard, like whatever was going on at school or at home during the day, I knew I'd be here soon and that things would be good here. Class became the safe place. So I'm kind of worried about not having that place no more. . . ." She shrugged as she trailed off, dropped her head, sipped her water, smiled at whatever she was thinking.

When Alex responded, he used a softer version of his classroom voice, with tones that rose and fell in a musical way but held a through line of assuredness. "Listen, there's no way to say this that doesn't sound a little made up. But hear me out. Exalt is not done with you all. I hope that you all are not done with Exalt. The cycle just ended. You all did great. You are ready to move on. But we will always be here. Office spaces change, staff changes, the cycles change. But the mission doesn't change and the mission is you all. You have a question about school? You call us. You looking for a job? Call us. You get in a little bit of trouble? Call us. You get in a lot of trouble? Call us *immediately*. You need a recommendation for anything, you need a semiquiet space to work and procrastinate, you want to practice interviewing, you have changes in your family or living situation, you have questions about careers—just come by. And I'm talking tomorrow or ten years from tomorrow. We don't have to be on speed dial, but keep us in your contacts. Someone will be there. All right?"

The words were a version of a speech that Alex made at the end of every cycle. He always hoped that the sentiment would be elicited by a rumination such as Nahla's rather than given as an unprompted soliloquy. When he would finish, someone would typically feign tears—such as Javi right now, dabbing at his eyes with a napkin and gasping, "That was so beautiful, man." Alex figured that they weren't entirely listening because their brains were too busy being glad for themselves, and hopeful. They deserved to be glad and hopeful in this moment. But he knew that in future days the hope would fade, blurred by the trials of their lives, and maybe wink out altogether at points. He didn't know if these present words would linger in their various memories and stand up against their pride; he didn't know if these kids, when challenged and even when they were no longer kids, would take out their phones and call for help. His own hope was that they would.

Their food came, unofficially concluding all further gravitas that evening. Instead, the kids ate while the adults marveled at how much the kids were capable of eating. The conversation assumed a greatest-hits rhythm to which everyone contributed: "Remember when Samantha wouldn't talk for three weeks straight?" "Remember when Javi got punked by Kyla?" "Remember when Hakeem got lost for an hour trying to find the bathroom?" "Remember when Ian won the typing contest and acted like it was the Super Bowl?"

The last remembrance was Nahla's, and it just slipped out. During the brief moment of awkwardness that followed, she thought about that innocuous moment in class and how Ian had preened because he'd typed something like thirty-three words per minute with 76 percent accuracy. They'd been five or six weeks into the cycle then, and she'd been surprised to learn that, beneath all of his posturing regarding Paterson and how fierce he was known to be there, he was kind of nerdy.

The rest of the table moved on to recounting the time Javi had been in the middle of an impression of Alex when Alex had entered the room and stood right behind him. Javi's glee was like a pure embodiment of childhood, and Alex said, "He did a pretty good impression of me, too."

*   *   *

IAN'S RETURN TO Paterson was commanded by the same system that had previously barred him from stepping foot in his hometown under penalty of imprisonment. In the middle of March, New York City closed its schools as a safeguard against the coronavirus. His aunt and uncle, responding to the increasingly alarming news coverage, began panicking over Ian's presence and potential threat as a virus carrier. The situation was untenable, and he called his parole officer to report the bind he was in. The PO told Ian that the city's probation system was facing upheaval, as the local juvenile justice system was continuing to hold arraignment hearings even though court trials had been suspended. Young people were still being processed into the system but were not being released. Populations in the city's two remaining detention centers (one of which was four blocks from where Ian was living in Brownsville) were climbing. The city's far broader network of group homes and community-based disciplinary centers were outsourcing to keep from being overrun. The probation network was static at the moment while preparing for a deluge once the courts began releasing as many detainees as they could, the way most major cities were doing. The PO was only projecting, but he assumed that, with hundreds of juvenile offenders streaming back into the city with no school and summer on the near horizon, the courts would subsequently be swamped with arrests.

Ultimately, the PO told Ian that outlying cases such as his were being vacated where possible. Some coordination with the New Jersey side of things would be necessary, and Ian would be placed under house arrest for some months, but the official who had spent more than half of a year counseling Ian on the many ways by which his life hinged on staying away from Paterson now certified that returning home would be in both New York City's and Ian's best interests. Ian himself wasn't listening closely enough to hear the details or think about the virus impelling all this activity. He was one person among billions of people whose lives were being rerouted right now, and he was probably one of the very few who were grateful for it.

Ten days later, Ian stood in the doorway of his home in north Paterson and dropped his duffel bag from his shoulder. He hadn't been here since the morning of the day he'd been arrested last May, as he'd gone from school to the police station, and from the station to juvenile hall, and eventually from juvenile hall directly to his relatives' in Brooklyn. The town house had a simple layout: a hallway front to back with a TV room, kitchen, and utility room off it, plus three small bedrooms upstairs. The space felt much narrower than it had before, or rather Ian felt much broader, though he hadn't been exercising since he hadn't been permitted to play sports. All the emotional zigzagging of late had left him very, very tired. He spent his first days at home just as he'd spent most of his days in Brownsville: on the couch, scrolling on his phone.

"You comfortable enough?" his father would sardonically ask. "Can I get you anything?"

Ian absorbed the jokes, which weren't wholly mean-spirited. He hadn't expected his father to be happy and accommodating, exactly; he'd cost the man far too much anguish to feel entitled to any nurturing gestures surrounding his homecoming. His status was the same now as it had been on the afternoon of his arrest eleven months earlier and every moment in between: he'd fucked up, and he'd damaged the love that people had for him. Failing to complete his Exalt cycle hadn't helped his cause, nor did the stress that COVID-19 was causing his father at work and the population generally. Ian was at least gratified by how glad his little siblings were to see him.

His house-arrest terms were strict but more or less ungovernable, as were the state's pandemic-related stay-at-home orders. He availed himself of illegal trips to the local delis, finding it hilarious that a few weeks ago a masked kid entering a store or just hanging out on neighborhood blocks would have triggered all sorts of mental and physical alarms. Now, a maskless kid anywhere had become a kind of symbol for the errant, destructive selfishness of youth. He began working out intensely: plyometric drills on the street outside, long runs circumnavigating the entire town, sprints up and down the Great Falls Park stairwells, thousands of old-fashioned push-ups and sit-ups. The exercise not only made him feel strong again, but helped him to tolerate the latent tension with his father at home and to fall asleep at somewhat decent hours. His parole check-ins now happened virtually. Certain friends hung out with him, while others had slipped quietly into his past. Spring went by, then summer.

Around the same time that he learned that his parole period was ending, he learned his senior year of high school would begin online. He was so inured to the insular structure of his life that the frantic, angry text threads he was a part of failed to rouse him. He was disappointed that there would be no sports this year and possibly ever again in his life, but was otherwise reconciled by the perspective that most every student in America was living with disappointment. His was not necessarily more urgent, nor was it more negligible, just part of the load he was to carry onward. He'd become well acquainted with its weight. He could handle it.

* * *

THE PARKING LOT was smaller than he remembered. One of his long runs unintentionally took him there. His strides had carried him for forty-five minutes through the nondescript tapestry of Paterson, lost in thoughts as aimless as his route, and then he'd recognized the office building and paused to wander into the rectangle of asphalt behind it. Everyone was still working at home, so no cars were in the lot. Weeds had grown knee-high through the cracks. It was a curiously unexceptional spot to be forever tied to the pivot his life had taken through the spontaneous, terrible act of asserting his supremacy over another human. Still panting from his run, he stood roughly in the area where that boy had come at him and Ian had dropped him so easily and then continued hurting him. Ian peered down at the ground and expected to feel regret, but he didn't. The violence that had occurred here was writ, fixed to a particular time and space in his little life.

The claustrophobia of home school and the angst of being a teenager had been activating some large ideas of late: he'd been thinking of just leaving, either striking back into New York City for no reason except that he knew some people and things were busier there, or maybe heading west to discover small, strange towns and maybe, ultimately, to find his mother in Arizona. These visions overlapped with earlier dreams he'd had, and they were mostly fantastical. The months ahead would more likely resemble quite precisely the months behind.

He felt that he was a better person than the one who had fought here—that he was a little smarter and more thoughtful and more restrained, definitely better able to factor consequences into decisions in real time. This growth manifested in acts as simple as picking up a couple lollipops for his siblings when he was buying food for himself, and doing his father's laundry when he was doing his own, and not often saying aloud exactly what was on his mind. He was on track to graduate from high school and then most likely find a job—maybe even at the port with his father. The parking lot would not always be here; the office building looked decrepit and primed to be replaced by the apartments rising throughout the gentrifying neighborhood. But what had happened here would always have happened here. All the events that it had engendered would always be a part of his experience and his consciousness. His mistakes would always trail him; the system and the societal constructs through which it operated and the human condition itself were designed to ensure that. He'd done those things, and he wasn't through paying for them. But he was young and some promise remained with him, too: the things he had not yet done.

He scuffed his soles across that bit of pavement, as if rubbing out a stain from the surface, and then he continued running the long route home.

Epilogue

◆

February 2022

THE HOME WAS modest, its beige-brick siding set back from a curving road amid a tract of other modest, beige-brick homes. Josiah Wright woke up inside, fixed himself breakfast, and dressed in slacks and a button-down shirt. His two roommates worked different hours and were still asleep. Josiah was waiting in the cold at the foot of his driveway when a coworker picked him up and drove him to work at an outdoor shopping center in Dover, Delaware, the state's small capital city. He worked at Kohl's, his eight-hour shifts spent alternately at the register and on the floor. After his shift, he ate at a fast-food pizza restaurant in the same shopping center and rode home. At night, he watched TV and played video games with his roommates and friends who came over to hang out. His days were long and uneventful. He didn't enjoy most of them very much, but he looked forward to the spring, when he was tentatively set up to volunteer as a lacrosse coach at a public high school in the afternoons. Assuming he didn't violate parole or get arrested, his record would be expunged in three to five years. He believed life would become richer then in all senses of the word.

About 175 miles north, Ian Alvaro also woke each morning and was driven to his job. When their shifts aligned, he rode with his father. They worked in different areas of Port Newark. Ian's position was low-tier and physically difficult. He helped secure shipping containers to the loader machines that would move them onto trucks, and he manually transferred smaller pallets of goods stored for longer terms in the warehouses—maybe electronics, maybe pet food, maybe bathroom tiles. During those grueling hours, he wore a thick leather belt around his lower back to keep the muscles from slipping out of place. At night, he often ate dinner with his family before walking to his own apartment two blocks away from his father's town house. He was often too exhausted to do much of anything besides send a few text messages and fall asleep. Like Josiah, he didn't enjoy his days very much. Also like Josiah, he looked forward to some undetermined future passage when he would feel more fulfilled.

*   *   *

AT THE OUTSET of this work, when I first began sitting with educators, administrators, counselors, social workers, and other adults orbiting the juvenile justice apparatus (this was before I gained permission to visit classrooms and meet the students with whom I would spend the bulk of my time), I was warned over and over about the proximity of death in this edge of the American fabric. Almost every adult I encountered in this space informed me—with unique supporting anecdotes but similar degrees of both certainty and deep sadness—that if I spent time in and around juvenile halls, then I would be exposed to young people dying. I would not witness it happen, they assured me, but I would at some point be in a classroom with a teenaged kid, watching that kid joke around and cause trouble and make expressive faces and be childish, and then, weeks or months or years later, I would learn that the same kid had departed this earth. Most likely, I would also learn that the end had been violent, pointless, and painful. Every one of the adults I worked with while writing this book, including those fairly new to the profession—some not even much older than the students they served— had experienced this crushing cycle numerous times.

While working on this book, I interacted directly with about eighty or ninety kids in the juvenile justice system. At this time, to my knowledge, five of those kids have died.

Josiah and Ian are both still living, and neither is currently in jail. As the author, I grant that this reportage does not make for the most rousing of finales: the primary characters are alive and free and leading undramatic, somewhat toilsome existences. As an observer and indirect participant in their stories and as someone who cares about them both, I hold that this current outcome—and the fact that they are both high school graduates—is an astonishing testament to their individual spirits and perseverance.

Josiah endured his incarceration in part by daydreaming scenarios in which he gloriously escaped jail alongside his friends, dethroned corrupt police and gang leaders alike, and reunited with the father who'd been completely absent from his life. In reality, he grew listless at home in Wilmington. With permission from his PO, he moved to Dover, about an hour south in central Delaware, with a girl he'd been seeing who was also eighteen years old. The state capital city was a sprawl of middle-class suburbia surrounding a major air force base and massive Nascar stadium. Both Josiah and his girlfriend worked part-time sales jobs in different shopping centers. She became pregnant over the summer, and Josiah was excited to be a father even though affording their rent was a struggle and their health insurance plans were basic. She miscarried in the fall. He grew depressed, stopped going to work reliably, and was eventually fired. He and his girlfriend broke up, and he found a new living situation in a house with roommates and another job in retail.

Ian continued to fantasize romantically about striking west after graduating from high school, which he did a little over a year after he dropped out of Exalt. The fantasy sustained him through Zoom school, cycles of COVID-19 surges, measured reopenings, and his high school graduation. He used map applications on his phone to plot various courses across the country at different latitudes, swiping his fingers to make random turns along the way, passing virtually town by town through Middle America. He imagined that this wandering method would be precisely how he would travel, if he had a car and a few months' worth of expendable cash. But Ian had neither of those commodities. He spent a portion of his free time scheming ways to gather both quickly, which ranged from contrived (a bender in Atlantic City) to outlandish (creating an online marketplace for collectors' edition sneakers). Ultimately, he procured a job at Port Newark through his father.

He worked manually in the transport chain while training to be certified to drive loader vehicles. With the global supply network in total upheaval throughout much of 2021, the work toggled unpredictably between periods of incredible strain and having very little to do. Ian hated that uncertainty, hated not knowing when he woke and rode to work with his father whether he was in for a fast-paced and arduous shift or hours spent snacking and talking. But because he had his father, he was always at work on time and his supervisors were pleased with him. He settled into the routine. He saved some money every month, though never as much as he felt like he should, and every paycheck made him think of that unit at Exalt, when his peers in Cycle 108 charted their expenditures next to their earnings and marveled at the tall red blocks of debt that formed. On the hardest days, when Ian might place upward of eight thousand pounds on his back cumulatively over the course of ten hours, he assured himself that he would head west as soon as he could. The Pacific Northwest appealed to him for some reason; the vision in his mind of verdant hills blanketed in mist sparked a certain yearning. But time kept passing and he kept deciding that he would be foolish to quit this job, with its strong union and relative security. Dozens of kids he finished high school with were unemployed. Ian remained in Paterson and continued working at the port. He eventually moved out of his father's home, but only to an apartment a few blocks away.

Their stories haven't ended. The portions involving incarceration and probation hopefully are concluded, but not even the boys themselves can make that declaration definitively. Either of them, really, could land back in jail on any day, because they are both still young, poor people of color in America. Incarceration never really ends anyway. Still, their lives continue on, flowing into new, not always satisfying shapes, often in a wearisome flatness punctuated with abrupt zigs and zags rather than distinguished, elegant arcs. And that is the task embedded in any individual life: to make an uneasy sense of these lines, and of the world as it unfolds; to try to form and sustain some novel vision for how to inhabit that world; to adapt that vision to unforeseen currents; above all to aspire for some idea of romance, maybe, and to avoid being doomed by all the warped logic, invisible burdens, and impossible loyalties that romance can hold. It's hard to follow the trajectories of young people in this manner, because those trajectories don't tend to proceed cleanly or with fanfare or on any sort of narrative bell curve. They don't often align with the one-note aspirational tropes that frame the stories we tell most habitually—stories like those that Woodside's Unit 7 students watched on video in that English language arts class in late 2019: Spielberg, Jobs, Winfrey, others of their ilk.

Neither Josiah nor Ian will grow up to resemble those figures, most likely. Nor will Bosley, Cassio, Sargent, Nahla, Kyla, Javi, or any of the young people who for different reasons felt willing to share their stories in these pages. Despite all the dreamy visualizing to the contrary in which they constantly took part during downtime—in which they described the glorious, exhilarating futures they had planned—they all had a sense that they wouldn't invent a world-altering technology or become a globally recognizable media brand. While I was learning their stories, that sense grounded the general sadness of educators and students alike: they all thoroughly knew that the lottery of birth and the structural racism and classism of the justice system—even as that system continues evolving for the better—had walled these particular kids into a very specific trajectory, and their own personal influences and decisions had only helped narrow their respective outcomes further.

Josiah attending college was supposed to upend that outcome, as was Ian graduating from Exalt, bending their pathways instead toward more pleasing locales of redemption and found happiness. Neither succeeded in those specific pursuits, and neither will ever forget not succeeding.

That is their primary commonality, and also their primary motivator in doing what they are both striving to do now: bear life's disappointments with a level of grace, control anger when possible, hold fast to love always, pay rent, not go to jail, survive, hope. Thus far, they're both doing all right in these respects. Most people who have cared about these boys consider them to be spectacular for doing all right.

Most people who have cared about them also agree that they are no longer boys, that the respective childhoods of Josiah Wright, Ian Alvaro, and all their erstwhile peers ended prematurely. It is a highly subjective task to identify the moment in which those endings occurred. Neither of the boys themselves, when asked, could point to a specific experience out of all the thousands of experiences each shared with me and declare it as the conclusion of childhood. An observer might be able to peer from a distance at certain formative instances—the first witnessing of severe violence, maybe, or the first night spent in a secure room in a locked facility—and assert that no one who has lived through such a trial could reasonably be labeled a kid. But I would add that one of the defining characteristics of childhood—perhaps the absolute defining characteristic—is the inability to peer at life from a distance. In a certain way, as of the writing of these pages in February 2022, Josiah and Ian are both still children in their own minds.

As children, they cling to a certain indomitable kind of wonder in the prospect of unlived years ahead: the further schooling, relationships, parenthood, promotions, tremendous leaps contained in the most innocuous of decisions.

* * *

THE ADULTS DEVOTED to these students are no more inoculated to the discordant rhythms of life, and no less subject to the bureaucracies of both the governments they work for and the emotions that course through their souls.

Chris Lanier requested a leave of absence from Woodside beginning in the fall of 2021 to realign his occupation and goals. He took a special assignment from the SFUSD assisting the special education sector, where he'd spent the majority of his career. School by school throughout the district, he visited with the administration, listened to them describe the shortcomings in the special ed programming, and then helped them devise a system within their unique community that would more thoroughly serve this subset of students. The work was episodic, engaging, and highly rewarding. The distance from Woodside was vital to his mental health, but he still planned to return to his leadership position in the second half of the school year—assuming there was still a position to which he could return.

There wasn't. In late January 2022, Megan Mercurio attended a regular staff meeting with Constance and David and the rest of their colleagues. At the end of the meeting, they were told abruptly that the Transition Age Youth program in the Woodside facility would not be continuing with its current level of educational support. Their jobs would be consolidated by the district at the close of the school year, and the new program for younger children in the system, which was still being designed by the Close Juvenile Hall Working Group, would have space—maybe—for two of them. They were all welcome to reapply, but they would need to procure an added certification in social work in order to do so.

Though stunned, Megan did a decent job of composing herself to continue her work with nineteen- and twenty-year-olds in quarantine at juvenile hall—including Lawrence, still confined in the building two years after he'd been remanded there for murder, who with her and Maceo Johnson's help had earned a year's worth of college credits. She struggled much more in untangling what her career would look like moving forward—whether she should acquiesce to the district administration and take whatever teaching job they assigned her, or actively pursue her work with juveniles at the discretion of the Working Group. Or maybe this was some kind of cosmic signal guiding her to exit this difficult sector of the American educational complex.

The decision was existential and vast and intimately related to her self-perceived purpose on earth, as well as the well-being of children in the justice system—children who might be strangers to her now, but whose passages could be softened in some small way by her role in their lives. For fourteen years at Woodside, her work had assumed a daily urgency and a significance that encompassed the living and dying of young people. For the same fourteen years, she'd been regarded by others as almost comically sensitive until a student or classroom necessitated fighting for, at which point she became ferocious. Now, she just needed time and quietude to discern whether those years represented a lifetime calling, or an enclosed chapter whose meaning wouldn't be lessened by its passing.

* * *

IN THIS KIND of work that I do—a form of immersion journalism, technically—I don't know how the stories I become involved in will end. With this particular project, I didn't know how they would unfold from week to week or day to day. A student might be excited to talk, and we would go through the somewhat arduous permissions procedures to secure a time and place to do so, and then that student might get in trouble, or the whole school might go on lockdown for the day due to some rumored contraband, or bad news from court might upend his life inside and outside of jail, or the student might wake up in a run-of-the-mill foul mood and decide to ignore me. Adults had similar volatility in their schedules and states of mind due to the ever-changing regulations under which they worked and the sadness and violence they witnessed constantly. The stories told here were just a few that emerged over a frenetic span of years. They were meaningful to me not because any specific drama felt particularly grand or timeless—all the nearly limitless drama I observed felt that way—but rather because of the opposite: Josiah, Ian, Megan, and their peers and colleagues remained so very much *themselves* throughout the messy markers of time documented in these pages that they all became a fixed, generous part of my own self.

At some point midway through the research for this book, my daughter, ten years old at the time and curious about my many weeks spent away with imprisoned children, asked me: "Do the kids you're with in these jails *like* you?"

I'd never overtly considered the stark terms of being liked or disliked in these spaces before. Of the dozens of kids with whom I crossed paths in the juvenile halls and diversion program, a number were particularly warm toward me, a few were overtly disdainful and wanted absolutely nothing to do with me, and the majority were simply indifferent. These kids were all well accustomed to having visitors observing their classes, such as school district representatives and probation officials. To most, I started out as just another white guy in a button-down shirt appraising them and the spaces they'd been placed in. As they learned that I wrote books, and that specifically I was there to write *this* book and to hear whatever stories they were willing to tell, some crowded me for attention and others scowled in paranoia and snuck glances at my notebook to make sure their names weren't recorded in it (I quickly ceased bringing said notebook to class, and I didn't list names). But most still remained too wrapped up in their own complicated interiors to register me or my work at all.

To my daughter, I replied, "Nobody really likes to be watched, because that feels the same as being judged. So when I'm first there, and kids think I'm just watching, they don't like me very much. But most people really like to be listened to. So once we get to talking, and they figure out that I'm just an awkward guy who thinks their experiences and their feelings matter enough to write a book about and hopefully make some strangers feel something for them and their situations, then some usually start to think I'm all right. And some still don't."

My daughter nodded, though she didn't seem fully satisfied with my slightly stammering, slightly circular response. You might not be, either. You might be a person with the view that it should never again be permissible for a white person to be entrusted with the stories of non-white people in this country. Or you might be among the many who simply cannot be moved by the story of any person who has perpetrated a violent crime, regardless of that person's age or circumstances. Or you might wish for a book of this nature to end with a clear, cost-effective solution to juvenile incarceration that has evaded centuries' worth of policy makers. No paragraph within these pages was written to invalidate anyone's perspectives on me or the work I do. Every paragraph was written to cast some angle of light into the somewhat impermeable spaces of the American justice system as it pertains to American children, and the way the human spirit adapts to and evolves within those spaces. In short, I spent time with these people in these places, and this is what happened.

I deeply, truly wish that Josiah had finished community college, and that Ian had completed the Exalt program. I don't maintain those wishes because they would have made for more heartening stories, but rather because the boys would have had a wider range of choices and supporters now. It also would have been nice to witness the particular smiles emerging their faces during those milestones.

Instead, Josiah and Ian carry on through different, less visible but no less vital milestones in young adulthood, and work, and family, and figuring out what it means to be a person. Through each one of those markers of time they are employing on various, often subconscious levels what they've seen and heard and learned during these past years: the years before, during, and after their time in jail. Those years were at turns grueling, painful, hilarious, triumphant, defeating, and strange. All that unfolded will continue to reside in their hearts, and in the hearts of those whose paths they've crossed, including mine.

I also hear from others whose paths I've crossed, such as from Darian Slay—the boy at Woodside who was over a hundred credits behind track in high school on the random day he spoke to David Malizia and Megan about his ambition to go to college and become a nurse. Later that same day, he was badly beaten up and then became emotionally withdrawn. While I was writing this epilogue, I learned that he had just graduated from high school. This was a little over two years after that afternoon I described. He sent a picture of himself tipped back in a kitchen chair with his braids splayed over his shoulders and a broad, slightly sheepish grin. One hand was nestled behind his head, and the other held up his diploma.

Throughout the intensive research I've conducted in these stories and the greater topics that they embody, I've found that the system of youth incarceration in America is convoluted, flawed, and above all intractably mired in generations of seesawing, opportunistic, naive, racist thought—but, for the time being, is incrementally improving and being redesigned, with deeper concern for the individual. Concurrently, I've found the humans within that system—both those tasked with operating its many layers and those subject to its labyrinthine laws—to be impassioned, benevolent, weary, admirable, and truthful. Above all, I've found young people incarcerated, even for truly heinous acts, to be redeemable—though that biblical word holds very different meanings to different people, such that I hesitate even to invoke it here on the last page.

I don't use the word to suggest what we owe to the most marginalized children among us, or what they deserve from us, or how this whole knotted province of justice could be suddenly idealized. The intention and the hope is simply to offer further nuance to what it looks and feels like to be cast aside at one of the tenderest junctures of life and then try—*try*—to reenter a society that, quite contrary to its long-held and oft touted ideals, is nothing if not grudging in its forgiveness.

A NOTE ON SOURCES

———————————◆———————————

THE EPIGRAPH TEXT was part of a Cincinnati judge's remarks made at the first national conference on juvenile court proceedings, held twenty-two years after the initial court's founding and sponsored by the U.S. Children's Bureau and the National Probation Association. The permanent record of this conference was published by the Department of Labor in 1922. It is a remarkable document.

For the history of the juvenile justice system in America, I am indebted to the websites of the Juvenile Law Center and the Center on Juvenile and Criminal Justice. I also learned a great deal from the books *Juvenile Crime, Juvenile Justice: Panel on Juvenile Crime Prevention, Treatment, and Control* (National Research Council and Institute of Medicine, 2001) edited by Joan McCord, Cathy Spatz Widom, and Nancy A. Cromwell; *A Century of Juvenile Justice* (University of Chicago Press, 2002) by David S. Tanenhaus, Margaret K. Rosenheim, Franklin E. Zimring, and Bernardine Dohrn; and *Juvenile Justice: Guide of Theory, Policy, and Practice* (SAGE Publications, 2017) by Steven M. Cox, Jennifer M. Allen, Robert D. Hanser, and John J. Conrad.

For statistical data recorded and aggregated from different eras, I am thankful to the Office of Juvenile Justice and Delinquency Prevention and the Prison Policy Initiative.

For discussions on various philosophical approaches to juvenile corrections over the past decades, I owe much to the above resources as well as the books *Rethinking Punishment in the Era of Mass Incarceration* (Routledge Studies in Contemporary Philosophy, 2017), edited by Chris W.

361

Suprenant; *Juvenile Justice: Policies, Programs, and Practices* (McGraw-Hill, 2019) by Robert W. Taylor and Eric J. Fritsch; and *School, Not Jail: How Educators Can Disrupt School Pushout and Mass Incarceration* (Teachers College Press, 2021), edited by Peter Williamson and Deborah Appleman (this book included chapters written by Megan Mercurio, Constance Walker, and Chris Lanier).

The *Newsweek* magazine article mentioned in Part I, entitled "Murder Town USA (aka Wilmington, Delaware)," was written by Abigail Jones and published on December 9, 2014.

Information regarding the Close Juvenile Hall Working Group in San Francisco, which included meeting agendas, minutes, transcripts, and often full Zoom recordings, was made publicly available by the City of San Francisco Human Rights Commission.

ACKNOWLEDGMENTS

◆

JOSIAH AND IAN, your families and advocates and support networks: thank you for the time and courage you gave to tell your stories. You shared your hearts to change the hearts of others.

Sarah Martin, Megan Mercurio, Chris Lanier, Alex Griffith: thank you for letting me into the private space of your classrooms and offices to gain insight into your difficult work. Each of you holds the magic and it was a gift to observe that magic happen.

At Ferris School and the Delaware Department of Services for Children, Youth & Their Families, and Youth Rehabilitative Services, a deep thanks to John Stevenson, Dr. Tanya Banks, Dr. Denise Purnell-Cuffe, Jen Rini, Glenroy Powell, Mr. Michels, Mrs. Stzrukza, Mr. Rezak, Ms. Darden, Mr. Dunn, Dr. Katherine Powers, Judge Andrea Rocanelli, Coach Carliss, Michaela Shuchman, and Newton Buchanan.

At San Francisco's Juvenile Justice Center, the San Francisco Unified School District, and the Juvenile Probation Department, thank you so much to Geoff Diesel, Constance Walker, David Malizia, Mr. Padilla, Mr. Laques, Ms. Rayukanti, Alyse Castro, Sam Janeway, Maceo Johnson, Ian Smith, "Sarge," Mama Rose Villalon, Cindy Alvarez, and Kodo Franklin.

At Exalt Youth in New York City, my gratitude will always reside with Gisele Castro, Brian Lewis, Kymare Hutchinson, Shalisia-Earth Hyman, Ikim Powell, Mai Brand, Rafelina Contrares, Frank Pettis, Julie Pastor, and everyone else in the office who worked so hard and tolerated my hanging around.

My deep and enduring gratefulness to Bosley, Cassio, Sargent, Crews, Little Axell, Araceli, Baby Ramsie, Slay, Perez, Mendoza, Lexi, Lawrence, Isaiah, Cynthia, Nahla, Kyla, Javi, Malachi, and Kensi. You all possess powerful hearts and powerful stories. Thank you for your patience and kindness toward me.

David Black, thank you for always guiding me through the years that this work takes with such a sharp mind and gentle spirit.

For the third time, I am grateful to my editor, Colin Harrison, for all his wisdom, insight, and faith in these stories—really, truly grateful.

At Scribner, I am thankful to Emily Polson, Nan Graham, Ashley Gilliam, Steve Boldt, Clare Maurer, Katie Rizzo, Jaya Miceli, and Brian Belfiglio for all of their time, effort, and kindness over the years.

Helen Thorpe, Kate Lloyd, Miranda Boe, Rebecca Rauth, John Molner, Will Schwalbe, Alex Kotlowitz, Martin and Sugar Goldstein, Steve Bumbaugh, Aubrey and Adam Siegel, Staci and Matt Eddy, Marty and Bellinda Scott, Mom and Dad: you've all helped so much in different ways in general life and in this particular project.

Lucy and Whit, writing this book about school while simultaneously teaching you school during the shutdown year will always be a (mostly) treasured memory. I really love you two.

Rebecca, thank you always, for everything. I really love you, too.

ABOUT THE AUTHOR

———————◆———————

Jeff Hobbs is the author of *The Short and Tragic Life of Robert Peace*, which won the Los Angeles Times Book Prize; *Show Them You're Good*; and *The Tourists*. He lives in Los Angeles with his wife and two children.